ASPECTS OF AVICENNA

Aspects of Avicenna

Robert Wisnovsky

EDITOR

Markus Wiener Publishers
Princeton

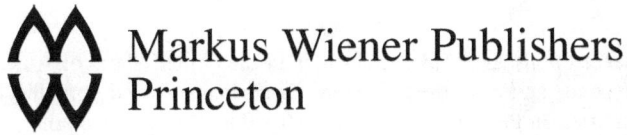

The cover is the negative of a cropped photograph of the first page of a manuscript, dating from 1082 AH/1671 CE, of the *Ilāhiyyāt* of Avicenna's *Kitāb al-shifā'*. The manuscript is owned by the Princeton University Library (Shelf Number 2[769]), and is listed as Number 1363 in R. Mach and J. Ormsby, *Handlist of Arabic Manuscripts (New Series) in the Princeton University Library*, Princeton, 1987. The editor is grateful to the Rare Books and Manuscripts Division of the Princeton University Library for permission to use a photograph of this manuscript as the cover of this volume.

Second printing, 2013

Reprinted from *Princeton Papers: Interdisciplinary Journal of Middle Eastern Studies*, Volume IX.

For information write to:
Markus Wiener Publishers
231 Nassau Street, Princeton, NJ 08542

Library of Congress Cataloging-in-Publication Data
Aspects of Avicenna/edited by Robert Wisnovsky.
Includes bibliographical references.
ISBN 978-1-55876-251-0 (alk. paper)
1. Avicenna, 980-1037.
I. Wisnovsky, Robert, 1964–
B751.Z7 A88 2001
181'.5—dc21 2001046832

Markus Wiener Publishers books are printed in the United States of America on acid-free paper, and meet the guidelines for permanence and durability of the Committee on Production Guidelines for Book Longevity of the Council on Library Resources.

Contents

Acknowledgments vi

A Note on Transliteration and Citation vii

Preface ix

DIMITRI GUTAS
Intuition and Thinking: The Evolving Structure of Avicenna's Epistemology 1

DAG NIKOLAUS HASSE
Avicenna on Abstraction 39

ABRAHAM D. STONE
Simplicius and Avicenna on the Essential Corporeity of Material Substance 73

DAVID C. REISMAN
Avicenna at the ARCE 131

Acknowledgments

I am grateful to the many people who, over the past several years, have helped bring this project to fruition. In particular, thanks are due to Bernard Lewis, General Editor of the *Princeton Papers*, who asked me back in 1997 to consider putting together a volume devoted to Islamic philosophy; to the Editorial Board of the *Princeton Papers*, who approved the volume's inclusion in the series; and to Bill Blair, the Managing Editor, and the staff at Markus Wiener Publishers, who helped enormously with the logistics of production. The contributors to this volume also owe a debt to the anonymous external readers for their very helpful criticisms and suggestions. Finally, I must express my gratitude to the authors: for putting so much hard work into their articles, for entrusting me with that work, and for remaining so patient while the wheels of publication ground slowly on. I hope they will be as satisfied with the result as I am.

A Note on Transliteration and Citation

Throughout this volume Arabic and Persian letters have been transliterated according to the system adopted by the *International Journal of Middle Eastern Studies*. The Greek long vowels have been transliterated as *ê* and *ô*, and the iota subscript as *-êi*, *-ôi*, and *-âi*. Each of the authors has been allowed to retain his preferred method of dealing with other transliteration issues, such as the rendering of *hamzat al-waṣl*, as well as with the citation of primary and secondary works.

Preface

The articles in this volume aim to further our understanding of the work and thought of the philosopher and physician Abū ʿAlī al-Ḥusayn ibn ʿAbdallāh ibn Sīnā (born before 370 AH/980 CE–died 428 AH/1037 CE), known in the West by his Latinized name Avicenna.

Now is a good time to be issuing a collection of articles on Avicenna. The explosion of work on Avicenna in the 1950s, sparked by the celebrations of his thousand-year (lunar) anniversary, was followed by a comparatively slow period. Partly this was because major projects initiated during the 1950s (such as the editing in Cairo of the *Kitāb al-shifāʾ*) and 1960s (such as the editing in Louvain of the medieval Latin translation of the *Shifāʾ*) took decades to come to fruition. But since the 1980s, by which time most of these new editions had become available, Avicenna scholarship has grown steadily. In addition to the newly available editions, the work done by Dimitri Gutas on Avicenna's intellectual biography, and Jules Janssens' annotated bibliography on Avicenna, have been especially helpful to those now plowing Avicennian fields.

The present volume, *Aspects of Avicenna*, is one of a number of collaborative projects undertaken recently. In September 2000, a special issue of the journal *Arabic Sciences and Philosophy* was published, consisting entirely of articles on Avicenna. The proceedings of a 1999 colloquium held in Belgium, entitled "Avicenna and his Heritage", are due to be published soon. An Avicenna conference whose participants were largely senior graduate students and junior scholars, took place at Yale in March 2001, and a collection of articles based on contributions to that conference is expected to appear in book form in 2002.

It seems to me that what much of the best new scholarship has in common, and what the articles in this volume aspire to, is a mature and subtle appreciation of the *history* of Avicenna's philosophy. By this I mean two things. First, the increasing availability of edited Avicennian texts has allowed scholars to examine a broader spectrum of passages about a particular topic than they were able to in the past. This, in turn, has made possible the recent and ongoing attempts to periodize Avicenna's philosophical career through the careful dating of individual works. Scholars now have to come to terms with the fact that there may not be a single Avicennian position on a given issue, but rather a history of positions, adopted at different periods of his life.

Second, many of the ancient commentaries on Aristotle, though available in the original Greek for a hundred years now, have only recently been translated into English. These translations, along with the new scholarly work on the commentators which has followed in their wake, have made a massive but heretofore forbidding resource for the history of late-antique and early-medieval philosophy easily accessible to specialists in Arabic philosophy. The more precisely we understand how Greek philosophy developed during the period between 200 CE and 600 CE, the better able we shall be to situate the theories of philosophers such as Avicenna in their intellectual-historical context.

In Chapter 1 of this volume, "Intuition and thinking: The evolving structure of Avicenna's epistemology", Dimitri Gutas argues for a developmentalist interpretation of Avicenna's ideas about intuition (*ḥads*). Intuition is a crucial element in Avicenna's epistemology, and Avicenna's ideas about the role intuition plays in intellection changed over time, according to Gutas, partly in response to the grilling he received from his students, as recorded in the recently re-edited *Mubāḥathāt* (*Discussions*). Avicenna seems to have had eschatological reasons for changing his mind about intuition, now distinguished more clearly from thinking (*fikr*) and assigned unambiguously to the human intellect rather than to the sensitive faculties of the animal soul. If intuition is a necessary component in intellection, yet is located in a ventricle of the brain with the animal soul's inner senses, the human rational soul, which survives the death of the body, will be unable to think about intelligibles after the body dies. This is because our intuition will have passed away when our brain, along with the rest of our body, passes away. An earlier analysis of Avicenna's theory of intuition figured prominently in Gutas' 1988 monograph, *Avicenna and the Aristotelian Tradition*; just as Avicenna's view of *ḥads* evolved from his "Middle" period, when he wrote his *Shifā'*, to his "Late" period, when he wrote his *Ishārāt* (*Pointers*), so Gutas' view of Avicenna's view of *ḥads* has evolved from his earlier work to the present article.

One of the underlying messages of Gutas' article is that the boundary Avicenna draws between the animal soul, which is tied inextricably to the body, and the human rational soul, which is not, is fuzzy. This is unsurprising considering the philosophical issues at stake. If, as a philosopher, my primary concern is to safeguard the human rational soul's separability after death, then I shall devote my greatest efforts to making a sharp ontological distinction between the intellectual faculties of the soul, which transcend the body, and the sensitive faculties of the soul, which are lodged in the body: the external senses in the sense organs, and the inner senses in the brain. If, on the other hand, my primary philosophical concern is to create a coherent account of the way we come to think about intelligibles, an epistemology in which humans play an active role in abstracting universal concepts from individual sense objects, I shall want to emphasize the connection, rather than the disjunction, between the sensitive faculty and the intellectual faculty.

The tug-of-war in Avicenna's thought between epistemology and the ontology of the soul is the issue Dag Hasse discusses in Chapter 2, "Avicenna on abstraction". Many scholars, according to Hasse, have assumed that for Avicenna, intellection consists in an almost entirely passive reception of emanated forms from the eternal Active Intellect, and that our role as thinkers is simply to dilate our intellects enough to soak up the gush of concepts. The criticism that Avicenna assigned such importance to the role of the Active Intellect that he robbed human intellection of genuine agency, is an old one, leveled by Thomas Aquinas in the 13th century and revived by Brentano in the 19th. As a result few scholars have investigated Avicenna's theory of abstraction (*tajrīd*), supposing that Avicenna's descriptions of how we construct intelligibles out of sensibles are nothing but a *façon de parler*, metaphorical shorthand for what is really an effect of the Agent Intellect. Hasse argues that this assumption is incorrect. Like Gutas, Hasse maintains that what appear to be inconsistencies in Avicenna's theory of abstraction may well reflect an evolution in his views. Nevertheless, by focusing on the language

Avicenna uses to describe the mechanics of conceptualization, Hasse detects two underlying themes in all the passages: that the process of abstraction is always dependent upon the activity of the human intellect and that the abstracted forms emanating from the Active Intellect ultimately derive from sense-data. The lesson from Hasse's article is that Avicenna scholars should not base their interpretations on the premise that in Avicenna's thought concerns about the soul's separability necessarily override concerns about issues such as abstraction; sometimes, it seems, epistemology trumps ontology.

In Chapter 3, Abraham Stone weighs Avicenna's ideas about what it is to be a body against those of the Neoplatonic Aristotle-commentator Simplicius. Stone is primarily interested in how Avicenna and Simplicius treat the problem of how the terms "corporeal" and "material" are related. Both corporeity and materiality appear to be the essential characteristics of natural substances, the subject of natural philosophy. Are corporeity and materiality ultimately the same thing, then? Or is there some way to distinguish them? Stone argues that Simplicius holds corporeity and materiality to be identical, while Avicenna holds corporeity to be a quasi-formal characteristic and thus different from materiality. Although Simplicius' and Avicenna's solutions to this problem differ, Stone finds that they share a tendency to treat issues such as this — originally a problem of natural philosophy — as part of the domain of metaphysics. By creating new metaphysical concepts ("corporeal form" is a good example) and carving new metaphysical distinctions, the two philosophers were trying to create deeper and deeper foundations of consistency on which their philosophical systems could rest.

The present volume also contains a valuable new resource to Avicenna scholars. When conducting research in Cairo, David Reisman discovered that the American Research Center in Egypt possessed a trove of photostats of Avicenna manuscripts, originally collected during the first half of the 20th century by the Orientalists Max Meyerhof and Charles Kuentz. Chapter 4, "Avicenna at the ARCE", is a detailed catalogue of those photostats, listed according to their shelf number at the ARCE Library. Many of the photostats are of compilations (*majmūʿāt*) of shorter philosophical and medical treatises, and Reisman provides details of their contents. He has also collated the photostats with Mahdavī's bibliography of Avicennian manuscripts, as well as with Janssens' bibliography of printed editions of Avicennian works. The ARCE's photostats appear, in fact, to constitute one of the world's most extensive collections of Avicenna manuscripts in a single location. With Reisman's catalogue in hand, scholars can now take full advantage of this exciting new resource.

Robert Wisnovsky
Cambridge, Massachusetts

Intuition and Thinking: The Evolving Structure of Avicenna's Epistemology*

DIMITRI GUTAS

The central position which Intuition (*ḥads*) and Thinking (*fikr*) occupy in Avicenna's epistemology — indeed, his entire philosophy — is not very clearly understood in all its ramifications and implications. The precise role which the central concept upon which they are based, finding the middle term of a syllogism, plays at the meeting point, or "interface," of his emanative cosmology, theory of the soul (including prophetology), epistemology, logic, eschatology, and that part of his scientific and medical approach that is empirical, has still to be delineated and defined. As with a number of other aspects of Avicenna's philosophy, however, providing a full and accurate account of it is not an easy matter. It concerns issues which were very dear to him and which he therefore revisited

* I wish to thank Robert Wisnovsky, David C. Reisman, and an anonymous reader for valuable suggestions and comments on earlier drafts of this paper. I have used the following editions of Avicenna's works: *Kitāb al-Shifā'*, ed. I. Madkour et al., 22 vols, Cairo 1952-83; *Avicenna's De anima, being the Psychological Part of Kitāb al-Shifā'*, ed. F. Rahman, Oxford 1959; *Kitāb an-Najāt*, Cairo 1331/1912; *Al-Ishārāt wa-t-Tanbīhāt*, ed. S. Dunyā, 4 vols, Cairo 1960-68; *K. al-Hidāya*, ed. M. ʿAbduh, Cairo 1974; *K. al-Ḥudūd*, ed. A.-M. Goichon, *Livre des définitions* [Mémorial Avicenne VI], Cairo (IFAO) 1963; *al-Mubāḥathāt*, ed. M. Bīdārfar, Qum 1413/1992; *Risāla fī māhiyyat aṣ-ṣalāt*, ed. A.F. Mehren, *Traités mystiques ... d'Avicenne*, Fasc. III, Leiden (Brill) 1894; *Fī Ithbāt an-nubuwwāt*, ed. M. Marmura, Beirut 1968; *al-Qānūn fī ṭ-ṭibb*, ed. Idwār [Eduard] al-Qashsh, Beirut (ʿIzz-ad-Dīn) 1413/1993.

repeatedly in his works, with occasional and inevitable shifts of emphasis and terminology over the years. Furthermore, Avicenna expressed himself in ways that differed both in style and emphasis or approach — this was also inevitable insofar as he did not only write for and respond to philosophical questions posed to him by his students, but he also tried to explain his position to a wider and less technical audience both as a result of requests by patrons and because of the inordinate interest which the concept generated. An overall and diachronically consistent picture of the role of these key concepts in Avicenna's philosophy will require more painstaking work and cannot be the purpose of this paper. I will try rather to provide further documentation on the subjects of Intuition and Thinking, as an appendix to my previous work and the questions it raised, and identify with greater sharpness some of the key problems which were faced by Avicenna and the solutions he proposed.[1] The order in which these passages will be given is roughly chronological, though certainty in this regard is quite impossible with our present knowledge of the chronology of Avicenna's works. The passages will be numbered sequentially beginning with number 9, following the 8 passages on Intuition given in my *Avicenna*. Some passages which were already presented there are either revised here or enlarged, and they bear the same paragraph number, followed by an asterisk.[2]

I

Avicenna formulated his theory of Intuition during what I call the transition period of his literary activity, the period when he was traveling in Jurjān until he went to Hamadān, roughly between 1013 and 1020.[3] In the earliest period of his philosophical activity he apparently had no clearly formulated epistemological theory, as we can judge by his *Compendium on the Soul* (*Maqāla fī n-nafs ʿalā sunnat al-ikhtiṣār*), from which **Text I** is taken. Avicenna adhered to his Intuition theory, more or less as originally formulated during the transition period, throughout both his middle period and that of his experimentation with what he called the philosophy of the Easterners. The writings of these periods include primarily *The Cure* (*ash-Shifāʾ*) but also *The Easterners* (*al-Mashriqiyyūn*, also known as *al-Ḥikma al-mashriqiyya*, *Eastern Philosophy*, in some later MSS), the section on the theory of the soul from which has survived intact,[4] *The Salvation* (*an-Najāt*), and *The Guidance* (*al-Hidāya*), to mention only the larger works. These works, to which I will be referring collectively as *The Cure* complex of writings, present a relatively unified view of Intuition, which may be called the "standard version."

To this standard view is opposed a "revised" one, which is met with in the writings of the late or final period of Avicenna's philosophical activity, primarily in *Pointers and Reminders* (*al-Ishārāt wa-t-tanbīhāt*), as well as in some portions from the *Discussions* (*al-Mubāḥathāt*). This latter work, an apparently posthumous compilation of his answers to questions posed by his students, provides valuable documentation for the discussions which led from the standard to the revised version.[5]

Briefly put, the standard version is the following. All intelligible knowledge, that is, all non a priori knowledge of universals that depends on syllogistic reasoning, is accomplished by the discovery of the middle term in a syllogism. The middle term can be acquired in two ways, through instruction or Intuition (*ḥads*), which is a movement of the Mind in its effort to hit spontaneously upon the middle term. Instruction is ultimately reducible to Intuition insofar as the theoretical first teacher, who had no one to instruct him, necessarily discovered the middle terms through his Intuition. All intelligible knowledge, therefore is acquired only through Intuition. This ability to hit upon the middle term varies in individuals; some can do it faster and more frequently, others slower or not at all. The person who is able to discover the middle term instantly and without thinking is characterized by Acumen (*dhakāʾ*). An extreme example of this ability and of Acumen is found in the prophet, who intuits all the intelligibles at once (see **Text 2**).

The revised version introduces two major modifications into this scheme. First, Intuition is no longer a movement of the Mind for the purpose of tracking down the middle term, but its instantaneous discovery; in other words, the function of Intuition is now restricted to that of what was formerly the definition of Acumen (*dhakāʾ*), mention of which is dropped from the revised formulation. Second, and because of the first (i.e., since all intelligible knowledge cannot now be acquired through the redefined Intuition), a second way of acquiring the middle terms and the intelligibles is introduced, in addition to Intuition. This is Thinking, which itself is now defined as a movement of the soul in search of the middle term, thus taking over a large part of the former definition of Intuition (see **Text 6**).

These are substantive changes and they are obviously due to sustained discussion both in Avicenna's own mind and with his disciples. It is possible to trace most of the elements of this exchange in the various questions and answers recorded in the *Discussions* (*Mubāḥathāt*).

II

The standard version of Avicenna's theory of Intuition generated some problems which gave rise to the search for a new formulation. To appreciate these problems it is necessary to start with some definitions, given by Avicenna himself in the Posterior Analytics part of *The Cure*, in the passage that parallels Aristotle's formulation which inspired Avicenna's theory of Intuition:

[**4***] From *ash-Shifāʾ*, *al-Burhān* 259.12-20, corresponding to Aristotle's *Posterior Analytics* 89b7-20

As for the discussion of Mind, craft, comprehension, wisdom, Acumen, and Intuition, most of it would more appropriately take place in other sciences, in the areas of Physics and Ethics, although their definitions should be given here.

Mind (*dhihn*) is a faculty of the soul that is ready and predisposed to acquire terms [of syllogisms] and ideas. Comprehension (*fahm*) is a complete readiness this faculty has to conceptualize whatever comes to it from others. Intuition (*ḥads*) is an accurate and spontaneous (*min tilqāʾi nafsihā*) movement of this faculty toward tracking down the middle term, as, for example, when one sees that the moon is bright, according to its phases,[6] only on the side that faces the sun, and his Mind tracks down a middle term by means of its Intuition, namely, that the cause of its brightness comes from the sun. Acumen (*dhakāʾ*) is accurate Intuition by this faculty, taking place in an infinitesimally short period of time. Thought (*fikra*) is the movement of the human Mind toward the principles of the problems [whose solution is sought] in order to work down from them to the problems. [There follow the definitions of craft (*ṣināʿa*) and wisdom (*ḥikma*).]

The important elements in these definitions are the following: The soul — Avicenna here does not specify whether he means the animal or rational soul — has many faculties or capacities. One of them is Mind, a predisposition to acquire terms of syllogisms and ideas. Intuition is a *movement* of the Mind when it is looking for the middle term of a syllogism. The definition here is similar to the one Avicenna uses in other parts of *The Cure*, especially in the *De anima* section (**Text 2**, §2), where he calls it not a movement but an act or function of the Mind (*fiʿlun li-dh-dhihni*). This movement of the Intuition is spontaneous, that is, the impulse to look for the middle term comes from this faculty, the Mind itself.[7] It is to be noted that the element of time does not enter into this definition of Intuition — the Mind can take as long as it wants to Intuit the middle term. Time becomes the distinguishing characteristic of a subcategory of Intuition, Acumen, which is Intuition in a very short time and without thinking.[8] Thought, finally, is another movement of the Mind, broader in scope than Intuition: the Mind moves first toward the principles of a problem so that, starting from them and traversing the entire cogitative process, the solution to the problem can be arrived at. The implication from **Text 4***, therefore, is that at one point, when in the solution of a problem it becomes necessary to discover a middle term, Thought (*fikra*) would include Intuition as defined here. Avicenna says this explicitly in another, shorter, work of his, *The Guidance* (*al-Hidāya*), which was written in 1023 during the lengthy period it took to compose *The Cure* (1020-27):

[**9**] From *al-Hidāya* 293-294 ʿAbduh[9]

Thought (*al-fikra*) sometimes Intuits (*taḥdisu*) the truth and discerns the good, though it varies in [both cases, Intuition and discernment,] with regard to increase and decrease. It is all accomplished by Intuiting the middle term without instruction (*taʿlīm*). It is not impossible, therefore, that one of the souls that shines with the sacred faculty should be constantly Intuiting

> things from beginning to end on account of its intense contact with the active intellects; for when there exists a lowest point [on the scale of increase and decrease], it is not far-fetched that there exist a highest point. This is prophecy with regard to the intelligibles.[10]

Thought, therefore, does include Intuition of the middle terms; it also includes discerning what is good, and thus performs a function for the practical intellect, something which has implications for conduct and ethics. To recapitulate, then, the standard theory of Intuition as depicted in the complex of works contemporary with *The Cure*: Mind includes at least two movements in its cogitative function; the broader in scope, Thought, involves the entire process starting from principles and arriving at solutions, while Intuition is the more restricted but epistemologically crucial capacity of seeking and hitting upon the middle terms in the construction of syllogisms. Intuition, in turn, includes Acumen as one of its kinds, the very fast one.

III

There is, however, a hidden problem in this account, a problem which created difficulties both for Avicenna's disciples and modern investigators; it became manifest in particular during the transition from the standard to the revised version of Intuition, as I will discuss later. The problem is, briefly put, whether Thinking, but also Intuition, both in the standard and revised versions, is a function of the animal soul, which is rooted in the human body and perishes with its death, or of the human, rational soul, which is immaterial and immortal. In the definitions in **Text 4*** from *The Cure* given above it is stated quite unequivocally that both Thought and Intuition are functions of the Mind, which in turn is a faculty of the soul. Avicenna does not specify which soul, animal or rational, though Mind (*dhihn*) in Avicenna always refers to the rational soul and it acts like the undifferentiated matrix upon which the various activities of the rational soul are registered or through which they take place.[11] In addition to this, in certain passages of the De anima part of *The Cure* it is quite unambiguous that Thinking is a function of the rational soul: Avicenna even uses the term *al-fikr an-nuṭqī*, "Thinking that pertains to reason," i.e., the intellect (*De anima* 175.9 Rahman), and has Thought (*fikra*) act as the mediator for the reception by the rational soul of the forms as they emanate from the active intellect (*De anima* 247.5 Rahman).

On the other hand, Thinking (*fikr*) and Thought (*fikra*), are clearly identified in a number of places with the "Cogitative faculty" (*al-quwwa al-mufakkira*), which is an internal sense of the animal soul, as will be discussed shortly. In the first place, Thinking, together with recollection (*dhikr*), is explicitly placed in the ventricles of the brain in *De anima* 268.6 Rahman. In another passage (170.7 Rahman), Thinking (*fikr*), together with Imagining (*takhayyul*), are said to be on occasion responsible for lodging a form in the Image-bearing faculty while the Mind (*dhihn*) is absent. This means that Thinking is contrasted to Mind, and if Mind refers to the rational soul, as discussed above, then Thinking must be the function of another faculty, i.e., the animal soul, since otherwise the rational soul would be doing two opposing things at the same time (being absent and lodging a form), which is impossible because the rational soul is immaterial and hence indivisible in its functions as in anything else. Finally, the word *fikr* in the plural (*afkār*) has on occasion an unrelated meaning in *De anima* (181.15-17 Rahman), where it means "worries," "cares" (*curae* in the medieval Latin translation). Clearly, therefore, there is ambiguity in Avicenna's use of terminology referring to Thinking, and a corresponding imprecision in his theory of the mechanism and locus of Thinking, which has consequently similar implications for Intuition. The problem whether to localize them in the animal or the rational soul is thus very real.

In a way it could be maintained that Avicenna inherited the problem from the material he had to work with, for it is possible to trace it to at least two factors, which need to be discussed at some length in order to bring out some of the creative tensions in Avicenna's thinking. The first is Avicenna's own extremely detailed and highly sophisticated analysis of the perceptive faculties of the animal soul, an analysis which is itself due to Avicenna's rootedness in the materialism of Aristotelian biology and Galenic medicine. The second is the indebtedness of his noetics to both Aristotle and its Neoplatonic developments, with the ensuing conflict between the two.

To start with Avicenna's materialistic analysis of the internal senses, including Thinking and Intuition: Avicenna divides the brain into three segments or ventricles, front, middle, and rear. Each one of these is the seat of one or two of the internal senses, which belong to the animal soul, and thus depend on the body for their function. The front ventricle is the seat of Common Sense (*ḥiss mushtarak*), which receives and properly perceives the forms of objects conveyed to it by all the senses, and of the Image-bearing faculty (*al-khayāl*, *al-muṣawwira*), which stores them. The middle ventricle is the seat of the Imagining and Cogitative faculty (*al-mutakhayyila*, *al-mufakkira*), which combines and separates sensory and conceptual images respectively, and of Estimation (*wahm*), which judges what the non-sensible connotations of objects are.[12] The rear ventricle, finally, is the seat of memory and recollection (*al-ḥāfiẓa*, *adh-dhikr*), which stores the connotative concepts (*maʿānin*, the medieval *intentiones*) of beings.

The operative, or active, faculties here are thus three: two in the middle ventricle, the Imagining/Cogitative one and the Estimation, and one in the front, Common Sense. The remaining two are merely storage areas for forms (Image-bearing) and connotations (memory). Among animals, Estimation (*wahm*) is the highest of these internal senses, insofar as it is a critical faculty, and the closest that they come to thinking. In humans, Estimation is the same as that in animals, but the Imagining faculty has an additional function. When the Imagining faculty (*al-mutakhayyila*) is employed by the animal soul of humans, it is the same as that in animals: it combines and separates images. But this faculty can also be employed by the human, rational soul, and in that instance it is called the Cogitative faculty (*mufakkira*) and its function is to think, that is, combine and separate conceptual images.[13] If the Thought (*fikra*) mentioned in **Text 4*** above is the function of this faculty, the *mufakkira*, then it is localized in the middle ventricle of the brain. And since, according to the standard version in *The Cure* passage (**Text 4*** above), Intuition is another motion of the Mind included in Thought, which is in the middle ventricle, Intuition also should be localized there. Avicenna in fact states this in his *Canon of Medicine*.

[**10**] From *al-Qānūn fī ṭ-ṭibb*, vol. II,6 and 8 Būlāq = vol. II (Book III), 810 and 813 al-Qashsh

1. The principles from which we arrive at a knowledge of the states of the brain consist of the sensory functions, the governing functions — i.e. recollection, Cogitation (*tafakkur*), Image-bearing (*taṣawwur*), and the strength of Estimation and Intuition — and the motive functions....

2. As for the governing functions, the strength of Estimation and Intuition indicates the strength of the temperament (mixture, *krasis*) of the brain as a whole, while their weakness indicates that there is a resident lesion in it until it is determined which of the other functions is [actually] impaired.

3. Among these [impaired other functions] is the loss of strength and lesion in the Image-bearing faculty (*al-khayāl wa-t-taṣawwur*). When this faculty is strong, it helps to indicate that the front [ventricle of] the brain is healthy. This faculty is strong only when the person is able to preserve fully the forms of sensible objects — like shapes, figures, sweetness, tastes, sounds, melodies and the like. The reason is that some people have such perfect capacity in this regard that the excellent geometer [for example,] can have a single look at a figure that has been drawn and its form and letters are impressed upon his soul; he then completes the proof to its very end without needing to have a second look at the figure....

4. Further among these [impaired functions] is the loss of strength in the Thinking and Imagining faculty (*al-fikr wa-t-takhayyul*). This takes either the form of complete loss, in which case [the disease] is called dementia (*dhahāb al-ʿaql*); or the form of weakness, in which case it is called stupidity, the origins of both being, for the most part as they say, a cold, dry, or humid front [ventricle of the] brain; or the form of change and disturbance, to the point that one thinks non-existent things and imagines what is wrong to be right, in which case it is called mental confusion....

5. Finally among them is a lesion in the faculty of recollection (*dhikr*) which causes either weakness or complete loss....[14]

Avicenna here clearly places Intuition, together with Estimation, in the brain. Because, however, he seems to imply that for proper Estimation and for Thinking by hitting upon the middle terms one needs all the other internal senses, Estimation and Intuition are said to be dependent on, and thus indicative of, the health of the entire brain, which is fair enough. Humoral imbalances, excesses of one or two of the four qualities (hot, cold, etc.), or lesions in any part of the brain impair the corresponding faculties, including those of Estimation, Thinking and Intuition.

So far, then, all of these activities of the Mind are brought into relation both with the internal senses of the animal soul (in humans) and the anatomy and pathology of the brain. This account of the perceptive and cogitative processes is thoroughly materialistic. As a matter of fact, in one passage Avicenna expresses himself in a way that gives no hint of the immaterial aspects of intellection. In the preamble to his short essay on prayer, he gives a brief account of the creation of man as microcosm in order later to explain the relation of prayer to the macrocosm, the supernal world. He says:

> [**11**] From *Fī māhiyyat aṣ-ṣalāt* 30-31 Mehren[15]
>
> God divided man's substantiality into body and spirit... Lastly He arranged (*hayyaʾa*) the human, rational soul in the brain, and He lodged it [the brain] in the highest location and most appropriate station. He adorned it [the brain] with Thinking (*fikr*), memory, and recollection, and gave the intellectual substance power over it, that it might be as it were commander with the faculties as soldiers and the Common Sense as courier ... who would then deliver [the information collected], sealed and enveloped, to the faculty of the intellect, to discriminate and choose what accorded with it, and to reject what was contrary to it.

The language throughout this brief essay is admittedly metaphorical, and the context is decidedly homiletic and expository rather than analytical, but even so, one might wish that less compromising words had been chosen. For it can hardly be denied that even a serious reading of the passage could easily come to the conclusion that saying that God *arranged* the rational soul *in* the brain and then *lodged* the brain *in* the highest part of the body is tantamount to saying that God *created* the rational soul *in* the brain, which would make the rational soul subsist through and in a bodily organ and thus contradict directly one of Avicenna's most cherished beliefs.[16] Avicenna, however, does not say "*created* in the brain" but "*arranged* in the brain." The word he uses is *hayya'a*, which literally means to make something ready, set it up, for a specific purpose or use. Thus what he says is that the rational soul was set up for operation in the brain — to control, that is, all the other faculties of the brain, as he says further down in the passage — and not that it was created with the brain as its substratum. Avicenna is referring here to his well-known position that the rational soul has two activities, the government (*siyāsa*) of the body and intellection.[17]

The second factor relating to the problem whether thinking is a function of the animal or rational soul is Avicenna's following, in this as in many other matters in his theory of the soul, Aristotle's text in the *De anima* within an emanationist noetics that derives from Neoplatonism. In the *De anima* Aristotle states that "the soul never thinks without an image," and "that which can think, therefore, thinks the forms in images" (43la16-17 and 431b2).[18] If, then, the thinking process inevitably involves images, and images can only be found stored in the front ventricle of the brain, in the *muṣawwira* or *khayāl*, the Image-bearing faculty of the animal soul, then thinking would appear to be related to, or somehow to be a function of, the animal soul. And this is what must have led Avicenna to identify the Imagining faculty (*al-mutakhayyila*), which is situated in the middle ventricle of the brain and whose function is to shuffle images — combine and separate them in order to arrive at new configurations — also as the Cogitative faculty (al-*mufakkira*) when used by the rational soul. But if the Cogitative faculty is conceived also as corporeal and as a faculty of the animal soul, the problem then becomes where it can find the intelligibles which are the indivisible thoughts of the active intellect and the intellects of the heavenly spheres. Avicenna himself posed this question in commenting upon the very passage from Aristotle's *De anima*:

[12] From *Marginal Glosses on Aristotle's De anima*, p. 110.13-18 Badawī.[19]

The Easterners said: [The answers to the following questions] should be sought from the books of the Easterners: 1)

> Whether (a) the contemplation (*mulāḥaẓa*) by the intellective soul (*an-nafs al-ʿāqila*) of the images [in the Image-bearing faculty] takes place with the help of the active intellect in the sense that it[20] receives the intelligibles from the Image-bearing faculty, or (b) the intellective soul becomes predisposed, by reason of the Image-bearing faculty and through somehow being acted upon by it, to receive[21] from the active intellect the intelligibles which correspond to those found in the Image-bearing faculty. 2) How it [the intellect][22] turns away from its intelligibles: either (a) because[23] they are stored in a storage place different from [the intellect] that asks to review them, as are the images [in the Image-bearing faculty], or (b) because the intellect comes into contact with the active intellect in a way that it is receptive [to some matters][24] while it withdraws from it in other matters.

This passage is a comment on the Aristotelian text in *De anima* III.7 which ends with the conclusion that the thinking faculty (*to noêtikon*) thinks the forms in images (431b2). Avicenna refers the reader to the Eastern texts, i.e., to his own book *The Easterners* where he discusses, in passages verbatim identical to those in *The Cure* and *The Salvation*, the questions he poses.[25] These questions are two, and in each case he gives two alternative and opposing solutions; in both cases the answer he favors is the second.

Avicenna identifies here the two most important questions in his theory of intellection: how intellection occurs, i.e., the precise mechanism of the thinking process, and the provenance, or locus, of the thoughts — the intelligibles — that are the objects of this process. It is best to start with the second which will lead us to the first.

In the De anima part of *The Cure*, which is the one work in which the process of intellection is described with the greatest detail, Avicenna follows an expository plan that proceeds from the material analysis of the soul to the immaterial, from the base to the nobler. In the second book he discusses the vegetative soul and then the animal soul and the senses except sight; in the third he discusses sight, singled out because it is more difficult to account for, because it is the highest of the senses, and because it provides an analogy to intellection. In the fourth book he discusses the internal senses, as described above, and finally in the fifth he discusses intellection. Certainly this progression is also to be found in Aristotle's *De anima*, but Avicenna's argument is much more tightly knit than that of Aristotle, at least in the state in which the latter's work has been historically transmitted. In the fourth book he discusses the internal senses and, in that context, the depositories of their objects: images are stored in the front part of the brain, connotative concepts in the rear, in memory. This is possible because the internal senses of Imagining and Estimation are faculties of the animal soul and hence have a physical substratum. In the fifth book, while discussing the intellect, the same question is raised with regard to the objects of intellection: where are the intelligibles stored?[26] Avicenna gives four possible solutions and then goes on to refute three of them. They cannot be "stored" in the human intellect because being stored in the intellect means that they are actually being thought by it; they cannot be stored in the body; and they cannot be independently subsisting, like Platonic ideas. This leaves as the only alternative that they are stored in the active intellect in the sense that it is always constantly intellecting them; this is what is meant by calling the active intellect pure actuality.[27] From this it follows that whenever the human intellect wants to think an intelligible, it will have to get it from the active intellect. This is the basis of Avicenna's concept of the emanation of the intelligibles — the "divine effluence" (*al-fayḍ al-ilāhī*) he keeps talking about — from the active intellect: *the philosophical problem behind it is trying to find a place for the intelligibles.*

If this is their storage place, this has consequences on how they are acquired, i.e., on intellection, which is the first of the two questions identified in his comment on the Aristotelian passage mentioned above. Intelligibles as propositions forming the conclusions of syllogisms can be acquired from the active intellect through hitting upon the middle term of the syllogism; i.e., through Intuition, as defined in the standard version.[28]

IV

This formulation, for all its merits in presenting an integrated epistemological theory that accounted even for prophecy within the

Aristotelian explanatory paradigm of the faculties of the soul, nevertheless lacked a certain precision in explaining the structure of the thinking process, generated the philosophical problem of the location of Thinking and Intuition (whether in the rational or animal soul), and even had serious consequences for eschatology, as follows:

1. If the intelligibles can be acquired only through obtaining the middle term of a syllogism (**Text 2**, §2), and if the middle term can be Discovered only through Intuition (**Text 2**, §2), then the intelligibles can be acquired only through Intuition.

2. If the intelligibles can be acquired only through Intuition, and if Intuition is included as part, or as the last stage, of the thinking process or Thought (*fikra*) (**Text 9**), then the intelligibles can only be acquired through Thinking.

3. If the intelligibles can only be acquired through Thinking, and if Thinking is a function of the Cogitative faculty of the animal soul (*mufakkira*) and hence a bodily faculty which dies with the body, then the intelligibles cannot be acquired after death.

But this conclusion is absurd, for the *only* thing that the rational soul does after the death of the body is to contemplate the intelligibles. Therefore, if this unacceptable conclusion is arrived at by considering Intuition as part of the Thinking process, then Intuition, *ḥads*, had to be dissociated from Thinking, *fikr*, and Thinking had to be better defined.

This very question, as stated in §3 above, was posed either by Bahmanyār or Abū-Manṣūr Ibn-Zayla, and answered by Avicenna along these lines, as follows:

[7*] From *al-Mubāḥathāt* §§234-238 Bīdārfar[29]

1. Question in the hand of [Bahmanyār or Ibn-Zayla]: The intellective faculty cannot avoid using Thought (*fikra*) when learning and remembering — and worse, even when intellecting that it has intellected! So how will it be able to perceive after the separation [of the soul from the body upon death), when this faculty [of Thought] ceases to exist?

2. Answer in the hand of [Avicenna]. God forbid that it [the intellect] should have to use the Cogitative faculty (*mufakkira*)

which searches for the middle term! The reason for this is that learning occurs in two ways: One is by way of Intuition, which consists of the middle term occurring to the Mind without search and thus being obtained, along with the conclusion [of the syllogism]; the second is through contrived means and [after] search.

3. Intuition is a divine effluence and an intellectual contact taking place without any act of acquisition at all. Some people may reach such a stage [of consummate Intuition] that they almost have no need of Thinking (*fikr*) in most of what they learn, and possess the sacred faculty of the soul.[30]

4. When the soul has reached a sublime stage, acquired the excellent [sacred] faculty, and separated from the body, it attains whatever is attained There, where all distractions vanish, faster than through Intuition: the intellectual world presents itself to the [soul] according to the essential, not temporal order of the terms of propositions and of the intelligibles,[31] and this takes place all at once.

5. There is need for Thinking (*fikr*) [in this world] only because the soul is turbid, or because it has had little training and is impotent to attain the divine effluence, or because of distractions. Were it not for this, the soul would obtain certain knowledge about everything to the farthest reaches of truth.

In all likelihood this exchange between Avicenna and his disciples marks the beginning of his transition from the standard version of his theory of Intuition to the revised one. It is to be noted that in describing the two ways in which learning can occur (§2) he does not identify the second; he merely says that it comes about through contrived means (*ḥīla*) and after search (*ṭalab*); in all likelihood he had not yet arrived at the unambiguous identification of Thinking as the second way which he gives in *Pointers* (**Text 6**, §3). "Contrived means" is general enough to accommodate, if necessary, both instruction, the second way of the standard version, and any activities that may fall under the general rubric of thinking. Furthermore, he appears to be unsure about "searching" (*ṭalab*) for the middle term, i.e., the conscious decision to go after it. Here he denies it to Intuition, perhaps as a first reaction to the question posed to him, in order to enhance the spontaneous and instantaneous nature of Intuition and thus better to differentiate it from Thinking. In Pointers, however, he is more modulated (and accurate), and recognizes two kinds of the redefined Intuition: one that includes search and one that apparently does not (**Text 6**, §8).

What Avicenna unambiguously does do in this exchange, though, is to differentiate clearly and forcefully between Thinking and Intuition (§§3, 5). That the motivation to do so was eschatological, as noted above, is clear from the detailed description of the soul's acquisition of the intelligibles after death (§4). Also what is effected in this new formulation is that the single way of the standard version to attain the middle terms, Intuition, is split into two, Intuition and Thinking (§2, "the Cogitative faculty which searches for the middle term"). This enhances the role of Thinking in the cogitative process and immediately raises anew and with greater urgency the problem of its nature (how Thinking works) and status (whether Thinking is a faculty of the animal or rational soul), especially as Avicenna appears to be using terminology relating to thinking interchangeably: the student asks about Thought (§1, *fikra*), Avicenna begins his answer (§2) as if he took Thought to be identical with the Cogitative faculty (*mufakkira*), and sums up his answer (§5) by talking about Thinking (*fikr*). A number of questions in the *Discussions* revolve around this issue. In the following exchange, a very similar question to the preceding one is asked concerning the status of Thinking in the context of eschatological concerns:

[13] From *al-Mubāḥathāt* §150-154 Bīdārfar[32]

1. Question in the hand of [Bahmanyār or Ibn-Zayla]: Granted that that which brings the [human] intellect from potentiality to actuality is an[other] intellect, as it has been Verified among us. But what is the proof that the [intellect] makes contact with it [i.e., the other, active intellect] after it separates [from the body]? For in this life, as it can be seen, it can barely make any contact with it except after careful examination of the forms in the Image-bearing faculty [*khayāl*] I and through application of Thought [*fikra*] — indeed, it seems as if Thought is what brings about a relationship between it and the separate [active intellect]. Why, then, is [the intellect] in such a state in this life and is

brought into actuality by [the active intellect] under this condition, while after it has separated [from the body] it will have dispensed with Thought?

2. Answer in the hand of [Avicenna]. Our intellect does not need the Image-bearing faculty every time it comes into contact with the separate [active intellect] but only when it seeks for the first time to acquire the primary universal concepts [*taṣawwurāt*]. On occasion it also seeks the assistance of the Image-bearing faculty with regard to some of its [the intellect's] activities by keeping it too busy to offer any opposition [to,] and in order to ensure its participation [in, its own project],[33] as [the intellect] does in the course of considering geometrical problems when it also carefully examines sensible figures.

3. This seeking of assistance, though, is useful, not necessary, and it concerns [only] questions that have to do either with real sensibles or a mixture [of sensibles and non-sensibles]. He who has a powerful intellect, however, may reject this and not seek the assistance of the senses, and sometimes he may even reject [the senses] together with the Image-bearing faculty and not individuate the concept [under examination] either as a sensible entity or an imaginable entity.[34] The person who constructs a syllogism all by himself[35] deals with the universal terms for his syllogism, definition, and description — terms that are not the objects of the Imagining faculty. The person who is granted a penetrating Intuition, the middle terms occur to him all at once, without search or Thinking (*fikr*), and without seeking the assistance of any faculties other than those of the intellect.

4. Not every contact [with the active intellect] comes about only through seeking the assistance of the Image-bearing faculty, nor does every human soul, upon separation [from the body], make contact with the separate [active intellect], but [only] when it has already acquired [during life] the capacity for this contact. The question of demarcating this capacity and when it occurs is considered somewhat difficult; perhaps [it occurs] when it has become easy for one to conceptualize all by himself[36] the concepts that are separate from matter.

Avicenna's answer here is important because it specifies the two different kinds of thinking that he was eventually to recognize, one in the animal soul and the other in the intellect. The student, first of all, asks him specifically about Thought (*fikra*), which he considers essential for the process of acquiring the intelligibles. Avicenna, however, in his answer talks almost exclusively about the Image-bearing faculty, *khayāl*. This would seem to indicate that he had in mind the operations in the animal soul of the Cogitative faculty (*mufakkira*), which is identical with the Imagining faculty (*mutakhayyila*), whose function is indeed dealing with the images in the Image-bearing faculty (*khayāl*). This kind of thinking by the Cogitative/Imagining faculty *in the animal soul* is important and useful in aiding the intellect to hit upon the intelligibles or middle terms, but it is not necessary. Some people with powerful intellects can think directly in terms of the universals, i.e., the intelligibles, without needing to "individuate" them, i.e., to represent them as particular entities and hence as sensible and imaginable entities. The example that Avicenna gives about geometry is telling, and he will use it elsewhere again (below, **Text 15**, §§2-3). One can think of the universal concept "circle" without having to look at an "individuated" circle drawn on the board. This person then can construct a syllogism "all by himself (*mustaqill*)," unaided by the senses and imagination, but dealing purely with the universal concepts that make up the terms of his syllogism and his definitions. This is a second kind of thinking and it takes place necessarily only in the rational soul, the intellect. As for Intuition, Avicenna defines it according to his revised version: it discovers the middle term all at once without search or any kind of Thinking (*fikr*), and without the help of any faculties other than those of the intellect. In this fashion Avicenna has clearly differentiated Intuition from Thinking in order to avoid the eschatological impossibility or impass mentioned earlier and asked about by the student.

The delineation of the two kinds of thinking in this and similar passages and the continuing imprecision in the terminology of thinking generated further questions in the minds of his students. One of them wanted to ascertain whether the second kind of thinking, that in the rational soul, was in fact a contact with the active intellect:

[**14**] From *al-Mubāḥathāt* §595 Bīdārfar

1. Question. If Thinking (*fikr*) is the search for perfect predisposition for contact with the [active intellect], in the sense that when [the rational soul][37] thinks and acquires knowledge it is up to it to effect this contact whenever it wishes, then how does error occur? how does it [the soul][38] withdraw from [the active intellect]? and how does it return to it?

2. Answer. Thinking (*fikr*) needs to come in contact with the principles[39] in order to bring forward (*iḥḍār*) definitions and to form concepts (*taṣawwur*) of them, and in order to bring forward the middle [terms]. But the function of combining (*tarkīb*) is up to it, and sometimes it does [it] well and sometimes badly.

This question would appear to have been occasioned by the passage in *Pointers* stating the revised version of Intuition (**Text 6**, § 7), where the variable success of thinking is mentioned. Avicenna's answer, however, is elliptical: what is the Thinking faculty combining? Combination (*tarkīb*) and separation of sensory and conceptual images are the proper functions of the Imaginative and Cogitative (*mufakkira*) faculty of the animal soul. The use of this word (*tarkīb*) here to explain where Thinking might err would suggest that Avicenna has in mind Thinking in terms of the animal soul. However, what is Thinking combining here? The immediate context would seem to indicate that it is combining these very terms which it "brought forward" from the active intellect in order to form conclusions. But these terms are intelligibles, i.e., universal concepts, and as such they cannot be thought by a faculty with material substrate like the Cogitative faculty of the animal soul. Either therefore the Thinking faculty referred to here belongs to the intellect (the rational soul), or else Avicenna is indeed talking about the Cogitative faculty of the animal soul, in which case he is not answering the question about errors concerning the intelligibles that the questioner asked. But it is clear that he is talking about the intellect's Thinking faculty: for he says that "Thinking needs to come in contact with the principles," and such contact, which means actually receiving the intelligibles, can only be accomplished by an indivisible and immaterial substance, the intellect or the rational soul. This is also indicated by his use of the word *taṣawwur*, forming concepts (by means of definitions), which together with *taṣdīq* (granting assent to a statement by means of a syllogism), constitutes all intelligible knowledge, as Avicenna never tires of repeating in his logical works.[40] What *taṣawwur* does is to bring to Mind definitions and terms; combining them to form syllogisms to whose conclusions one would give assent would appear to be the implication of the second half of the sentence, and it is here that Thinking may go wrong. All this activity of combining terms would naturally be the proper function of the rational soul, as stated in **Text 13**, §3. This point is also made explicitly in another passage in the *Discussions*, §10 below:

[**15**] From *al-Mubāḥathāt*, §§107-112 Bīdārfar[41]

1. Among [the questions raised by al-Kirmānī] is his statement about Intuition and his insistence that middle terms can only be found by means of Thinking (*fikr*). This is erroneous in many ways.

2. First, consummate (*bāligh*) Intuition is the appearance of a middle term [in the Mind] all at once without the [rational] soul searching for it by rummaging among images of others, until it is led to it in some fashion. This determination is something which is established by experience; most frequently it becomes obvious to skilled geometers.

3. The reason is that people vary in [their ability to] figure things out. [3a] There are those to whom the middle term at times appears unexpectedly, as they are setting up the problem, and they find the solution. [3b] At other times they may have [set up the problem and] spent some time passing in mental review images of thought, and they failed, so they tended to relax and ease off, when all of a sudden the middle term appeared to them. [3c] At still other times they may not even have set up a problem when all of a sudden there appeared to their souls a concept, which arranged itself in association with a term [of a syllogism] and became a conclusion, as if it were a gift from God that had not been asked for.

4. Another class of people need to do little Thinking and need to spend little time among images.

5. Another class need to do a lot of Thinking before they can

perceive.

6. Yet another class need someone to instruct them from outside, and even then their Thinking produces no results except rarely.

7. Now these classes [of people] do exist; it is just inexperienced people who would deny them. For only experience is sufficient for [settling] something which requires experience to be resolved.

8. Second, [al-Kirmānī's position is wrong] because he made the fatigue which he experiences when thinking (*tafakkur*) into an argument valid for the [entire] world. In this regard he is nothing else but like the person who can digest only with the help of digestive medication and so comes to the conclusion that the [rest of the] world also can digest only with the help of digestives.

9. Third: Even if we were to grant that there is no way for us in this world of ours to perceive anything except through learning or Thinking, this would not necessitate that such is the practice of the [rational] soul[42] in its every [form of] existence. Perhaps as long as the soul is with the body it has an adversary in the Imagining faculty (*takhayyul*) with regard to everything that it engages in,[43] and if it [the soul][44] seeks to be partners with it in whatever relates to its [own] activity, it will be easy for it to remain engaged in its proper activity — and on occasion the [adversary] might even help — but if it does not seek to be partners with it in whatever relates to its [own] activity, it will be distracted and hindered — just like the rider of a recalcitrant animal. It thus needs to seek its partnership and the help of its company. But when it separates [after death] from the partner who had been a hindrance, having acquired the positive disposition [*malaka*] to perform [its proper activity], it will be entirely independent of others. No attention, therefore, should be paid to this [issue] at all; rather what should be asked is whether the [rational] soul in itself can act or be acted upon and receive a form, and for which reason it proceeds from potentiality to actuality. If this is correct [i.e., if the rational soul does have its own proper activity], then no attention need be paid to any concomitant impediments and

opposition. If it is not correct, then the matter remains unresolved, unrelated to whatever [the rational soul] may undergo from its partnership with the Imagining faculty, but rather is dependent only on irrefutable proof invalidating [the claim] that the soul has no proper activity.

10. Finally, you must know that combining (*tarkīb*) universal terms [as propositions of a syllogism] is not something that is apt to be done through faculties or organs of the body, even if the ready willingness of these faculties to imitate this [combining] by means of particular images — as geometers do with their boards and stylus — is useful.

The last paragraph here makes it quite certain that the combining (*tarkīb*) that Avicenna mentions in the preceding passage (**Text 14**, §2), the one which can go wrong, is in fact done by the intellect.[45] The reason is that the combining, or any handling, of intelligibles cannot be done by a corporeal faculty — the reference here is to the Cogitative faculty (*mufakkira*) — or an organ of the body, i.e., the middle ventricle of the brain, because the substratum of the immaterial intelligibles can be neither material, nor divisible, nor finite.[46] So what Avicenna is necessarily doing here (as he did also in **Text 13**) is *setting up two parallel processes of thinking*, one in the rational soul and the other in the animal. The function of the former is to combine universal propositions or terms to form syllogisms[47] and reach conclusions — essentially, what we call plain reasoning — only that it takes place necessarily in the intellect because of the immaterial nature of the concepts involved, the intelligibles. The function of the second process in the animal soul, that of the Cogitative faculty, is to combine conceptual images of particulars *in imitation of* (*muḥākāt*) the process in the intellect for the purpose of aiding it. Particulars and their images are always at hand, whereas the intelligibles are not; one therefore starts with what is available — like the geometer drawing his diagrams — in order to proceed to correct conceptualization and reach the abstract solution. The function of the Cogitative faculty thus is useful, as Avicenna says, like the geometrical diagrams, but it is imitative and hence derivative; the real thinking with the real intelligibles takes place in the rational soul.

The reference to the geometers in this passage (as in **Text 13**, §2 and in **Text 10**, §3) provides interesting clues for the development of Avicenna's thinking on these issues. It would appear from his detailed description of the experience of geometers in the process of solving their problems that it was his own experience with geometry that gave him the original idea, if not of Intuition immediately, then at least of the basic concept that some things occur to us "out of the blue," as it were. In other words, regardless of what he may have read in Aristotle, his experience with finding the geometrical proof all of a sudden and unexpectedly – his description of someone giving up and then having the solution occur to him suddenly is telling – may have been the deciding factor for him to formulate his theory, for which he then found happily the authority of Aristotle in the *Posterior Analytics*. As he says in his Autobiography,

> As for the *Elements* of Euclid, I read the first five or six propositions with him [an-Nātilī], and thereafter undertook on my own to solve the entire remainder of the book. Next I moved on to the *Almagest* and when I had finished its introductory sections and reached the geometrical figures, an-Nātilī said to me, "Take over reading and solving them by yourself"... Then ... I occupied myself on my own with Determining the Validity of books, both original texts and commentaries, on Physics and Metaphysics, and the gates of the Philosophical Sciences began opening for me.[48]

This experience of having something occur to him "out of the blue" may also be at the basis of his theory of the active intellect as the locus or "storage area" of all the intelligibles (mentioned above at the end of Section III). The experience is indeed startling: one has a problem; after hours of work he gives up and moves on to something else; some time later, when he may have even forgotten about the problem, the answer just occurs to him. Where did the answer come from? This is more difficult to account for than any other kind of conceptualization like axiomatic truths (they are so obvious that the question of their provenance is not immediately problematic) or abstraction (one starts from a concrete specimen and then can almost hear himself think through to the abstract concept). The answer then obviously came out of the blue, and Avicenna had no difficulty identifying the "blue" with the active intellect, given the noetic ontology of the emanationist schema with which he was working. He almost says as much in *Philosophy for ʿAlāʾ-ad-Dawla* (*Dāneshnāma*, **Text 5**, §3): "There may also be a person ... who can attain whenever he wishes the sciences from beginning to end in order of Intuition without a teacher and in very little time ... and *therefore believes that this knowledge is being poured into his heart from one place*;" i.e., the experience is so strong that the only explanation would appear to be that the knowledge is coming from somewhere else, and, by elimination, the somewhere else must be up above; and Avicenna concludes, "and perhaps this is what the truth is."

To return to the discussion about thinking: the dual process of thinking, conducted both by the rational soul and the animal soul, is explicitly stated by Avicenna in an answer to a related question, a question which spells out the very reasoning given by him in **Text 15**, §10:

> [**16**] From *al-Mubāḥathāt* §§252-255 Bīdārfar
>
> 1. Question in the hand of [Bahmanyār or Ibn-Zayla]. Which faculty other than the intellect employs constantly the Cogitative faculty (*al-mufakkira*) so that it will not slacken from its movement? For I estimate that none other than the intellect employs this faculty. The reason is that concepts with which this faculty [the Cogitative] deals are not things that come about in bodily faculties: things like opinions (even if they are false), consideration of consequences, affection toward relatives, managing particular activities, and dealing with premisses which pertain to the Estimative faculty. Now all these in reality do not come about in a bodily organ, so how could there come about in such an organ our beliefs that everything created-in-time must be preceded by time, that death does not apply to the soul, and that the individuals of every species — as well as the species itself — exist after (in a temporal sense) not having existed before? These are [all] universal concepts to which a bodily faculty does not apply; and if there is another faculty that is appropriate, then this one also is not bodily.
>
> 2. Answer in the hand of Avicenna. When the intellective fac-

ulty desires an intelligible form, by nature it entreats the donor principle [i.e., the active intellect]. If the form flows upon it by way of Intuition, then it is spared the trouble; otherwise it has recourse to movements of other faculties whose nature it is to prepare it to receive the effluence. This is on account of a special influence which they [the other faculties] have upon the soul and of a similarity between the soul and some of the forms which exist in the realm of effluence [i.e., the celestial spheres]. Thus it acquires after much trouble what [otherwise] would not have been acquired except through Intuition.

3. If by 'Thinking faculty' (*al-quwwa al-fikriyya*) is meant the one that searches, then it is the rational soul[49] as the dispositional intellect (*in habitu*), especially when its purpose with going beyond[50] the [state of] positive disposition is to attain perfection. But if what is meant by it is the faculty that presents the forms and is in motion,[51] then this is the Imagining faculty insofar as it is in motion upon the instigation of the intellectual faculty.

By this stage the revised version of Thinking and Intuition is fully in place. Intuition is now reserved only for what was formerly Acumen, the immediate discovery of the middle term, which spares the person who has it the trouble of going through the thinking process. Thinking, by contrast, is the discovery of the middle term by the rational soul as a result of search, while Thinking in terms of the Cogitative faculty of the animal soul is preliminary movements among conceptual images at the instigation of the rational soul. In this way the animal soul is again assisting the rational soul, as Avicenna describes in detail in *The Cure* (*De anima* 221-222 Rahman). It is important to notice that Thinking by the rational soul is the process which leads to the discovery or reception of the middle term, i.e., what brings about the contact with the active intellect. In the standard version of the Intuition theory, contact with the active intellect meant discovering the middle term, and it was defined only as Intuition (**Text 2**, §§2-3), which varied in speed and frequency according to the individual; in the revised version, contact with the active intellect still means discovering the middle term, but in this case it is defined both as the result of Intuition, redefined as instantaneous discovery of the middle term, *and* as the result of Thinking, the laborious process for those who do not have Intuition. In essence the two versions say essentially the same thing, viz., all intelligible knowledge comes from the acquisition of the middle term; the difference is in the redefined, more restricted concept of Intuition, which does not involve Thinking, and the enlarged role assigned to Thinking. The change was brought about by Avicenna, as mentioned earlier, in order to dissociate thinking from Intuition and allow for the possibility for the trained soul to contemplate the intelligibles after death without having to think.

A major development in the revised version, in the sense that it had never been explicitly expressed by Avicenna before, is the statement in **Text 16**, §3 above that Thinking belongs to the intellect at the level of dispositional intellect (*in habitu*). In other words, what brings the dispositional intellect to the level of acquired intellect (i.e., to the "perfection" Avicenna is referring to in this passage) is precisely Thinking. In the standard version, it is understood that this was done by Intuition (**Text 2**, §1). As already mentioned, the difference is only terminological because Thinking in the revised version does most of what Intuition did in the standard, i.e., hit upon middle terms. But it is nevertheless a very significant difference in emotional appeal and philosophical clarity. Intuition, regardless of its technical definition, is a difficult concept upon which to build an entire epistemological system, which may also explain why it was never fully appreciated by both medieval and modern scholars. Thinking is not; it is the most human of our faculties and one which is expected to lead the way in any epistemology.

The enhanced role which Thinking assumes in the revised version also required numerous explanations by Avicenna in order to specify its precise nature. A final passage from the *Discussions* gives a very detailed account of Thinking, again at the request for precision by a disciple.

[**17**] From *al-Mubāḥathāt* §§599-601 Bīdārfar

1. Question. In some passage [Avicenna] made the determination that when the [rational soul] is divested of the body and has no more connection with anything but its own realm, the activities and ideas which it has then are only those which are appropriate for that realm — which is the realm of the soul's con-

tact with the principles which contain the configuration (*hay'a*) of all existence. This realm is imprinted on the soul, which does not need any longer to engage in any activity such as Thinking (*fikr*) or remembering in order to attain perfection thereby — as a matter of fact the impression of all existence is imprinted on it so that the soul does not need to seek any other impression. What is the explanation of this?

2. Answer. Middle terms and what is analogous to them are not acquired by means of Thinking (*fikr*) in the same way as one acquires something whose location and method [of acquisition] are known, but rather in the way in which one prepares a snare to track down whatever may happen to fly in the vicinity of the possible; the instruction provided in the book of syllogisms[52] is instruction for preparing the snares and approaching[53] the place where one expects [the middle terms to lie]. Had [their acquisition] come about in the former way [mentioned above], then one would have been able to reach the middle terms whenever one wished. To the contrary, Thinking is a kind of entreaty which paves the way for the response, or for the reception of the effluence which corresponds to the two extreme terms [of a syllogism] represented in the Mind, or their likes. Middle terms come only from the divine effluence. Sometimes they come through Intuition, without Thinking having inspected any [such] correspondences, and sometimes they come without any attention having been paid even to the two extreme terms.

3. The less a soul travels in the realm of the intelligibles, the less it can track down middle terms and their likes, while the more practice it has with such traveling, the more successful it is with tracking them down and the easier it is for them to come suddenly upon the soul. This impeding [of the soul from tracking down the middle terms] comes only from the body; it is to be expected, then, that when the predisposition [to hit upon the middle term] becomes perfect and the impediment disappears, it will be most easy.

4. This tracking down is nothing else but a kind of contact of the soul with the principles.[54] Sometimes it is easy for a single

> soul to perceive a number of middle terms simultaneously. So it is not unlikely that a happy soul might accomplish unobstructed contact with the separate [active intellect], because obstruction occurs either on account of loss of predisposition [for contact] or on account of something that impedes. As for the substance that is being acted upon [i.e., the human rational soul] and the substance that acts [i.e., the active intellect], [in themselves] they do not bring about necessarily any obstruction; and whenever there is no impediment, perfect contact occurs and [the human intellect] receives something like the impression of [the active intellect].

Noteworthy in this passage is the striking image of the snares that Avicenna introduces to represent the Thinking that is done by the intellect. Preparing syllogisms, i.e., identifying the extreme terms, major and minor, in order to figure out the middle term, is likened to setting snares to catch the prey. This tracking down of the prey, the process of Thinking which discovers the middle terms, is itself a kind of contact with the active intellect (§3). The other kind is Intuition, which catches the prey without Thinking. As in the *Pointers* passage of the revised version (**Text 6**, §8), there are two sorts of Intuition. One is the result of a search for the middle term: the extreme terms of a syllogism have been set up but no further Thinking has taken place; the other occurs without even a search. These two kinds also correspond to the levels in §3a and §3c in Avicenna's example from geometry in **Text 15** (and §3b is presumably of the same category as either the one or the other). The revised version of Avicenna's theory of Intuition thus shows remarkable consistency in the passages that have been discussed in this study. It also appears, finally, in Avicenna's last work, *On the Rational Soul* (**Text 8**, §3); and this leads us to the final subject that needs to be discussed.

V

The evolution of Avicenna's thought about Intuition and Thinking as presented in the preceding pages has an interesting relevance to the chronology of Avicenna's works. What I have called the standard and revised versions are clearly incompatible and they cannot both be maintained simultaneously; they are sequential. All the evidence analyzed from the *Discussions* points to an internal development of the theory that follows the sequence I have laid out: first the standard version in *The Cure* complex of works, and then the revised version in *Pointers*, a sequence which is also conformable to the traditional dating of *Pointers* after *The Cure*. In recent works, J. Michot has argued that *Pointers* antedates *The Cure*, or at least some parts of it, dating it before 1020.[55] If this is true, then the revised version would be prior chronologically, and the standard version subsequent. Such an assumption, however, goes against the nature of the discussions in the *Discussions*. Had the revised version been prior, in which Avicenna clearly states that Thinking and Intuition are separate, there would have been no point to the questions posed by the students, as discussed above. Similarly, since Avicenna's answers in the *Discussions* consistently represent the revised version in *Pointers*, and if *Pointers* is to be dated before 1020, then the *Discussions* also is to be dated before 1020, which would be quite difficult to accept.

More decisive, however, is the congruence on the subject of Intuition between *Pointers* and Avicenna's last work, *On the Rational Soul*. They both say virtually the identical thing (cf. **Text 6**, §§7-8 with **Text 8**, §3). Now *On the Rational Soul* is dated unambiguously to Avicenna's last few years.[56] Since *Pointers* and *On the Rational Soul* agree on the subject of Intuition, i.e., they both have the revised version, then if *Pointers* is dated to before 1020, this would mean that Avicenna first held the revised version, then switched to the standard version, and at the end of his life switched back to the revised version. This is quite unacceptable, and the traditional late dating of *Pointers* stands.

VI

Avicenna fully subscribed to the reality of the active intellect as the eternal substance, ontologically prior to us, which makes our potential powers of thinking actual by being itself incessantly an actual thinker and hence the real "locus" of all intelligibles, or all thoughts actually being thought. The principle behind this idea is that for something to exist potentially in something it must exist actually in something else — a principle which Avicenna uses in connection with prophecy in the *Proof of Prophecies*[57] — and it is analogous to his core conception of necessary and contingent being: just as we are contingent beings because there is a necessary being — and in *that* sense being emanates to us therefrom — so also are we potential thinkers because there is an actual thinker — and in *that* sense thoughts emanate to us therefrom.

This is the ontological basis for our capacity to think; but valuable as it is for what it does, it was never meant by Avicenna to substitute for the psychological and epistemological accounts of *how* we think, as some modern interpreters tend to believe. The cognitive processes described by Avicenna as "preparatory" for the reception of the intelligibles are not mere metaphors, and neither is one of them, abstraction, a *façon de parler*.[58] For Avicenna just as certainly also subscribed to the reality, and indeed, necessity, of the cognitive processes: these range from Thinking in terms of images in the animal soul, through abstraction, through Thinking in terms of universals in the rational soul, and culminate with hitting upon the middle terms, with Intuition and Acumen. All these are real and necessary processes, given our corporeal existence, and indeed, the only available processes for thinking.

All these cognitive processes arc necessarily real in Avicenna for at least two reasons. First, without them we would have been unable to acquire the intelligibles at all, emanation or no emanation; our corporeality makes it impossible for the rational soul to acquire intelligibles unaided by thinking (**Text 7***, §5), except in the very rare case of prophets. Also, emanation, precisely because it is an ontological principle and not a psychological or epistemological one, is inert; it must be "activated" by thinking.[59]

The second reason is eschatological. Thinking gives meaning to punishment after death. An evil person follows his Estimation in pursuing false goals and as such never trains his rational soul to acquire the intelligibles which actualize it or perfect it. After death, when only the rational soul survives, it realizes its shortcomings and wishes to undo the damage:

But this happens to the [rational] soul when the instruments used

> to attain the acquired intellect, such as the external and inner senses, Estimation, memory, and Thinking, have been corrupted. The individual thus remains longing for the soul's natural activity of acquiring the things by which it realizes its essence [i.e., the intelligibles], at a time when none of the instruments for such an acquisition exists. What greater calamity can there be, particularly that the [rational] soul continues eternally in this state?[60]

This passage, together with §4 of **Text 13**, give the context within which to understand Avicenna's objection (in **Text 7***, §2) that the rational soul does not need Thinking after death in order to come into contact with the active intellect. This is true *only if* the rational soul has already acquired, while in the body, the capacity for this contact (**Text 13**, §4); otherwise, it is too late and nothing can be done about it. This means (a) that this contact (*ittiṣāl*) is not automatic, *regardless of emanation*, even after death, when there is no body to encumber the rational soul, much less before, and (b) that even for the rational souls which acquired the capacity for this contact, Thinking was a necessary precondition for them to get to that stage (with the exception of the prophets), again, regardless of emanation. Thinking, therefore, both in the rational and animal soul, is absolutely essential in Avicenna's epistemology also from the point of view of eschatology.

It would have been a cruel joke indeed on humans if acquiring the intelligibles — which is the prerequisite for a happy rational soul after death — depended on, or was initiated by, the emanation from the active intellect and then the individual person was punished after death for not having acquired the intelligibles! Thus thinking, and acquiring the intelligibles through one's free will while one still has the instruments wherewith to accomplish this, is what gives meaning to Avicenna's eschatology and ensures the bliss of the soul after death, adding a twist to the Aristotelian concept of happiness (*eudaimonia*).

Neoplatonist ontology, Aristotelian psychology and ethics, and eschatology are but three of the disparate elements which are here amazingly synthesized to create a consistent epistemological theory based on Thinking and Intuition. The philosophy of Avicenna is capacious and inclusive, to say nothing about rigorous; so must our thinking about it be.

Notes

1. See D. Gutas, *Avicenna and the Aristotelian Tradition*, Leiden (Brill) 1988, 159-176, and the collection of passages on 161-166. Some of these questions are raised explicitly by M. Marmura in his review of my book (see his "Plotting the Course of Avicenna's Thought," *Journal of the American Oriental Society* 111 (1991) 333-342 at 336-337), and, indirectly, by H.A. Davidson's one-sided account of Intuition and Thinking in his *Alfarabi, Avicenna, and Averroes on Intellect*, Oxford (OUP) 1992, 99-102; however, only those questions directly relating to the structure and function of Intuition and Thinking can be discussed at this time. Goodman's discussion of Avicenna's epistemology in his *Avicenna*, London (Routledge) 1992, 129-149, written from the vantage point of the history of Western epistemology, does not go into the details of Intuition.
2. All bold face **Text** references are to these passages, the 8 that appeared in my *Avicenna* and the rest in this paper. Here I will follow again the convention of capitalizing in English those words which were used as technical terms by Avicenna.
3. For the chronology of Avicenna's life see my "Biography" of Avicenna in the *Encyclopaedia Iranica* III, 69b; the periodization of his literary production is given in my *Avicenna* 145. Most of the material pertaining to the chronology of Avicenna's life and works, together with the various views about it, have been recently collected in a booklet by M. Cruz Hernández, *La vida de Avicena como introducción a su pensamiento*, Salamanca (Anthema Ediciones) 1997, which also contains a new text and Spanish translation of the autobiography and biography.
4. See my "Avicenna's Eastern ('Oriental') Philosophy: Nature, Contents, Transmission," *Arabic Sciences and Philosophy* 10/2 (2000), 159-180.
5. The discrete responses by Avicenna in the *Mubāḥathāt* that are discussed below have an inner progression made apparent by the trend and direction of the argument. It should be noted, however, that this progression is not necessarily in itself, nor presented here as being, identical with the precise chronological sequence of the individual responses in that work, assuming such can be ascertained. It is chronological only in the sense that the initial states of the argument preceded the final ones, while the sequence of the intermediary states can be only roughly surmised, due to indeterminable factors: the responses by Avicenna were given over a lengthy period of time to at least two, if not more, students (Bahmanyār and Ibn-Zayla) who may have had different abilities, questions, and levels of access to Avicenna's favors. By the same token, however, the rough chronology indicated by the progression of the argument here is also a key factor in controlling any strict

chronological sequence of the individual discussions in the *Mubāḥathāt* that may be established by independent means. See now the discussion of the chronology of the *Mubāḥathāt* by D.C. Reisman, *Al-Mubāḥathāt: The Making of the Avicennan Tradition*, Leiden (Brill) 2002.

6. For the expression *ʿalā ashkālihi* used here cf. Avicenna's definition of the moon, *min sha'nihi an yaqbala n-nūra mina sh-shamsi ʿalā ashkālin mukhtalifatin*, "whose nature is to receive illumination from the sun according to various phases;" *Ḥudūd* no. 21, p. 27 Goichon. Cf. further the translations of this passage by Marmura and Hasse given in D.N. Hasse, "Das Lehrstück von den vier Intellekten in der Scholastik: von den arabischen Quellen bis zu Albertus Magnus," *Recherches de Théologie et Philosophie Médiévales* 66 (1999) 21-77 at 36 and note 37.
7. The spontaneous, according to Avicenna (following Aristotle's *Physics* II.6), is that whose beginning is natural (*mā bad'uhu ṭabīʿī*), i.e., inheres in the natural subject, and entails no will or volition: *ash-Shifā', as-Samāʿ aṭ-ṭabīʿī*, ed. S. Zayed, Cairo, 1983, 66.7-9.
8. Reflecting the Greek of Aristotle in the *Posterior Analytics, en askeptôi khronôi*, 89b10-11.
9. Cf. the French translation of this passage by J.R. Michot, *La destinée de l'homme selon Avicenne*, Louvain (Peeters) 1986, 83, note 91.
10. Avicenna is saying the same things here as he is in the contemporary passage from *The Cure*, **Text 2**. For the concepts of increase and decrease and highest and lowest points, and prophecy through intelligibles cf. §3 in **Text 2**. "Sacred faculty" refers to the material intellect in humans when it possesses the strongest possible predisposition to receive the intelligibles; see §1 in **Text 2**. A soul that "shines" (*mushriqa*) with the sacred faculty is thus one that is most apt to Intuit, through hitting upon the middle terms, all the intelligibles by itself. This is the meaning of *mushriqa* here (cf. *an yashtaʿila ḥadsan* in **Text 2**, §3, "blazes with Intuition"); Michot mistranslates the intransitive verb, "illuminées par la puissance sainte," which implies an outside divine agent illuminating the soul.
11. For example, in *De anima* 221.19 Rahman, Avicenna says that the senses provide the rational soul (*an-nafs an-nāṭiqa*) with particulars, and the Mind (*dhihn*) then "extracts from the particulars the individual universals;" here Mind is clearly identified either with the rational soul as a whole or with one of its functions, intellect. This is stated explicitly in the Metaphysics of *The Cure* where the same power to abstract universals from particulars is attributed to the intellect, *ʿaql*: (*Ilāhiyyāt* 205). In *De anima* 247.18 Rahman, he practically identifies Mind with intellect (*ʿaql*) by saying that an intelligible (*maʿqūl*) is "present in his Mind and depicted in his intellect;" see also **Text**

2, §2 (the Mind Discovers the middle term) and §3, first sentence. In *Pointers* (*Ishārāt*, **Text 6**, §4), Mind is identified with the acquired intellect because he describes it as when "the intelligibles come about actually in [the rational soul], observed and represented in the Mind;" and similarly in the same **Text 6**, §8, etc. Cf. also A.-M. Goichon, *Léxique de la langue philosophique d'Ibn Sīnā*, Paris (de Brouwer) 1938, No. 263, although the final paragraph of this entry would seem to place *dhihn* in the animal soul.

12. On Estimation see D. Black, "Estimation (*Wahm*) in Avicenna: The Logical and Psychological Dimensions," *Dialogue* 32 (1993) 219-258, and now D. Hasse's chapter in his *Avicenna's De anima in the Latin West: the Formation of a Peripatetic Philosophy of the Soul, 1160-1300* [Warburg Institute Studies and Texts 1], London (The Warburg Institute) 2000.
13. *De anima* 166.3-4 Rahman. It would appear that *mufakkira* here stands for Aristotle's *dianoia* (*Metaphysics* E4, 1027b3O), to which the function of combination and division are attributed: *hê sumplokê estin kai hê diairesis en dianoiai*. The Arabic translation has, *fī l-fikrati immā tarkībun wa-immā tafṣīlun* (p. 737.7 Bouyges), precisely the terms used by Avicenna. Cf. Rahman, *Avicenna's Psychology*, Oxford 1959, 105, note to p. 55,7.
14. Avicenna's account of the diseases of the brain and its Galenic background are discussed by D. Jacquart "Avicenne et la nosologie Galénique: l'exemple des maladies du cerveau," in *Perspectives arabes et médiévales sur la tradition scientifique et philosophique grecque*, ed. A. Hasnawi, A. Elamrani-Jamal, M. Aouad [Orientalia Lovanensia Analecta 79], Leuven-Paris (Peeters) 1997, 217-226.
15. English translation adopted, with modifications, from A.J. Arberry, *Avicenna on Theology*, London (John Murray) 1951, 50-51.
16. See the English translation of the *Najāt* in Rahman *Psychology* 46-54, a text reproduced by Avicenna from *The Cure, De anima* V,2, pp. 209-221 Rahman.
17. *De anima* 220.6-7 Rahman; Rahman *Psychology* 53.26-29.
18. This concept in Aristotle himself is not without its own problems with regard to the duality it poses between the corporeal sensible and the incorporeal intelligible, problems which prefigure those in Avicenna. See the discussion in D. Frede, "The Cognitive Role of Phantasia in Aristotle," in M.C. Nussbaum and A.O. Rorty, eds., *Essays on Aristotle's De anima*, Oxford (Clarendon) 1992, 279-295.
19. *At-Taʿlīqāt ʿalā ḥawāshī Kitāb an-nafs li-Arisṭāṭālīs*, ed. in ʿA. Badawī, *Arisṭū ʿinda l-ʿArab*, Cairo 1947.
20. I.e., the intellective soul; read *taqbala* for *yaqbala* in Badawī's text. The ms

(Cairo, Dār al-kutub, Ḥikma 6M) has no dots for the third person prefix.

21. Reading *li-an taqbala* with the ms for *li-annahu yaqbalu* in Badawī's text; again the ms has no dots for the third person prefix.

22. Here the text switches to the masculine, although it still refers to the feminine "intellective soul;" but the intellective soul is the same as the intellect, *ʿaql*, which is masculine.

23. Reading *<a>* or *<immā>* *li-annahā* for *illā li-annahā* in Badawī's text. The ms has *illā annahā* in the text, corrected to *li-annahā* in the margin; the introductory *<a>* or *<immā>*, answered by *aw li-annahu* in the second half of the sentence, was omitted in the process.

24. Perhaps *al-ittiṣāl al-qābilī <li-umūrin>* is to be added to the text.

25. See the tables of correspondence between the texts of the *Shifāʾ* and the *Mashriqiyyūn* in my article referred to in note 4 above.

26. Avicenna asks, poignantly, *fa-mā-dhā naqūlu l-āna fī l-anfusi l-insāniyyati wa-l-maʿqūlāti llatī taktasibuhā wa-tadhhalu ʿanhā ilā ghayrihā*? "What, then, are we to say now about the human souls and the intelligibles which they acquire and then ignore, moving on to another?" *De anima* 245.5-247.2 Rahman.

27. In the *Ishārāt* Avicenna even establishes the existence of the active intellect by arguing that there must be "something external to our substance in which the intelligible forms exist essentially;" 3rd *namaṭ*, *faṣl* 13; ed. S. Dunyā, vol. II, 400-401.

28. For a discussion of Avicenna's theories about the acquisition of primary intelligibles see Hasse "Vier Intellekte" 32ff.; for the acquisition of intelligibles as universal concepts through abstraction see his essay in this volume.

29. This revised translation of the version in my *Avicenna* is partly made necessary by the more reliable text in Bīdārfar's edition. Cf. also the French translation by Michot, "Cultes, magic et intellection: l'homme et sa corporéité selon Avicenne," in C. Wenin, ed., *L'Homme et son univers au Moyen Age* [Philosophes Médiévaux XXXVI], Louvain-la-Neuve (Institut Supérieur de Philosophie) 1986, pp. 220-233 at 231-232, §§6-8.

30. I.e., the material intellect which is so strong that it is actually like an intellect *in habitu* and can acquire through intense Intuition all the intelligibles by itself; see the formulation (and the corresponding Arabic text) in **Text 2**, §1 and §3, last sentences, and cf. note 10 above. The reading should accordingly be, *wa-yakūnu lahu quwwatu n-nafsi l-qudsiyyatu*, not *al-qudsiyyati*, as read by Michot and mistranslated as "la puissance de l'Ame Sainte", which theologizes the context. The same passage is also mistranslated by Davidson *Intellect* 101 ("the power of [a] holy soul") — apparently inde-

pendently of Michot — although on the following page, 102, he translates the parallel passage from *The Cure* correctly, "holy faculty."

31. The correct text is as given by Bīdārfar (*adh-dhātī*, instead of *adh-dhātiyya* in Badawī) and as translated both by Michot "Cultes" 232 and in my *Avicenna* 166; my note 45 on that page should be deleted.
32. Cf. the French translation by Michot "Cultes" 230-231. It is, however, based on Badawī *ʿArisṭū ʿinda l-ʿArab* 227-228 (§457), which both follows a different recension of the *Mubāḥathāt* and has misleading vowelling and punctuation.
33. I.e., the Image-bearing faculty would inadvertently oppose whatever the intellect is doing if it were to engage at the same time in other, unrelated projects. Michot understands the sentence differently.
34. I.e., thinking in terms of the geometry example just cited by Avicenna, drawing a figure to solve a problem means "individuating" it as a sensible and imaginable entity.
35. I.e., unaided by the senses and the images in the Image-bearing faculty.
36. Reading *al-istiqlāl bi-taṣawwur* instead of *al-istiqlāl yu/tutaṣawwaru* in Bīdārfar and Badawī respectively. The meaning is the same as above, §3: unaided by sense perception and images.
37. The text has a feminine verb, which could only refer to the soul, although the word is never used.
38. Reading *tazūlu* and *taʿūdu* in the feminine for the masculine verbs printed in Bīdārfar.
39. I.e., the active intellect and the intellects of the spheres.
40. Cf., e.g., *Najāt* 3.
41. Cf. the French translations by Michot "Cultes" 232-233 (§§9-13) and also his "La Réponse d'Avicenne à Bahmanyār et al-Kirmānī," *Le Muséon* 110 (1997) 143-221 at 187-189.
42. Even though Avicenna uses the unqualified term *nafs* in these passages, it is clear from his reference to the soul's separation from the body that he is referring to the rational soul, or intellect.
43. Reading the feminine pronoun, *tataʿāṭāhu*, as in Badawī and Michot, for the first person plural form printed in Bīdārfar.
44. From here on the text has the masculine pronoun throughout to refer to the (rational) soul (*nafs*). This is relatively common in the mss of Avicenna's works. If it is not scribal error, it would indicate that he was thinking all along of intellect, *ʿaql*, a masculine noun.
45. This fact has eluded most scholars who assume that Thinking in Avicenna,

in the sense of combining and separating intelligible forms, is done only by the Cogitative faculty of the animal soul. See Davidson *Intellect* 95ff., and especially D. Black, "Avicenna on the Ontological and Epistemic Status of Fictional Beings," *Documenti e Studi sulla Tradizione Filosofica Medievale* 8 (1997) 425-453 at 448: "Combining and dividing themselves are functions of the cogitative faculty, which is an internal sense power and thus a part of the cluster of faculties that make up imaginative soul." §10 in **Text 15** flatly contradicts such claims and, in this case, invalidates Black's argument here. Strangely, Black refers in her note 62 on pp. 448-449 to this very passage in the *Mubāḥathāt* (in Badawī's edition, §468) in support of her position!

46. See Avicenna's extensive arguments in this regard in *The Cure* and *The Salvation*, translated by Rahman *Psychology* 41-54.

47. Thus the word *ḥudūd* in §10 in **Text 15** clearly refers to terms of a syllogism, not to 'definitions,' as in Michot 'Réponse" 189: "la composition des définitions universelles."

48. Gutas *Avicenna* 26-27.

49. Reading, with ms L in Bīdārfar's apparatus, *fa-hiya n-nafsu n-nāṭiqatu* instead of *fa-hiya li-n-nafsi n-nāṭiqati* printed in the text.

50. Reading *bi-mā jāwaza* (literally, "with what goes beyond"), as in some mss and in Badawī's edition (*ʿArisṭū ʿinda l-ʿArab* 232, §468) instead of *fa-mā jāwaza* printed in Bīdārfar's text.

51. "And is in motion" (*al-mutaḥarrikata*) here refers to the Thinking/Imagining faculty and not to the forms, as erroneously translated by Black, "Fictional Beings" 449 note 62, "moving forms;" this is obvious from the next phrase in the Arabic text: *wa-in ʿuniya bi-hā (bi-l-quwwati l-fikriyyati) l-ʿāriḍata li-ṣ-ṣuwari, al-mutaḥarrikata, fa-hiya l-mutakhayyilatu min ḥaythu tataḥarraku maʿa shawqi l-quwwati l-ʿaqliyyati*. That it is imagination/thinking that is in motion and not the forms is in any case a doctrine that Avicenna received from Aristotle, *De anima* III.3, 428b10-17: *hê de phantasia kinêsis tis dokei einai.*

52. Avicenna uses here the plural form, *Kitāb al-qiyāsāt*, which would indicate that he is using a descriptive term for the book rather than its exact title, which is in the singular, *al-Qiyās*. He is referring either to Aristotle's *Prior Analytics* or to his own version of it in *The Cure*.

53. Reading the variant reading *muqāraba* in some manuscripts listed in the apparatus instead of *muqārana* printed in the text.

54. I.e., the active intellect and the intellects of the spheres.

55. Michot "Réponse" 161-163.

56. See Gutas *Avicenna* 72 (where the reference in the introductory passage should be to §11 and not to §1), and 82.

57. See M. Marmura, "Avicenna's Psychological Proof for Prophecy," *Journal of Near Eastern Studies* 22 (1963) 49-56.

58. As the vast majority of students of Avicenna claim; see the references cited by Dag Hasse in this volume. To those also add R.C. Taylor, who cites with approval Davidson's views in his review, *Journal of Neoplatonic Studies* 5 (1996) 89-105. Cf. in general Goodman's more balanced and insightful discussion of this question in his *Avicenna* 143-149, and in particular Dag Hasse's detailed article here.

59. Avicenna is explicit: emanation occurs only *bi-ḥasabi ṭalabi n-nafsi* (*De anima* 245 Rahman, last line), "in accordance with the request of the [rational] soul," the "request" being, of course, a metaphor for the thinking process of the rational soul (see *ṭāliba*, "the one that searches," in **Text 16**, §3).

60. "On the Proof of Prophecies," translation adopted, with minor modifications, from M. Marmura, "Avicenna: On the Proof of Prophecies," in R. Lerner and M. Mahdi, *Medieval Political Philosophy*, New York 1963, 112-121 at 119. Arabic text in Avicenna's *Ithbāt an-nubuwwāt* §38.

Avicenna on Abstraction

DAG NIKOLAUS HASSE

The theory of abstraction is one of the most puzzling parts of Avicenna's philosophy. What Avicenna says in many passages about the human intellect's capacity to derive universal knowledge from sense-data seems to plainly contradict passages in the same works about the emanation of knowledge from the active intellect, a separately existing substance. When he maintains that "considering the particulars [stored in imagination] disposes the soul for something abstracted to flow upon it from the active intellect",[1] he appears to combine two incompatible concepts in one doctrine: either the intelligible forms emanate from above or they are abstracted from the data collected by the senses, but not both.

The standard reaction to this problem among modern interpreters is to believe Avicenna on emanation and to mistrust him on abstraction: abstraction is "only a *façon de parler*"[2] for emanation of intelligibles, it is "not to be taken literally":[3] "intelligible thoughts ... flow directly from the active intellect and are not abstracted at all";[4] Avicenna "was unable to explain intellectual abstraction in knowledge"; the activity of the human intellect "can only dispose the mind to be receptive of new concepts".[5] This certainly is not only a well-established line of interpretation, but also a powerful one: it measures Avicenna's theory against a systematic concept of abstraction, as we know it from intellectual history, and finds that it falls short of the criteria and hence cannot be properly called a theory of abstraction.

Nevertheless, I think this interpretation cannot stand as it is. One of its unpleasant consequences is that Avicenna would not have achieved what he thought to have achieved, namely the development of a theory of abstraction. With good philosophers such as Avicenna, who knows his Graeco-Arabic sources, this is a dangerous hermeneutical standpoint. In addition, one wonders whether Avicenna also falls short of speaking properly about emanation: the active intellect makes the forms flow upon the human intellect, but it does so by serving as a mediator in the process of intellectual perception, as a kind of immaterial light which helps the soul to see;[6] hence, concluded Anne-Marie Goichon some sixty years ago, "en rigueur de termes" the intelligibles are neither abstracted by the soul nor given to it by the active intellect.[7]

If one wants to avoid this negative double conclusion, it seems advisable, first, to focus again on Avicenna's own usage of terms from the semantic field "abstraction" — as some previous interpreters did before they decided that Avicenna should not be taken literally. Admittedly, this presupposes some intuition about what we are looking for — i.e., some notion of "abstraction" — but this notion may be taken broadly as referring to every transformation of sense-data into intelligibles. Secondly, it appears sensible to attempt a developmental explanation of Avicenna's theory: an explanation that does not consider his philosophy a system but follows the formation of the theory from the writings of his youth to that of his age. This approach is possible because, since Dimitri Gutas' study of Avicenna's oeuvre and its subsequent discussion by Michael Marmura and Jean Michot, there exists a basic scholarly consensus about the relative chronology of Avicenna's philosophical works (with the exception of *al-Ishārāt wa al-tanbīhāt*, *Ḥāl al-nafs* and the autobiography).[8] Ideally, a developmental interpretation would start with the sources which Avicenna had at his disposal, but that would transgress the boundaries both of this article and of my competence, given that the history of the concept of abstraction has not yet been written. The important article "Abstraktion" in the *Historisches Wörterbuch der Philosophie* of 1971 remains the best survey available, being particularly strong on the Western Middle Ages, but less so on Arabic philosophy.[9] Still, one of Avicenna's predecessors on the topic shall briefly be discussed because his theory is sometimes compared to that of Avicenna: Abū Naṣr al-Fārābī (d. 339 AH/950 AD).[10]

II

Al-Fārābī's standpoint may be illustrated by reference to two works of his, the "Principles of the Views of the Citizens of the Best State" *(Mabādiʾ ārāʾ ahl al-madīna al-fāḍila)*, a major and influential treatise of comprehensive philosophical character written towards the end of his life, and his earlier, short tract "On the intellect" *(Fī al-ʿaql)*. The *Mabādiʾ* do not contain much more than one sentence on the subject of abstraction, which on the one hand is not surprising since the book touches upon many philosophical areas without going into detail, but which on the other hand shows us that abstraction is not a topic important enough to be given a section of its own in this late work (as is the case with, for instance, the various members of the body). Al-Fārābī assumes, just as Avicenna after him, that the active intellect is a separately existing substance, the tenth and last of the incorporeal intelligences of the universe. Using the Peripatetic comparison of this intellect to the sun, he explains that, due to the influence of the active intellect, potentially intelligible things become actually intelligible. And he proceeds:

> When, then, that thing which corresponds to light in the case of sight arises in the rational faculty from the Active Intellect, intelligibles [arise] at the same time in the rational faculty from the sensibles which are preserved in the faculty of representation *(al-quwwa al-mutakhayyila)*.[11]

One may note that al-Fārābī does not describe the rational faculty as an active participant in this process, and that the terminology used to describe the transformation of sense-data into intelligibles is restricted to intransitive verbs: intelligibles arise from *(ḥaṣala ʿan)* the sensibles, the intelligibles in potentiality become *(ṣāra)* intelligibles in actuality. Terms such as 'discovering/deriving' *(istanbaṭa)*, 'abstracting' *(jarrada)*, 'divesting' *(afraza)*, or 'extracting' *(intazaʿa)*, that Avicenna half a century later would use with respect to the intellect, do not appear in this context in *al-*

Mabādiʾ. The phrase *al-instinbāṭ* is used when al-Fārābī comes to speak about rational actions following upon the appearance of the intelligibles: then "a desire to find out things" arises.[12]

If one cannot say that there is anything close to a coherent theory of abstraction in this treatise, the case is different with the earlier *Fī al-ʿaql*. One must bear in mind, however, that this work does not necessarily present al-Fārābī's own philosophy but rather different usages of the term "intellect" among ordinary people, theologians and Aristotle. It is in the section on Aristotle's *De anima* that al-Fārābī mentions the abstracting activity of the human intellect: one of the definitions of the potential intellect, al-Fārābī says, is that its essence is disposed or able "to extract *(intazaʿa)* the quiddities of all objects and their forms from their matter".[13] He comes back to this when speaking about the second of Aristotle's intellects, as al-Fārābī understands them, the intellect in actuality:

> When we say that something is known for the first time, we mean that the forms which are in matter are extracted *(intazaʿa)* from their matter and that they receive an existence different from their previous existence. If there are things that are forms to which does not belong any matter, then this essence [i.e., the intellect] does not need to extract *(intazaʿa)* them from matter at all but finds them as something abstract *(muntazaʿ)*.[14]

In this passage, Al-Fārābī takes up a doctrine stemming from Aristotle about the difference between those objects of thought that are in matter and those that are not.[15] Apart from this, we can see that al-Fārābī takes a view on the issue of the intellect's activity of "extracting": the form of something is separated from its matter and in virtue of this enters a new mode of existence. Alternative positions would be, for instance, that the forms in matter are imitated in the intellect (as Avicenna once mentions) rather than put into a new mode of existence, or that intelligibles arise from sense-data, as al-Fārābī says himself in the *Mabādiʾ*, or that the active intellect is involved in the process, as again in the *Mabādiʾ*. It is true that al-Fārābī has an elaborate passage on the separate active intellect in *Fī al-ʿaql*, but as to its role in the process of abstraction he maintains no more than that the active intellect makes potential intelligibles become actual intelligibles.[16] He never in this treatise explicitly connects the abstracting activity of the human intellect with the influence of the separate active intellect. Hence, one cannot say that according to *Fī al-ʿaql* the light of the active intellect "enables the human intellect to abstract".[17] Alfarabi also keeps silent about the transformation of sense-data, presumably because sense-perception falls outside the scope of this treatise on the intellect. In sum, al-Fārābī's remarks about abstraction remain sketchy and are in danger of being overinterpreted.

III

Compared with his Arabic predecessor, Avicenna appears a champion of abstraction theory. This is already apparent in a very early treatise, with which he began his career as a writer, the *Maqāla fī al-nafs ʿalā sunnat al-ikhtiṣār* or *Compendium on the Soul* (dating probably 386/996–387/997).[18] The work certainly does not present Avicenna's mature thoughts on the topic of abstraction, but it contains *in nuce* several pieces of doctrine that are later developed into fully-fledged theories, such as the cooperation between the intellect and the internal senses (and the limits of this cooperation); the distinction between common and special, accidental and essential forms; the involvement of a separate universal intellect in the intellective process; the thesis that all perception, sensual as well as intellectual, is the abstraction of forms from matter; the comparison of the different modes of abstraction in the senses and in the intellect. And in general we encounter a notable interest in the transformation of sense-data into intelligibles:

> The faculty which grasps such concepts *(i.e. intelligibles that are not self-evident)* acquires intelligible forms from sense-perception by force of an inborn disposition, so that forms, which are in the form-bearing faculty *(scil. common sense)*[19] and the memorizing faculty, are made present to [the rational soul] with the assistance of the imaginative and estimative [faculties]. Then, looking at [the forms], it finds that they sometimes share forms and sometimes do not, and it finds that some of the forms among them are essential and some are accidental. An example of the

sharing of forms is that the forms[20] 'man'[21] and 'donkey' — in someone forming concepts[22] — share life, but differ with respect to reason and non-reason; an example for essential [forms] is 'life' in both of them, an example for accidental [forms] is 'blackness' and 'whiteness'.

When it[23] has found them being forms in this way, each of these essential, accidental, common, or special forms becomes a single, intellectual, universal form by itself. Hence it discovers by force of this natural disposition intellectual kinds, species, differences, properties and accidents. It then composes these single concepts by way of first particular and later syllogistic composition; from there it concludes derivations from conclusions. All this [the rational soul is able to do] with the service of the animal faculties and the assistance of the universal intellect, as we will explain below, and with the mediation of necessary, intellectual axioms[24] that naturally exist in it.

Even though this faculty receives help from the faculty of sense-perception in DERIVING *(istinbāṭ)* intellectual, single forms from sense-perceived forms, it does not need such assistance in forming these concepts in themselves and in composing syllogisms out of them, neither when granting assent to, nor when conceiving the two propositions, as we will explain below. Whenever the necessary corollaries have been DERIVED *(istanbaṭa)* from sense-perception through the afore-mentioned natural disposition, it dispenses with the assistance of the faculties of sense-perception; instead it has enough power by itself for every action dealt with by it.

Just as the faculties of sense-perception perceive only through imitation of[25] the object of sense-perception, likewise the intellectual faculties perceive only through imitation of the object of intellection. This imitation[26] is the ABSTRACTION *(tajrīd)* of the form from matter and the union with [the form]. The sensible form, however, does not come about when the faculty of sensation wishes to move or act, but when the essence of the object of sensation reaches the faculty either by accident or through the mediation of the moving faculty; the ABSTRACTION *(tajarrud)* of

> the form [occurs] to the faculty because of the assistance of the media which make the forms reach the faculty. The case is different with the intellectual faculty, because its essence performs the ABSTRACTION[27] of forms from matter by itself whenever it wishes, and then it unites with [the form]. For this reason one says that the faculty of sense-perception has a somehow passive role in conceiving [forms], whereas the intellectual faculty is active,[28] or rather one says that the faculty of sense-perception cannot dispense with the organs and does not reach actualization through itself, while it would be wrong to apply this statement to the intellectual faculty.[29]

The first thing to note about this passage is that its terminology of abstraction can hardly be read as a *façon de parler* for emanation of intelligibles. Avicenna uses much transitive vocabulary: the rational faculty acquires *(istafāda)*, finds *(wajada)*, derives *(istanbaṭa)* and abstracts *(jarrada)* intelligible forms; they do not "arise" in it, as al-Fārābī put it in *al-Mabādi'*. In addition, Avicenna plainly states that in contrast to sense-perception, the rational faculty is an active faculty which can perform *(fa'ala)* the abstraction of a form at will. The power to form concepts is innate.

Nevertheless, Avicenna also mentions that the intellect needs the help of the senses, of the universal intellect and of naturally inborn axioms (the latter are needed for syllogistic forms of reasoning).[30] Later in the *Compendium on the Soul*, he elaborates upon the axioms and also adds a sentence on the separate intellect's role in intellection, when invoking the traditional analogy of light: Light is similar to this intellect in that it enables the faculty of sight to perceive without, however, providing it with the perceived forms:

> This substance *(i.e. the universal intellect)*, in turn, supplies by the sole force of its essence the power of perception *(idrāk)* unto the rational soul, and makes the perceived form arise *(ḥaṣṣala)* in it[31] as well, as we have said above.[32]

The cross-references in this passage and in the previous quotation ("as we will explain below") make it plausible that these remarks about perceived forms refer to the same forms that were before said to be abstracted. Here, then, is the core of the problem which troubled so many interpreters of Avicenna, the collaboration of two very different powers in the process of abstraction, the human intellect and the separate universal intellect. But even if the rather casual sentence on the supplying activity of the separate intellect is taken very seriously — it reminds one of al-Fārābī and is certainly much less original than the long passage on the human intellect — it does not allow us to make the separate intellect the main protagonist in the process of intellection. For the relation between the human and the universal intellect is clearly described as an act of "assistance" *(aʿāna)*: "All this [the conceptualizing faculty is able to do] with the service of the animal faculties and the assistance of the universal intellect". Without doubt, in this early version of Avicenna's theory of abstraction, it is the powerful abstracting force of the human intellect which is the focus of the theory. The senses are indispensable, for they provide the necessary sense-data. The universal intellect is indispensable as well; its function is hardly described at all but seems to consist in somehow providing the necessary intellectual surrounding for the activity of the rational soul, in a manner similar to light with respect to the human ability to see. Hence both the senses and the universal intellect are necessary accompanying conditions rather than powers active in the process.

IV

In later writings of Avicenna — in the mature works of his middle period[33] — one can observe that one part of abstraction theory receives a formulation that Avicenna obviously considered perfect: it appears in four different works in almost identical wording: *Ḥāl al-nafs al-insāniyya* ("The State of the Human Soul", also called *al-Maʿād*, "The Destination"), the *De anima* part of *al-Shifāʾ* (dating probably 412/1022-414/1024),[34] *al-Najāt* ("The Salvation"), and the *Mashriqiyyūn* ("The Easterners").[35] This piece of Avicennian philosophy treats four different degrees of abstraction in sense-perception, imagination, estimation and intellect.

Two other doctrines familiar from the *Compendium on the Soul* are developed identically in these four treatises: the theory that the animal faculties assist the rational soul in various ways and especially in abstraction, and, connected with it, the theory that a soul with much acquired knowledge can dispense with the assistance of the senses.

Significantly, the case is different with the doctrine of the separate active intellect and its participation in the abstraction process: the treatises *Ḥāl al-nafs al-insāniyya* and *al-Najāt* do not go much beyond the *Compendium on the Soul* but similarly state that a power is issued from above and that imaginable forms become intelligible forms. Avicenna obviously felt the need to reformulate and develop the doctrine, for both in *De anima* and in the *Mashriqiyyūn* he gives a long and famous explanation of the active intellect's mediating role in intellection.

It is characteristic of Avicenna's working method that these three groups of doctrines (degrees of abstraction — assistance by the senses — function of the active intellect) that once were treated together in a single passage of the early *Compendium*, have now become fully-fledged theories of their own which are only loosely connected with each other. The increasing theorization of Avicenna's philosophy is accompanied by fragmentation. In *Ḥāl al-nafs*, for example, the three theories are treated in chapters three, six and twelve, in *De anima* they appear in chapters II,2, V,3 and V,5.

What then is the effect of this development on the content of Avicenna's theory of abstraction as present in the works of the middle period? The passage on the four degrees of abstraction, to start with the first group of doctrines, is too long to be given in full; the reader may be referred to the translation by Fazlur Rahman.[36] For the present purposes, suffice it to quote the beginning (on abstraction in general) and the end (on intellectual abstraction) only:

> It seems that all perception is but the grasping of the form of the perceived object in some manner. If, then, it is a perception of some material object, it consists in an apprehension of its form by ABSTRACTING *(tajrīd)* it from matter in some way. But the kinds of ABSTRACTION are different and their degrees various. This is because, owing to matter, the material form is subject to

certain states and conditions which do not belong to [the form] by itself insofar as it is this form. So sometimes the ABSTRACTION *(naz')* from matter is effected with all or some of these attachments, and sometimes it is complete in that the concept[37] is ABSTRACTED *(jarrada)* from matter and from the accidents it possesses on account of the matter.[38]

[...]

(There follows the example of the abstraction of the concept "human being" and the description of the increasingly higher degree of abstraction among sense-perception, imagination and estimation.)

The faculty in which the fixed forms are either the forms of objects which are not at all material and do not occur in matter by accident,[39] [or the forms of objects which in themselves are not material but happen to be so by accident],[40] or the forms of material objects though purified in all respects from material attachments — such a faculty obviously perceives the forms by grasping them as ABSTRACTED *(mujarrad)* from matter in all respects. This is evident in the case of objects which are in themselves FREE *(mutajarrad)* from matter. As to those objects which are present in matter, either because their existence is material or because they are by accident material, this faculty completely[41] ABSTRACTS *(intaza'a)* them both from matter and from their material attachments and grasps them in the way of ABSTRACTION; hence in the case of 'man' which is predicated of many, this faculty takes[42] the unitary nature of the many, DIVESTS *(afraza)* it of all material quantity, quality, place, and position. If[43] [the faculty] did not ABSTRACT *(jarrada)* it from all these, it could not be truly predicated of all.[44]

It is obvious that important parts of the doctrine have changed since the *Compendium on the Soul*. First, in the early *Compendium*, the main difference between sense-perception and intellection is described in terms of passivity and activity: the senses are not able to grasp a form at will, as is the intellect. In the later formulation of the doctrine, the difference lies in the faculties' widely diverging powers to divest forms of their material attachments. Second, there is no explicit link to the theory of the separate active intellect in the passage from the middle period. Third, no mention is made of "imitation" or "assimilation" *(tashabbuh)*, as was the case in the *Compendium*. Fourth, Avicenna now connects the fully abstracted status of a form with its predicability of many. Fifth, the terminology of "form" and "matter", though present in the *Compendium* ("This imitation is the abstraction of the form from matter"), had not yet served to develop a theory about the ontological status of concepts, which is a major concern of Avicenna's in his works of the middle period. What Avicenna means when he speaks of abstraction from matter, is once illustrated with an example: the rational soul divests the concept of man of "all material quantity, quality, place and position". Hence, the soul distinguishes between what is accidental to the form and what belongs to the form "insofar as it is this form" — which shows us that the discussion of concepts here is a development of the distinction between the essential and the accidental made in the *Compendium*.

Avicenna calls these accidents "material" because they occur to the form only in virtue of its presence in matter in an externally existent object. But what exactly is the nature of this form, which is the object of abstraction? It is with respect to this topic that Avicenna adds an important feature to his abstraction theory (in a sentence not yet quoted in the above doctrine of the four degrees of abstraction):

> To give an example: the form or essence *(māhiyya)* of man is a nature in which all the individuals of the species share equally, while in its definition it is a single unit: although it is merely by accident that it happens to exist *(wujida)* in this or that individual and is thus multiplied.[45]

Multiplicity is only accidental to the form. This theory clearly touches upon the metaphysical topic of the nature of intelligible forms and the distinction between essence and existence,[46] which Avicenna spins out in greater detail in the *Metaphysics* and the *Logic* part of *al-Shifāʾ*, written also in the middle period.[47] There is one passage in the *Metaphysics* which directly tackles the issue of abstraction in the context of the theory of forms; here he explains that both universality and particularity are accidents to the intelligible form. This passage is a good illustration of what

Avicenna says in other works on abstraction, but it is an illustration only; Avicenna himself does not treat both theories — of abstraction and of forms — together, probably because he considered them to belong to different disciplines, psychology and metaphysics:

> The single form in the intellect is related to a multiplicity, in this respect being universal, while being a single concept in the intellect; there is no variation in its relation to whatever animal you perceive. That is, the form of every animal is made present in imagination with some disposition, then the intellect EXTRACTS *(intazaʿa)* an ABSTRACTION *(mujarrad)* of its concept from the accidents, [and] this form itself comes about in the intellect. This form is what derives from the ABSTRACTION *(tajrīd)* of animality from some individual [form in] imagination, which is grasped from an object outside (or something similar to an object outside), although it is not found itself outside but is created by imagination. This form, though universal with respect to the individuals, is particular with respect to the particular soul, being one of the forms in the intellect.[48]

Avicenna here says more clearly than in his psychological works that neither multiplicity nor particularity belong to the form as such. Embedded in this theory is a lucid description of the process of abstraction: the intellect works on data presented to it by the senses and stored in imagination; these data themselves are not imported from outside but are creations of the senses. The form that is in the intellect is a single concept only with respect to the intellect; it is universal with respect to the objects outside, and in itself it is neither universal nor particular, since — and here the distinction between essence and existence is involved again — it is independent of its existence outside and inside the intellect: as Avicenna says in his psychological works, it is the "unitary nature of the many" or "a nature in which all the individuals of the species share equally".

One may with some justification call this — the doctrine of the four degrees of abstraction plus the related discussion of intelligible forms in the *Metaphysics* — Avicenna's classical formulation of the process of abstraction: classical in the sense that he himself repeats it in several works and in that it was influential historically.[49] With respect to intellectual abstraction, the human rational faculty appears as fully capable of performing the act of abstraction by itself: a comparatively broad range of transitive vocabulary is employed to describe its abstracting and divesting activity *(intazaʿa, jarrada, afraza).*

One does not hear anything, however, about a collaboration with other entities involved in abstraction, neither with respect to the senses nor with respect to the separate active intellect. This collaboration is the topic of the two other groups of doctrines that Avicenna developed in the works of the middle period. The passage on the role of the senses appears identically in the four works mentioned above. Despite its brevity, one can easily spot that its roots lie in the early *Compendium*:

> The animal faculties assist the rational soul in various ways,[50] one of them being that sense-perception brings to it particulars, from which four things result in [the rational soul]: One of them is that the mind[51] EXTRACTS *(intazaʿa)* single universals from the particulars, by ABSTRACTING *(tajrīd)* their concepts from matter and the appendages of matter and its accidents, by considering what is common in it[53] and what different, and what in its existence is essential and what accidental. From this the principles of conceptualization *(taṣawwur)* come about [in] the soul: and this with the help of its employing imagination and estimation.[53]

The passage contains much that is already familiar: the use of the terminology of "form" and "matter" (but not the language of "essence" and "existence"); the explanation of the process of abstraction as the distinction between the common and the special, the essential and the accidental; the abstraction of forms as the starting-point for further intellectual activities such as the combination of concepts, and, most importantly, the usage of the term "assist" *(aʿāna)* for the role played by the senses. In this text as well as in the *Compendium*, it is the human intellect which is the active force in the process of abstraction, while the senses' main function is auxiliary: to present particulars, i.e. sense-data, to the intellect. The intellect is even said to "employ" or "govern" *(istaʿmala)* the internal senses in this operation. One sees that Avicenna has not changed the basic features of his theory since the *Compendium* with regard to the intellect's relation to the senses. Instead, he has added new material. After the above quoted passage Avicenna adds two pieces of doctrine: the first maintains that the intellect returns to the senses only when forced to acquire an intelligible form not yet known to it — which is Avicenna's important distinction between the first acquisition of forms and their later reacquisition; for the latter, it suffices to reconnect to the active intellect[54]; the second is the example of the riding animal *(dābba)* which ceases to be useful when the place of destination is reached, just as there is no need for the senses when one has attained the intelligibles needed for further reasoning.[55]

If this group of doctrines does not undergo a revision in Avicenna's major writings, the opposite is true of the third topic, which concerns the role of the active intellect in the process of abstraction. One recalls that the *Compendium* contained very brief statements (reminiscent of al-Fārābī) about the universal intellect having an assisting function in the process: the active intellect supplies the power of perception and makes the forms arise in the human intellect. In two of Avicenna's later works, *Ḥāl al-nafs* and *al-Najāt*, the doctrine reappears without much alteration; it follows upon the standard Peripatetic analogy with light issuing from the sun:

> Likewise, there emanates from the active intellect a power and proceeds to the imaginable things that are potentially intelligible, in order to make them intelligible in actuality and to make the intellect in potentiality an intellect in actuality.[56]

What is missing, though, is the terminology of "assistance" which Avicenna had retained when explaining the function of the senses. This may simply be the effect of the increasing fragmentation of Avicenna's philosophy, that is, of the development of separate sets of doctrines (on abstraction and on the active intellect) loosely connected with each other, but when one turns to two other works of the middle period, the *De anima* of *al-Shifāʾ* and the *Mashriqiyyūn*, one finds that Avicenna, significantly, has substituted "mediation" for "assistance". These latter works, in fact, present a fully-fledged theory of the roles of the soul and the separate active intellect in abstraction, a theory of which there is not yet any sign in *Ḥāl al-nafs* (and *al-Najāt*, which has the same text); this may indicate that *Ḥāl al-nafs* was composed earlier than *De anima*.[57] Avicenna obviously felt the need to revise what he had said earlier on the topic, and, even more, to give a proper theoretical foundation to a key doctrine of Peripatetic philosophy: the role of the active intellect in intellection. He tackles this problem at great length in chapters V,5 and V,6 of *De anima*, which present Avicenna's most important treatment of the issue in his entire work, given that he never returns to it with the same detailed attention and systematic approach (as will appear below).

On the basis of the evidence from earlier Avicennian writings laid out above, it can be demonstrated that the first part of chapter V,5 is not simply about the active intellect but about its involvement in abstraction (in contrast, the section on intuition in chapter V,6 does not employ abstraction terminology).[58] The passage in V,5 not only contains — in sequence — the analogy of light (pp. 234-5) and the theory about the transformation of sense-data into intelligibles (p. 235), but also the doctrine that the human intellect separates the essential from the accidental (p. 236), and the theory that the concept "man" is a single concept with respect to the human intellect and a universal concept with respect to the objects outside (pp. 236-7). Without doubt, these are by now familiar ingredients of Avicenna's theory of abstraction. The last doctrine even contains an explicit reference to the *Metaphysics* passage translated above, which touches upon abstraction in the context of the theory of forms. A developmental interpretation of Avicenna's oeuvre, therefore, should make us very sceptical that this passage in *De anima* V,5 can be called in as principal witness for the "façon de parler" thesis: one can, of course, still claim that the vocabulary of abstraction in this passage should not be taken literally, but it seems impossible to claim that this is how Avicenna wanted to be understood, since the same vocabulary appears in the same doctrinal contexts in earlier or contemporary works of his which clearly deal with abstraction (and some of which do not mention the active intellect at all).

Let us turn to the crucial part of chapter V,5, the passage on the transformation of sense-data into intelligibles (p. 235); it contains the well-known sentence cited at the opening of the present article, in which Avicenna appears to combine incompatible notions of abstraction and emanation:

(1) When the intellectual faculty considers the particulars which are [stored] in imagination and the light of the above-mentioned active intellect shines upon them in us, then the [particulars] are transformed *(istaḥāla)* into something ABSTRACTED *(mujarrada)* from matter and from the [material] attachments and get imprinted in the rational soul, (2) but not in the sense that the particulars themselves are transferred from imagination to our intellect, nor in the sense that the concept buried in [material] attachments — which in itself and with regard to its essence is ABSTRACT *(mujarrad)* — produces a copy of itself, but in the sense that looking at the particulars disposes the soul for something ABSTRACTED *(al-mujarrad)* to flow upon it from the active intellect. (3) For thoughts and considerations *(al-afkār wa al-taʾammulāt)* are movements which dispose the soul for the reception of the emanation, just as the middle terms in a more certain way dispose [it] for the reception of the conclusion (although the two happen in different ways, as you will understand later). (4) When some relation towards this form occurs to the rational soul through the mediation of illumination *(bi-tawassuṭi ishrāq)* by the active intellect, then from [the form] something comes about in the soul, [something] of [the form's] kind in some way and not of its kind in another way — just as when light falls upon coloured things, it produces in vision an effect which is not of its nature[59] in all aspects. The imaginable things, which are intelligible in potentiality, become intelligible in actuality, though not themselves, but that which is COLLECTED *(iltaqaṭa)* from them. Or rather:[60] just as the effect, which is transmitted through the medium of light from the sense-perceptible forms is not identical with these forms but something different, related to them, [something] which is generated through the mediation of light in the corresponding receiver, likewise when the rational soul looks at these imaginable forms and [when] the light of the active intellect makes contact with them in some way, [the rational soul] is disposed to have appear in it, due to the light of the active intellect, uncontaminated ABSTRACTIONS *(mujarradāt)* from these forms.[61]

Compared with the brief remarks in Avicenna's previous works, or with what we know from al-Fārābī, or with the passage in Aristotle's *De anima* III,4-5 which is at the origin of the problem, this is an impressively systematic theory of the active intellect's role in abstraction. The basic assumption of all three authors is that the active intellect renders potentially intelligible thoughts actually intelligible; in addition, they somehow connect this with the difference between intelligibles in matter and intelligibles freed of matter. Al-Fārābī added that it is the sensibles stored in an internal faculty from which arise the intelligibles through the influence of the active intellect. Avicenna does not leave it with this: section one in the above quotation gives a more precise description of the process by saying that the particulars stored in the faculty of imagination are "transformed" *(istaḥāla)* into something "abstracted" from matter and hence are imprinted in the intellect. Avicenna also mentions two conditions for this process: the human intellect needs to consider the particulars and the light of the active intellect needs to shine upon them. Note that he does not speak of "assistance": both intellects seem equally important for a successful transformation.

This is comparatively precise, but it is not yet Avicenna's main contribution to the discussion, which follows in section two. Here he distinguishes between three different possibilities for such a transformation: either the particular imaginable form travels from imagination to the intellect, or a copy is produced of its immaterial core, or an abstraction of it comes from the active intellect, for which the soul is disposed through its consideration of the particulars. Avicenna chooses the third and last possibility and justifies it in the long section four (after a brief explanation of what is meant with disposition). The abstracted form which arrives in the human intellect is partly of the kind of the imaginable form and partly not: it is not the imaginable form itself which becomes intelligible, but something taken or collected *(iltaqaṭa)* from it. Avicenna compares this process to vision: the effect produced in the receiver and transmitted through the medium of light is "different" from the sense-perceptible form of the object, but "related" to it. There cannot be much doubt that Avicenna here tries to pin down the exact meaning of intellectual abstraction — the Latin *abstractio*/"drawing from" is a very apt translation in this case — and to distinguish it from other possible forms of the transformation of sense-data: no simple transportation of them to the intellect, and no imitation *(mithl)* either – remember the term "imitation" *(tashabbuh)* in the *Compendium* – but a kind of derivation.

What are the respective roles of the human and the active intellect in this process? Note the terminology employed to describe the active intellect: its light "shines upon" the particulars in imagination; something abstracted "flows from" it *(fāḍa)* upon the soul; the forms occur to the soul "through the mediation of" its illumination; its light "makes contact with" the imaginable forms; abstractions of these forms appear in the soul "due to the light of the active intellect". The human intellect, in turn, "considers" the particulars stored in imagination; "looking at" (*ṭālaʿa)* the particulars disposes the soul for an abstraction; thoughts and considerations are "movements" which dispose the soul for the reception of the emanation; the form "occurs to" or "comes about in" (*ḥadatha)* the rational soul; it "looks at" the imaginable forms and hence is "disposed" *(istaʿadda)* to have "appear in it" abstractions from these forms.

A number of points need to be underlined: first, in contrast to the senses, which remain powers with an auxiliary function only, the active intellect is granted a more important role than in earlier writings of Avicenna: its traditional role was to give the power of intellectual perception to the rational soul and to make the intelligible forms arise in it – which is a Peripatetic version of Aristotle's idea that thinking needs to be triggered, needs to be turned from potentiality to actuality; its function now, much more specifically, is to make abstractions appear in the human intellect which are derived from the particulars stored in the soul's imagination. Second, the rational soul still is the main protagonist, even though there is a notable increase in passive vocabulary ("occurs to", "comes about in", "appears in" or "flows upon"). While the active intellect assumes the function of an indispensable intellectual surrounding and mediator, the human intellect is the power in action: it considers the particular forms stored in imagination and produces "thoughts and considerations", which eventually lead to the acquisition of a new intelligible form. Third, although Avicenna speaks of emanation and illumination, the vocabulary of light does not serve a theory of illumination in the strict sense: the light of the active intellect does not make contact with the human intellect only and not even primarily; rather, it shines upon the particulars stored in imagination and thus creates a connection between imagination and human intellect. Hence, the analogy of light is employed for the specific purpose to explain the role of the active intellect in the process of abstraction. When Avicenna maintains in section two that an abstraction emanates from the active intellect upon the soul, then this is an abbreviation — describing the entire process from one end of the process only, namely the human intellect — for the sentence in section four which maintains that abstractions from the imaginable forms appear in the soul due to the light of the active intellect.

In the traditional reading of the translated passage, the human intellect's attention towards the imaginable forms *only* disposes *(aʿadda)* the soul for receiving an emanation of intelligibles from above. This emphasizes the limitation of the soul's power of abstraction,[62] which, however, is not Avicenna's point. There is no "only" in the text.[63] As shown above, the core of the argument runs: no transportation of the imaginable form, no copying, but an abstraction mediated by the active intellect. The disposition of the soul is part of the theory, but it is not the gist of it, and there is no indication that Avicenna conceives of the soul's power of abstraction as something limited. One of the impossible consequences of the traditional line of interpretation is that — on account of the analogy used by Avicenna — the soul also would not *see* in the proper sense of the word, because turning towards the object only disposes the eye to have visible forms appear in it due to the light of the sun; which is clearly not what Avicenna means.

It is not correct to say that for Avicenna "human intelligible thought comes directly from the active intellect", or that "intelligible thoughts ... flow directly from the active intellect and are not abstracted at all".[64] Apart from the fact that this interpretation rests on a misunderstanding of the term *fikr* ("reasoning") as referring to one of the internal senses only,[65] it is countered by Avicenna's explicit statement in section three: "thoughts" *(al-afkār)* are movements of the human intellect produced before the reception of abstract forms. When Avicenna speaks about abstraction and emanation, he means the acquisition of an intelligible "form" (*ṣuwar*) such as "man", not of thought in general. Moreover, as shown above, Avicenna unambiguously states that intelligible forms ultimately derive from the particulars in imagination and still resemble them:

they are partly of their kind and partly not. It is true that one often finds in Avicenna's works the expression that the intelligibles flow from the active intellect, especially in the context of the reacquisition of a form which had been intellected before; but when the phrase is used with respect to the first acquisition of a form, it should not be misunderstood as excluding abstraction. On the contrary: to have given a clear definition of abstraction, to have described the function of the active intellect in it and to have distinguished abstraction from other modes of transforming sense-data, counts among Avicenna's major contributions to the history of epistemology.

V

For the present purposes, the late period of Avicenna's oeuvre shall be defined as comprehending works which postdate the psychological section of *De anima* and which present a theory of abstraction not identical with the version of the middle period. The *Najāt* and the *Mashriqiyyūn*, though clearly written after *De anima*, advance the same theory and thus belong to the middle period, considered from a doctrinal point of view. This is different with three later works which do not simply copy the doctrine: the *Dāneshnāme* (written in Iṣfahān between 414/1023 and 428/1037),[66] *al-Ishārāt wa al-tanbīhāt* ("Pointers and Reminders") and *al-Mubāḥathāt* ("Discussions").

These treatises are of very different character: the *Dāneshnāme* is a summary of philosophy written in Persian for the ruler ʿAlā ad-Dawla; the *Ishārāt* is traditionally considered Avicenna's last *magnum opus*, peculiar for its style of giving hints and pointers rather than fully-fledged arguments; the *Mubāḥathāt* are a loosely organized series of answers to miscellaneous questions concerning Avicenna's philosophy. It is characteristic of these treatises that they treat abstraction less systematically and less comprehensively than the works of the middle period. The relevant passages are shorter and state a doctrine rather than argue for it. What makes them interesting for the present investigation, is that they show us what Avicenna considered worth selecting or altering, be it for the readership of a ruler or of an intellectual élite.

We meet two familiar groups of doctrines in the *Dāneshnāme*, on the degrees of abstraction and on the participation of the active intellect in abstraction. The topic of the senses' assistance seems to be dropped; what is left, is the passage on the senses becoming a hindrance to the intellect, including the example of the riding animal.[67] With respect to the degrees of abstraction, Avicenna takes over the basic features of what was called above the classical formulation of the doctrine: the faculties' varying powers of abstraction, the omission of any reference to the active intellect, the language of "form" and "matter", the interest in the ontological status of concepts. He has reduced, however, the vocabulary of abstraction itself, shifting the focus towards different modes in which forms are perceived — rather than abstracted.[68] Another significant alteration concerns the metaphysical doctrine of forms, which Avicenna had woven into his theory of abstraction in various passages of the middle period. That multiplicity and particularity are extraneous to the form, is not a topic discussed in relation with abstraction theory in the *Dāneshnāme*.

If the section on the various degrees of abstraction (or, rather, perception) is a digest of the mature version of the doctrine — which is not surprising, given the addressee of the book — the same holds true of the passage on the active intellect. Here we meet with a number of features clearly taken from *De anima* (or *Mashriqiyyūn*): the light of the active intellect falls upon the imaginable forms; abstractions are taken from these forms; they are presented to the (human) intellect. Remember that in *Ḥāl al-nafs* and *al-Najāt* Avicenna had only spoken of imaginable forms being made intelligible in actuality. Avicenna has, however, skipped the entire discussion of the various possible ways of the transformation of sense-data; only the third possibility is left, which is abstractions from imaginable forms. No mention is made of the intellect being disposed to receive these forms.[69]

It is in the *Ishārāt* that one finds the most important development of the theory in Avicenna's late period. The *Mubāḥathāt*, in contrast, do not contain anything close to a *theory* of abstraction, to the best of my knowledge.[70] Of course, one finds various pieces of doctrine deriving from the thematic groups of the middle period, such as: imagination does not grasp concepts completely abstracted from matter (p. 177); the bodily senses can be compared to a riding animal (p. 232); consideration of what is stored in imagination is needed to receive an emanation from above; this consideration consists in thoughts and reasonings that prepare the soul for the emanation (p. 239). It is tempting but hermeneutically hazardous to combine these scattered sentences to a coherent picture of Avicenna's theory in *Mubāḥathāt*; the collection of responsa obviously is not meant to offer a systematic treatment of philosophical questions. The same *caveat* should be kept in mind when sentences from *Mubāḥathāt* are used to explain Avicenna's position in other works of his without proper consideration of context and the precise nature of the question asked.[71]

Turning to the relevant passages in the *Ishārāt*, one finds that the text has much in common with the *Dāneshnāme* (which corroborates the late dating of the *Ishārāt*):[72] it has about the same length; it does not say much on assistance by the senses but all the more on degrees of abstraction and on the active intellect; it does not use the terminology of "multiplicity" and "particularity" of forms; it draws on *De anima* for the theory of the active intellect in abstraction but omits the discussion of the exact nature of the transformation of imaginable forms. The first passage is the following:

> Sometimes a thing is perceived [via sense-perception] when it is observed; then it is imagined, when it is absent [in reality] through the representation of its form inside, just as Zaid, for example, whom you have seen, but now is absent from you, is imagined by you. And sometimes [the thing] is apprehended intellectually when the concept 'man', for example, which exists also for other people, is formed out of Zaid. When [the thing] is perceptible to the senses, it is found covered by things which are foreign to its essence and which, if they had been removed from it, would not affect its core essence *(māhiyya)*. As, for instance, with place, position, quality, and quantity itself: if something else had been imagined in their place, it would not affect the reality of the essence of its humanity.
>
> Sense-perception grasps [the concept] insofar as it is buried in these accidents that cling to it because of the matter out of which it is made without ABSTRACTING *(jarrada)* it from [matter], and it grasps it only by means of a connection through position

> [that exists] between its perception and its matter. It is for this reason that the form of [the thing] is not represented in the external sense when [sensation] ceases. As to the internal [faculty of] imagination, it imagines [the concept] together with these accidents, without being able to entirely ABSTRACT it from them. Still, [imagination] ABSTRACTS it from the afore-mentioned connection [through position] on which sense-perception depends, so that [imagination] represents the form [of the thing] despite the absence of the form's [outside] carrier.
>
> As for the intellect, it is able to ABSTRACT *(tajrīd)* the essence which is enclosed[73] in extraneous accidents that individuate it,[74] securing it as if [the intellect] were acting upon the sense-perceptible [form] in a way that would make it intelligible.[75]

This is, indeed, a very dense fusion of various strands of abstraction theory as present in Avicenna's works of the middle period. It starts off, just as in the *Dāneshnāme*, with a distinction between different kinds of perceptions rather than abstractions. But shortly afterwards Avicenna touches upon the familiar doctrine of forms: imagine (and this is the more speculative tone of the *Ishārāt*) that one would give a different place, position, quality etc. to the essence of humanity, the essence itself would not be affected in any way. Avicenna here gives a new expression to the distinction between the forms' essences and their existence and even invokes the corresponding vocabulary, without however mentioning the forms' existential independence also of the intellect.[76]

There follow the three increasing degrees of abstraction; they are reduced from four to three by omitting estimation from the scala. Although this is a heavily abbreviated version of the doctrine, the vocabulary *(jarrada, tajrīd)* and line of argument show that the topic is the same as in the middle period: the difference between external senses, internal senses and intellect with regard to perception is explained in terms of varying powers of abstraction. A development of doctrine can be seen in the prominence given to the phrase "connection through position" *(ʿalāqa waḍʿiyya)* existing between perception and matter, that is, the fact that there is no sense-perception if the object is not present. In earlier versions, Avicenna had also mentioned a "relation" *(nisba)*[77] between object and perceiver as characteristic of sense-perception, but he had not yet spoken of this relation as something necessarily "grasped" by the senses and "abstracted" by imagination. We see him here elaborating a theoretical concept not yet fully developed in the middle period in order to create the highly condensed doctrine of the late *magnum opus*.

The passage in the *Ishārāt* ends with a sentence on intellectual abstraction which sounds just as a conclusion to the present article: the explicit use of abstraction terminology, the transformation of sense-perceptible forms into intelligible forms, the invoking of essentialist vocabulary with respect to the abstracted forms, and, above all, a reference – present in Avicenna's work since the early *Compendium* – to the very active part played by the human intellect: abstraction means that the intellect "acts upon" *(ʿamila bi)* the sense-perceptible form "in a way that would make it intelligible".

If the human intellect's activity is a constant feature of Avicenna's theory, this is not true of the role of the separate active intellect which changes from assistance to mediation, as we have seen. The *Ishārāt* give a final twist to the story:

> The multiplicity of the soul's occupations with sense-perceptible imaginable forms and connotational images,[78] which are in the form-bearing and the remembering [faculties respectively], with the help *(istikhdām)* of the estimative and cogitative faculty, makes the soul obtain a disposition for the reception of ABSTRACTIONS of them [i.e., of the imaginable forms and images] from the separate substance through some kind of relationship between the two. Observation and inspection of the issue verify this. These occupations [with imaginable forms and images] are those which give [the soul] a perfect disposition that is specific for [the reception of] each individual form, though an intellectual concept may [also] provide this specific [disposition] for [the reception of] another intellectual concept.[79]

One recognizes elements of doctrine central to Avicenna's abstraction theory since his earliest works: for instance, the role of "assistance" performed by the internal faculties; the soul's consideration of sense-data. But what is missing, is the analogy of light and, with it, the doctrine of the active intellect as a mediator — not to speak of an assisting factor — in the process of abstraction. In this *al-Ishārāt* differ from all other works treated, including the *Dāneshnāme*; it may be an indication of Avicenna's gradual emancipation from the Peripatetic tradition. The result, from a doctrinal point of view, is a theory that appears to reduce the consideration of imaginable forms to a mere preparation for an emanation of abstractions. Upon closer inspection, however, this interpretation does not hold: for Avicenna has taken over from *De anima* (or *Mashriqiyyūn* or *Dāneshnāme*) the phrase "their abstractions" *(mujarradātihā)*, that is, abstractions from the afore-mentioned forms stored in imagination and memory. Even in the *Ishārāt*, no doubt is left about the origin of these intelligible forms: they ultimately derive from sense-data. The concept of the active intellect as mediator is still in force.

One also notes that there is only one active power in the process, the human intellect: it turns towards the imaginable forms and acts upon them — which is the sense of *taṣarrufāt fī*, "occupations with". These occupations give to the intellect a particular disposition to acquire a specific form; they particularize or "customize" *(mukhaṣṣiṣa)* the intellect for its reception. In other words, by looking through the many data furnished by the senses, the intellect assumes a focus that allows for the discernment of a specific intelligible form. Clearly, the protagonist in abstraction remains the human intellect.

VI

Is Avicenna's language of abstraction a *façon de parler* for emanation, and should we hence refrain from taking him literally in this context? Does he himself negate the reality of abstraction as a cognitive process? Or is he simply unable to explain intellectual abstraction in knowledge? *Pace diligentiae* of those who have given affirmative answers, mine can only be negative. It seems impossible to deny that Avicenna was convinced of the human power of abstraction, that he meant what he said and that he was fully capable of developing a theory of impressive quality, if measured against al-Fārābī's or those of his thirteenth-century Latin readers.[80]

Modern interpreters have perhaps been too impressed — and thus misguided — by some salient features of Avicenna's philosophy: the ample usage of emanation terminology, the fact that the active intellect is not part of the soul but nevertheless plays an essential role in human intellection, and the denial of intellectual memory, or rather the attribution of this function to the active intellect. It seemed impossible to integrate an actively abstracting human intellect into such a system — which however is exactly what Avicenna did. He achieved this not by turning one or the other of his discourses into a metaphorical, non-literal one, but rather by giving a new sense to transmitted vocabulary and a new explanation to traditional doctrines. Since abstraction is a complex phenomenon and since Avicenna developed his position gradually, one can find passages relevant to the topic in many different contexts of Avicenna's oeuvre. Combining these passages does not yet give us a clear picture of the theory: the increasing complexity of his philosophy makes it difficult to decide which pieces of doctrine are interrelated and which are not. This is why it seems advisable to attempt a developmental interpretation by describing the gradual transformation of groups of doctrines.

It is an entirely different question — and certainly not an interesting question for everybody — whether Avicenna's theory of abstraction deserves its name if compared to a systematic concept of abstraction derived from the longue durée of intellectual history. In view of the fact that Avicenna is a major factor in the historical shaping of the concept, one feels reluctant to believe that he falls short of speaking properly about it.

Notes

1. Avicenna, *al-Shifāʾ, al-Ṭabīʿiyyāt, Kitāb al-nafs*, edited by F. Rahman (London: Oxford Univ. Press, 1959) (quoted as: *De anima*, ed. Rahman), ch. V,5, p. 235, line 7.
2. F. Rahman, *Prophecy in Islam: Philosophy and Orthodoxy* (London: George Allen and Unwin, 1958), p. 15. Cf. L. Gardet, *La Pensée religieuse d'Avicenne* (Paris: J. Vrin, 1951), p. 151: 'Il n'y a donc pas abstraction proprement dite'.
3. H. A. Davidson, *Alfarabi, Avicenna, and Averroes on Intellect* (New York, Oxford: Oxford Univ. Press, 1992), p. 94.

4. Davidson, *Alfarabi*, p. 93.

5. J. A. Weisheipl, "Aristotle's Concept of Nature: Avicenna and Aquinas", in *Approaches to Nature in the Middle Ages*, edited by L.D. Rogers (Binghamton, N.Y.: Center for medieval and early Renaissance studies, 1982), p. 150. Cf. D. Black, "Avicenna on the Ontological and Epistemic Status of Fictional Beings", *Documenti e studi sulla tradizione filosofica medievale* 8 (1997), p. 445: '... he denies the reality of abstraction as a cognitive process'. Cf. as probable sources for this line of interpretation, F. Brentano, *Die Psychologie des Aristoteles* (Mainz: Kirchheim, 1867), p. 14 ('das Sinnliche hört auf die Quelle des geistigen Erkennens zu sein') and Thomas Aquinas, *Summa contra gentiles*, 2.74, and idem, *Summa theologiae*, I.84.4.c.

6. Avicenna, *De anima* V,5, ed. Rahman, pp. 235-6.

7. A.-M. Goichon, *La Distinction de l'essence et de l'existence d'après Ibn Sīnā* (Paris: Desclée de Brouwer, 1937), p. 309: "Mais l'intelligible est-il abstrait par l'âme ou donné par l'Intellect actif? En rigueur de termes, ni l'un ni l'autre".

8. See D. Gutas, *Avicenna and the Aristotelian Tradition* (Leiden: E. J. Brill, 1988), pp. 79-145; M. Marmura, "Plotting the Course of Avicenna's Thought", *Journal of the American Oriental Society* 111 (1991), pp. 334-336; J. Michot, "La Réponse d'Avicenne à Bahmanyār et al-Kirmānī", *Le Muséon* 110 (1997), pp. 153-163. Cf. also Michot's earlier book *La destinée de l'homme selon Avicenne* (Louvain: Peeters, 1986), pp. 6-7, and L. E. Goodman, *Avicenna* (London/New York: Routledge, 1992), pp. 1-48.

9. See P. Aubenque, T. Kobusch, L. Oeing-Hanhoff et al., "Abstraktion", *Historisches Wörterbuch der Philosophie* (Basel: Schwabe and Co, 1971-), vol. 1, pp. 42-65. On Thomas Aquinas's distinction between *abstractio* and *separatio* see J. F. Wippel, "Metaphysics and *Separatio* in Thomas Aquinas", in idem, *Metaphysical Themes in Thomas Aquinas*, Washington, D.C.: The Catholic University of America Press, 1984, pp. 69-82. Cf. also (on Alexander of Aphrodisias, Boethius, Abelard and Avicenna): A. de Libera, *L'art des généralités. Théories de l'abstraction* (Paris: Aubier, 1999).

10. For comparisons of al-Fārābī and Avicenna on abstraction see F. Rahman, "Ibn Sīna", in *A History of Muslim Philosophy*, edited by M. M. Sharif (Wiesbaden: Harrassowitz, 1963), vol. 1, p. 495, and Davidson, *Alfarabi*, p. 93. For the late Greek and early Arabic tradition see Arnzen's commentary on Ibn al-Biṭrīq's paraphrase (extant in a revised version) of Aristotle's *De anima* in R. Arnzen, *Aristoteles' De anima: eine verlorene spätantike Paraphrase in arabischer und persischer Überlieferung* (Leiden: E. J. Brill, 1997), pp. 335 and 451-2.

11. Al-Fārābī, *Mabādiʾ arāʾ ahl al-madīna al-fāḍila*, edited and translated by R. Walzer (Oxford: Clarendon Press, 1985), pp. 202-203.

12. Al-Fārābī, *al-Mabādiʾ*, pp. 204-205.

13. Al-Fārābī, *Risāla Fī al-ʿaql*, edited by M. Bouyges, Bibliotheca Arabica Scholasticorum, Série arabe 8,1 (Beirut: Imprimerie catholique, 1938), p. 12. Cf. the Latin translation, *De intellectu et intellecto*, edited by E. Gilson, "Les sources gréco-arabes de l'augustinisme avicennisant", *Archives d'Histoire Doctrinale et Littéraire du Moyen Age* 4 (1929), p. 117: "... vel aliquid cuius essentia apta est abstrahere quidditates omnium quae sunt et formas eorum a suis materiis".

14. Al-Fārābī, *Risāla Fī al-ʿaql*, p. 20, line 6. Cf. Latin tr., *De intellectu et intellecto*, p. 120, line 185.

15. Aristotle, *De anima* III.4, 430a2-6.

16. Al-Fārābī, *Risāla Fī al-ʿaql*, p. 27, line 6. Cf. Latin tr., *De intellectu et intellecto*, p. 122, line 265.

17. As maintained by Davidson, *Alfarabi*, p. 93.

18. The early dating is well established: see S. Landauer, "Die Psychologie des Ibn Sīnā", *Zeitschrift der deutschen morgenländischen Gesellschaft* 29 (1875), pp. 336-9; Michot, *La destinée*, p. 6; Gutas, *Avicenna*, pp. 82-4; Marmura, "Plotting", p. 341.

19. For textual comments the following abbreviations are used: La = Landauer's edition, Ah = al-Ahwānī's edition, A = manuscript A in Landauer, B = manuscript B in Landauer, tr. Al = Alpago's Latin translation, tr. La = Landauer's German translation in "Die Psychologie" (full references in footnote 29). The phrase 'form-bearing' translates *al-mutaṣawwira* (La, Ah, tr. Al: *informativa*); this does not refer to the rational soul and its power to form concepts, but is an alternative term for common sense in the *Compendium* (cf. ed. Landauer, p. 352, line 13, p. 359, lines 4-5). In later writings, Avicenna uses the term *al-muṣawwira* for the faculty of imagination, the storing-place of sense-data (see the *Lexiques* in S. Van Riet, editor, *Avicenna Latinus. Liber de anima seu sextus de naturalibus IV-V* (Louvain: Éditions orientalistes/Leiden: E. J. Brill, 1968), pp. 244-245).

20. 'forms': *ṣuwar* (Ah); 'form': *ṣūra* (La), *formae vel speciei* (tr. Al).

21. 'man': *insān* (B, Ah); *zayd* (A, La); *Platonis* (tr. Al).

22. 'in someone forming concepts': *fī mutaṣawwir* (La, Ah); 'wenn man an den Begriff ... denkt' (tr. La); *in forma* (tr. Al).

23. 'it': *wajadat-hā* (conj. La), 'inuenit eas' (tr. Al); *wajadnā-humā* (A, La, Ah); *wajada-humā* (B).

24. 'axioms': *al-badā'ih* (B, La, tr. Al: *principiis*); *bidāya* (A, Ah).
25. 'the object of sense-perception ... imitation of': om. Ah.
26. 'assimilation': *al-tashabbuh* (B, La, Ah); *al-tashbīh* ('comparison': A).
27. 'performs the abstraction': *taf'alu ... tajarrud* (La, tr. Al: *operatur ... denudando*); *ta'qilu ... bi-tajrīd* ('knows the abstraction': Ah).
28. 'For this reason ... active'; om. tr. Al.
29. Avicenna, *Compendium on the Soul*, edited by Landauer, "Die Psychologie", p. 362, line 16; edited by A. F. al-Ahwānī, *Aḥwāl al-nafs* (Cairo: el-Halaby and Co., 1952), p. 169, line 10; Latin translation by A. Alpago, *Compendium de anima* (Venice: Giunta, 1546, repr. Farnborough: Gregg International, 1969), p. 23v; alternative English translation by E. A. van Dyck, *A Compendium on the Soul* (Verona: Nicola Paderno, 1906), p. 72.
30. On Avicenna's theory of axioms and primary intelligibles see D.N. Hasse, 'Das Lehrstück von den vier Intellekten in der Scholastik: von den arabischen Quellen bis zu Albertus Magnus', *Recherches de Théologie et Philosophie médiévales* 66 (1999), pp. 31-36.
31. 'in it [scil. the rational soul]': *fī-hi* (La with footnote: "suffixum masc.?"; Ah); cf. tr. Al: "in ea", scil. *virtus rationalis*, tr. La: "in ihr", scil. "denkende Seele".
32. Avicenna, *Compendium on the Soul*, ed. Landauer, p. 371, line 9; ed. al-Ahwānī, p. 177, line 3; Latin tr., *Compendium de anima*, p. 34r, line 6.
33. For matters of chronology in general, see the references in n. 8 above.
34. Gutas, *Avicenna*, pp. 41 and 103-106; the earliest possible dating for *De anima* is 1015, but since in 1021 only 20 folia of the section on natural philosophy had been finished (as reported by Jūzjānī, Avicenna's secretary; see the translation in Gutas, ibid., p. 41), the later dating (1022-4) is more probable. Michot argues for a dating earlier than 1021; see his 'La Réponse', p. 157, n. 58.
35. Avicenna, *Ḥāl al-nafs al-insāniyya*, ed. al-Ahwānī, *Aḥwāl* (as in n. 29 above), pp. 69-73; Avicenna, *De anima* II,2, ed. Rahman, pp. 58-61 (= the Latin *Liber de anima seu Sextus de naturalibus*, ed. Van Riet, pp. 114-20); Avicenna, *al-Najāt* (2nd edition: Cairo, 1357/1938), pp. 168-71; Avicenna, *al-Mashriqiyyūn*, MS Istanbul, Ahmet III 2125, fols 665v-666v.
36. F. Rahman, *Avicenna's Psychology. An English Translation of Kitāb al-Najāt, book II, chapter VI* (London: Oxford Univ. Press), pp. 38-40.
37. 'concept': *al-ma'nā* (*De anima*, *Mashriqiyyūn*); om. (*Ḥāl*, *Najāt*).
38. Avicenna, *Ḥāl al-nafs al-insāniyya*, ed. Ahwānī, p. 69; = *al-Shifā': De anima*, ed. Rahman, II,2, p. 58, line 4; = Latin tr., ed. Van Riet, p. 114, =

Mashriqiyyūn MS Ah, fol. 665v, = *Najāt*, ed. Cairo, p. 168, line 22, translation by Rahman, slightly modified, p. 38.

39. 'by accident': *lā ya'riḍu* (*Ḥāl, Najāt*); *lā 'araḍa* (*De anima, Mashriqiyyūn*).
40. [...]: *Ḥāl, Najāt, Mashriqiyyūn*; om. *De anima.*
41. 'completely': *min kulli wajhin* (*Ḥāl, Najāt, Mashriqiyyūn*); om. (*De anima*).
42. 'takes': *fa-ta'khudhu* (*Najāt*); *fa-ya'khudhu* (*Ḥāl*); *wa-ḥattā yakūna qad akhadha* (*De anima, Mashriqiyyūn*).
43. 'if': *wa-law* (*De anima, Mashriqiyyūn*); *thumma* (*Ḥāl, Najāt*).
44. Avicenna, *Ḥāl al-nafs al-insāniyya*, ed. Ahwānī, p. 72; = *al-Shifā': De anima*, ed. Rahman, II,2, p. 61, line 5; = Latin tr., ed. Van Riet, p. 120, = *Mashriqiyyūn* MS Ah, fol. 666r-v, = *Najāt*, ed. Cairo, p. 170, line 20, translation by Rahman, slightly modified, p. 40.
45. Avicenna, *Ḥāl al-nafs al-insāniyya*, ed. Ahwānī, p. 69; = *al-Shifā': De anima*, ed. Rahman, II,2, p. 58, line 11; = Latin tr., ed. Van Riet, p. 115, = *Mashriqiyyūn* MS Ah, fol. 665v, = *Najāt*, ed. Cairo, p. 169, line 4, translation by Rahman, p. 38 (slightly modified).
46. On these doctrines see Rahman, "Ibn Sīna", pp. 483-6.
47. For the *Logic* part see: Avicenna, *al-Shifā', al-Manṭiq, al-Madkhal* (Eisagoge), edited by G. C. Anawati et al. (Cairo: Imprimerie nationale, 1952), ch. I,12, pp. 65-9 (on particularity and universality as accidents to the essential concept).
48. Avicenna, *al-Shifā': al-Ilāhiyyāt*, edited by G. C. Anawati and S. Zayed (Cairo: Imprimeries Gouvernementales, 1960), V.1, p. 205 (= Latin tr., *Liber De Philosophia prima sive Scientia divina*, edited by S. Van Riet, 3 vols, Louvain/Leiden: E. Peeters/E. J. Brill, 1977-83, vol. II, p. 238).
49. At present state of research, the influence has only been documented for the Latin tradition; see the references to Dominicus Gundissalinus, anonymous *De anima et de potentiis eius*, Jean de la Rochelle, Alexander of Hales, Albertus Magnus, Vincent of Beauvais, Petrus Hispanus and Anonymous (MS Siena) in D.N. Hasse, *Avicenna's De anima in the Latin West*, Warburg Institute Studies and Texts 1 (London/Turin: The Warburg Institute/Nino Aragno Editore, 2000), pp. 200-203 and Index Locorum II.2.b-g.
50. The *Mashriqiyyūn* write: 'The rational soul, however, sometimes employs the help of the animal faculties: they assist it in various ways'.
51. 'mind': *dhihn* (*De anima, Mashriqiyyūn*); *nafs* (*Ḥāl, Najāt*).
52. 'in it': *fī-hi* (*De anima, Mashriqiyyūn, Najāt*); *fī-hā* ('in them': *Ḥāl*).
53. Avicenna, *Ḥāl al-nafs al-insāniyya*, ed. Ahwānī, p. 87 (= *al-Shifā': De anima*, ed. Rahman, V,3, p. 221, line 17, = Latin tr., ed. Van Riet, p. 102, =

Mashriqiyyūn MS Ah, fol. 685r-v, = *Najāt*, ed. Cairo, p. 182, tr. Rahman, pp. 54-55).

54. Cf. Rahman's translation in *Avicenna's Psychology*, p. 56: "When not so diverted, [the soul] does not need the lower faculties for its special activity, except in certain matters wherein it specially needs to refer once more to the faculty of imagination for finding a new principle in addition to what had already been obtained, or for recalling an image" (for references to the Arabic text see next footnote). The theory of acquisition and reacquisition is discussed most fully by Avicenna in *De anima* V,6, esp. p. 247; it is put in context in Hasse, *Avicenna's De anima in the Latin West* (as in n. 49), pp. 174-89, esp. pp. 186-7.
55. Avicenna, *Ḥāl al-nafs al-insāniyya*, ed. Ahwānī, p. 89, line 4 (= *al-Shifā': De anima*, ed. Rahman, V,3, p. 223, line 8, = Latin tr., ed. Van Riet, p. 105, = *Mashriqiyyūn* MS Ah, fol. 685v, line 18, = *Najāt*, ed. Cairo, p. 183, line 7, tr. Rahman, p. 56). Some of these editions or manuscripts erroneously read *dhāt* instead of *dābba* (*Ḥāl*, *Najāt* and *Mashriqiyyūn*; corrected on the basis of better manuscripts by Rahman, *Avicenna's psychology*, p. 125). The example of the riding animal is briefly discussed by Davidson, *Alfarabi*, p. 104.
56. Avicenna, *Ḥāl al-nafs al-insāniyya*, ed. Ahwānī, p. 112; = *Najāt*, ed. Cairo, p. 193, = translation by Rahman, p. 69.
57. Gutas argues for an early dating of *Ḥāl al-nafs*; see his *Avicenna and the Aristotelian Tradition*, pp. 99-100. See Michot, *La destinée de l'homme*, pp. 6-7, n. 29, for the contrary opinion.
58. Such terminology is also missing in the Avicennian treatise on prophetic knowledge called *Fī ithbāt al-nubuwwāt*, edited by M. E. Marmura (Beirut: Dār Al-Nahār, 1968).
59. *jumla* here means 'gist', 'essence', not 'all', 'whole' (the Latin has *similis*).
60. 'or rather': *bal* (*De anima*); om. (*Mashriqiyyūn*).
61. Avicenna, *De anima* V,5, ed. Rahman, p. 235, line 2; = Latin tr., ed. Van Riet, p. 127; = *Mashriqiyyūn* MS Ah, fol. 688v.
62. Cf. Weisheipl, 'Aristotle's Concept of Nature', p. 150: "According to Avicenna, human teachers and books can only dispose the mind to be receptive of new concepts from the dator formarum, the 'agent intellect'"; and Davidson, *Alfarabi*, p. 93: "Activity leading up to the ostensible act of abstraction thus does not come to fruition in a true act of abstraction. It rather prepares the way for the reception of abstract concepts from the emanation of the active intellect".
63. *Pace* Rahman, who translates (in *Prophecy in Islam*, p. 15): "... but only in

the sense that its consideration prepares the soul so that the abstract form should emanate upon it from the Active Intelligence" (my emphasis).

64. Davidson, *Alfarabi*, pp. 102 and 93.

65. Davidson takes *fikr* ("reasoning", "cogitation") to refer only to the cogitative faculty *(al-mufakkira)*; see his *Alfarabi*, pp. 95-102. In fact, Avicenna's use of the term is varied and it refers to reasoning processes both in the animal soul, where the cogitative faculty resides, and in the rational soul. At one point in the *De anima* (IV,2, p. 175, line 9) he even implies that intellectual reasoning *(al-fikr al-nuṭqī)* is hindered by the imaginative/cogitative faculty of the animal soul. Further, one of the key passages for Davidson's interpretation (*Alfarabi*, p. 96) is *Mubāḥathāt* (edited by A. Badawī, *Arisṭū ʿinda l-ʿArab*, Cairo: al-Nahḍa al-Miṣriyya, 1947, pp. 122-239) p. 199, line 12, where it is said that *fikr* consists in seeking the perfect disposition to make contact with the active intellect. But this passage is adopted from *De anima* V,6, p. 247, line 3, where the term is not *fikr* but *taʿallum*: "acquiring knowledge", or "acquiring an intelligible form". See also the article by Dimitri Gutas in this volume.

66. Gutas, *Avicenna*, p. 114, suggests the year 1027; Michot, *Destinée*, p. 7, and 'La Réponse', p. 161, places it between 1030 and 1034.

67. Avicenna, *Dāneshnāme*, edited by S. M. Meshkāt (Tehran, 1974), vol. 2, pp. 125-6; cf. the French translation by M. Achena and H. Massé in *Avicenne: Le Livre de science* (2nd edition: Paris: Les belles lettres/Unesco, 1986), p. 79.

68. Cf. the first sentences of the doctrine in its classical formulation (translated above, reference in n. 38) with the opening paragraph in *Dāneshnāme*, ed. Meshkāt, p. 102, tr. Achena/Massé, p. 66: "Toute connaissance que nous acquérons est la quiddité, l'idée et la forme de telle chose que nous appréhendons. L'on saisit de diverses manières la forme d'une chose. A cette fin, prenons comme exemple l'humanité".

69. Avicenna, *Dāneshnāme*, ed. Meshkāt, vol. 2, p. 124, tr. Achena/Massé, p. 78: "Mais tant que tout d'abord les sensations et les imaginations n'existent pas, notre intelligence ne vient pas à l'acte. Et quand les sensations et les imaginations viennent à l'existence, les formes se mêlent à des accidents qui leur sont étrangers, et elles sont alors voilées comme les choses qui se trouvent dans l'obscurité. Mais ensuite le rayonnement de l'intelligence active tombe sur les imaginations, de même que celui du soleil tombe sur les formes [des choses] qui se trouvent dans l'obscurité. Puis, partant de ces imaginations, les formes ABSTRAITES se présentent à l'intelligence, de même qu'à cause de la lumière les formes visibles se présentent dans le miroir ou dans l'oeil: comme ces formes sont ABSTRAITES, elles sont universelles; en effet, si tu

retranches de [la perception] d'humanité les parties superflues, il en reste le concept général, tandis que les particularités individuelles disparaissent".

70. The references are to the edition of Badawī, *Arisṭū* (as in n. 65 above). A similar case is Avicenna's *Marginal Notes on the De anima* (edited by Badawī in the same volume, pp. 75-116): it is doubtful whether a collection of passages employing abstraction terminology (e.g., *Marginal Notes*, pp. 96.4, 110.4, 111.7-8) or an analysis of key passages (such as p. 110, lines 10-12, on the light of the active intellect falling upon forms stored in imagination with the effect of their abstraction) will offer us more than heterogeneous pieces of a theory which Avicenna treats systematically elsewhere.

71. Cf. n. 65 above.

72. The anonymous Longer Bibliography, which is based on a list by Jūzjānī, calls it "the last and best work he wrote on philosophy, to which he held steadfastly", edited and translated in W. E. Gohlman, *The Life of Ibn Sina* (Albany, N.Y.: State University of New York Press, 1974), pp. 96-97. Gohlman dates the book to 1024-37 (ibid., p. 154); Gutas, *Avicenna*, p. 140, argues more specifically for the years 1030-34. Michot, 'La réponse', pp. 153-163 — against his earlier view on the problem (cf. *La destinée*, p. 7) — prefers a date as early as 1016, but acknowledges that the *Ishārāt* postdate the *De anima* and the logic part of *al-Shifāʾ*, which was begun in 1015 at the very earliest and completed in 1027. However, in view of the enormous scale of *al-Shifāʾ* and of its intellectual complexity, which would demand a longer period of composition, and on the basis of the internal evidence laid out in the present article, the traditional dating seems much more probable.

73. 'enclosed': *maknūfa*; cf. the passage in *De anima* II.2, p. 61, line 4: *maknūfa bi-lawāḥiqi al-mādda* (Latin tr.: 'stipatam accidentibus materiae').

74. 'that individuate it': *mushakhkhaṣ* (misprint in Dunyā: *mushakhkhash*).

75. Avicenna, *al-Ishārāt wa al-tanbīhāt*, edited by S. Dunyā, 4 vols (Cairo, 1960-68), vol. 2, p. 367. Cf. the French translation by A.-M. Goichon, *Avicenne: Livre des Directives et Remarques, traduction avec introduction et notes* (Beirut/Paris: J. Vrin, 1951), p. 314.

76. On the object of perception see also the preceding paragraph in *al-Ishārāt*, ed. Dunyā, vol. 2, pp. 359-66 (tr. Goichon, *Livre des Directives et Remarques*, pp. 311-12).

77. Avicenna, *De anima* II,2, ed. Rahman, p. 59, lines 11-12.

78. 'connotational': *al-maʿnawiyya* (Dunyā; ='intentional', refers to the objects of estimation); *al-maʿqūla* (Goichon: 'intelligibles').

79. Avicenna, *al-Ishārāt wa al-tanbīhāt*, ed. Dunyā, vol. 2, p. 403; cf. Ṭūṣī's comment, ibid., footnote 1. Cf. tr. Goichon, *Livre des Directives et*

Remarques, p. 333.

80. For general information on the history of abstraction theory, see notes 9 and 49 above. See also J. Rohmer, "La Théorie de l'abstraction dans l'école franciscaine d'Alexandre de Halès à Jean Peckham", *Archives d'Histoire Doctrinale et Littéraire du Moyen Age* 3 (1928), pp. 105-184.

Simplicius and Avicenna on the Essential Corporeity of Material Substance*

ABRAHAM D. STONE

Avicenna and Simplicius are, broadly speaking, part of the same philosophical tradition: the tradition of Neoplatonic or Neoplatonizing Aristotelianism. There is probably no *direct* historical connection between them, however, and anyway I will not try to demonstrate one in this paper. Nor, similarly, will I attempt a historical comparison between their views and the true views of Aristotle, whatever those may be. It is in general very difficult, and also, often, of limited importance, to determine exactly what Aristotle really means; it is usually both more important and easier (though by no means trivial) to determine how his interpreters understand him. I will therefore limit myself to explaining and comparing the closely related, but ultimately quite different, accounts of corporeity, and in particular of the essential relationship between corporeity and materiality, that Simplicius and Avicenna put forward in Aristotle's name.

The problem they both face in this respect is as follows. There is a certain genus of substances which forms the subject matter of the science of physics.[1] I will refer to the members of this genus as the physical substances. On the one hand, all and only these physical substances are bodies; on the other hand, all and only they are material — that is to say, are

* Thanks are due to R. Wisnovsky and to an anonymous reviewer, both of whom read earlier versions of this paper with great care and made many helpful comments, criticisms, and corrections.

composed of form and matter.[2] This in itself is not problematic. It is often the case that all and only the members of a certain genus or species share several characteristics, and the reason that these characteristics are connected to one another may be unclear. For example, all and only human beings are rational, and all and only human beings have the capacity to laugh. A problem arises, however, because Simplicius and Avicenna take it that both materiality and corporeity are essential to physical substances as such.

The *essence* or *quiddity* of a thing is that which is signified by its definition.[3] An essential predicate is therefore one which belongs to the members of a certain genus or species by definition: something without which they cannot be conceived.[4] "Rational," for example, according to most if not all Aristotelians, is essential to humanity: a human being is by definition a rational animal. In contrast to this are other predicates which, although they belong to all and only the members of a certain genus or species, are not essential, but mere "concomitants" of the essence: characteristics which must always attach to the members of that genus or species in reality, but without which they can nevertheless be conceived. If either corporeity or materiality were merely concomitant to the physical substances, then it would be possible to understand one without the other, and in particular it would be possible not to know why these two characteristics are always and only found together. If, however, physical substances are essentially both corporeal and material, then either these two characteristics must be identical (i.e. "corporeal" and "material" must, in the relevant senses, be synonymous), or, if they are different, there must be a conceptually unavoidable connection between the two. Simplicius, as we will see, argues for the former option, and Avicenna for the latter. To understand their respective positions, and the particular difficulties which they are designed to solve, it is necessary first to say a few words about matter and body as they are understood in the Aristotelian tradition.

Matter

Aristotelian matter fulfills two distinct functions — I will call them the "physical" and "metaphysical" functions.

Matter in its physical role is a permanent substrate of change. Both Plato and Aristotle were driven to introduce such a substrate because change, strictly speaking, is between opposites. Something not-white, say, becomes white. But the not-white cannot literally become white: when the white arrives, the not-white as such must already have departed. This paradox is solved by assuming that, in every change, there is something that remains constant, and which takes on each of the opposites in turn. What changes is the form; what remains is the matter.[5]

In its metaphysical role, on the other hand, matter is the subject of determination. The quiddity of a composite, that which is indicated by its definition (i.e. by a list of essential predicates), that which determines something to be such-and-such, is its form. The matter, in contrast, is the undetermined which receives this determination.[6]

Both of these functions require that matter itself be formless. Physical matter, as the substrate which can receives two opposites, must not as such possess either of them; metaphysical matter, as the subject of determination, must not as such have either the determination in question or its opposite. It must be, in itself, "the indeterminate [*aoristos*], before it is determined and participates in some form."[7]

These two kinds of formlessness are in most cases equivalent. What is determined, by a form, as either white or not-white, must not in itself possess either of these determinations, and similarly what serves as the substrate for a change from one to the other. But the formlessness in such a case is merely relative: the matter must not be white or not-white, but it may be determined in other ways. The difference between the two becomes apparent only if we focus on prime matter, which is purely matter, absolutely without form.[8] *Absolute* formlessness means different things, depending on whether matter is physically or metaphysically construed. Since the physical distinction between matter and form is merely a distinction between what remains and what does not remain in the course of some change, there is no absurdity in supposing that the ultimate physical matter has its own positive character, so long as it is conserved under all changes. Metaphysical prime matter, on the other hand, must be without positive intrinsic predicates. "By matter," says Aristotle,

> I mean that which per se is said neither to be a quid nor a quan-

> tum nor any other [thing] by which being is determined. For there is something of which each of these is predicated, the essence of which [*hôi to einai*] is other than each of the predicates.[9]

Though nothing positive can be said about metaphysical prime matter, it can be truly described by a kind of negation. Plotinus makes a show of disagreeing with Aristotle about the explanation for this: whereas Aristotle says that negations belong to matter only per accidens, Plotinus argues that "infinite" and "indeterminate," at least, are essential to it, and that this is allowable because to predicate a privation of something is not to assert that there is some form in it.[10] But in truth their positions are identical. What Aristotle calls a negation per accidens is really just an example of Plotinus' indeterminateness. Matter is not per se not-white, for example, in the sense that it does not have some inherent characteristic which excludes whiteness — i.e., matter is not some *other* color. Matter, rather, is not-white per accidens, in the sense that its nature is different from that of the white, i.e. does not include whiteness. But if "not-white" is itself taken to mean just that, "not-in-itself-determined-as-white," then it names an *essential* characteristic of prime matter, in the sense that prime matter is not conceptually separable from that indeterminacy. Prime matter does not have an essence, properly speaking, since a proper essence would have to consist of a finite number of *positive* characteristics; it therefore has no proper definition, and is "unknowable per se."[11] But, because negative predicates of intedeterminacy are nevertheless essential to it, a kind of per accidens definition of it, and hence a kind of per accidens knowledge about it, is possible by way of the *via negationis*. That is how Simplicius understands both Aristotle's statement that we know prime matter "according to analogy"[12] and Plato's that it is "insensibly tangible by a certain bastard reason":[13]

> This knowledge "according to analogy" Plato called bastard reason, because it comes to be not by the impression of form, but by stripping-off and negation of forms; and reason sees matter as if with its eye closed.[14]

The idea of an essential, but purely privative, characterization of prime matter suggests one way to make sense of Aristotle's assertion that matter is a kind of substance.[15] There are, it is true, other passages where Aristotle distinguishes between matter, on the one hand, and substance, on the other, or even denies outright that matter is a substance.[16] Many interpreters have concluded that, when he *does* refer to matter as a substance, he is using the term in a derivative or secondary sense — that matter, for example, is *potentially* a substance, but not a substance strictly speaking.[17] It goes hand in hand with this interpretation that matter is not, strictly speaking, a "kind" of substance, in the sense of falling, in a strict sense, under the category of substance as its genus.[18] Avicenna, however, takes Aristotle's statements that prime matter is a kind of substance quite literally.[19] If prime matter really is a kind of substance, however, in a strict rather than a derivative sense, then it belongs to a genus, the genus of substance; because, moreover, not every substance is prime matter, it must also have a differentia. But this genus and differentia are predicates, and predicates, one would think, require a subject — i.e., are forms in matter, in the metaphysical sense. Prime matter qua substance therefore seems not to be prime matter after all. As Avicenna puts the argument:

> Someone might ask, and say: hyle, too, is composite, and that is because it is in itself hyle, and a substance in actu [i.e., that is its genus], and it is also adapted [*mustaʿidd*] [to receive form] [i.e., that is its differentia].[20]

Let us, however, look more closely into the definition of substance, or rather its description.[21] A substance, in the primary sense of the term, is something which "neither is said of any subject nor is in any subject."[22] What bothers the commentators about this description is precisely what will help us: it is purely negative. If the other categories are all described as categories of accidents — of things that are "in a subject" — then why not define substance positively, as the ultimate subject of all such accidents? "Because," says Ammonius, "not every substance is a subject: for the primary and divine substances are not subjects."[23] But this must apply, not only to "divine" (intelligible, immaterial) substances, but to prime matter, as well: it must not, properly speaking, be a subject.

This point requires some explanation. Aristotle not only often refers to matter (and presumably to prime matter) as a "subject" (*hupokeimenon*), but in fact often uses "subject" as a synonym for "matter," implying that prime matter is, so to speak, the subject par excellence. Nevertheless, Avicenna states in no uncertain terms that prime matter is *not* a subject in the relevant sense of the word: it is indeed called "subject" (*mawḍūʿ*), but "the sense [*maʿnā*] of 'subject' here is not the sense which we took in logic as part of the description of substance; the hyle is not, in that sense, a subject at all."[24] His reason for maintaining this, in the face of so much prima facie textual evidence to the contrary, is precisely the *Categories* definition of substance. For substantial form is in prime matter, so that, if prime matter is a subject, substantial form is in a subject; but substantial form is a kind of substance, therefore not in a subject: a contradiction.

There are various ways of approaching this problem. The favored modern option is to leave the contradiction unresolved: to admit, that is, that the *Categories* (perhaps because it is an early work) simply puts forward a different doctrine of substance than does *Metaphysics Z*. This option is not, of course, available to traditional interpreters. They do have the related option of claiming that the *Categories* is an introductory work, in which Aristotle therefore does not speak very precisely. They would generally prefer, however, to resolve contradictions completely, and the move which Avicenna makes here is one obvious way of doing so: if prime matter is not a subject at all, then substantial form fits the description of substance perfectly. The textual problem is then resolved by claiming that, when matter *is* called a "subject," that is a secondary or equivocal use of the term. "By 'subject,'" in the *relevant* sense, Avicenna explains, "is meant that which has become existent [*qāʾim*] in itself and in its specificity, and then became a cause that there be constituted in it [another] thing, not as a part of it."[25] The upshot is that "substance," insofar as it is predicated of matter, is not a positive predicate or determination at all.

> The meaning [*maʿnā*] of [matter's] substantiality is nothing other than that it is something [*ʾamr*] which is not in a subject. Now the affirmation here is "that it is something," whereas "that it is not in a subject" is a negation. But it does not follow, from "that it is something," that it is any singular thing [*shayʾ muʿayyan*] in actu, because this is a universal, and a thing [*shayʾ*] does not become a

> thing [*shay'*] by something general [*bi-'amr al-'āmm*] which does not have a differentia to specify it [*faṣl yakhuṣṣuhu*].[26]

As for the differentia, there is an apparent disagreement between Avicenna and Simplicius. Avicenna says that the differentia in question is "that it is adapted for every thing [*shay'*],"[27] whereas Simplicius says that matter "has no differentia at all relative to anything, since every differentia is a formal quality."[28] But, once again, the disagreement in language masks an agreement in doctrine. Normally, a differentia is a determining predicate, and must therefore be a form in (metaphysical) matter. The Plotinian essential "predicates" of pure indeterminacy which apply to prime matter, however, are not true predicates in this sense, and therefore do not imply any such form/matter distinction:

> The property [*idiotês*] of it [i.e., matter] is nothing other than what it itself is [*ouk allo ti ê hoper esti*], and the property is not added [to it], but is rather in the relation [*skhesis*] to other [things], that it is other than them.[29]

"Adapted to every thing," however, as it applies to prime matter, is just such a predicate. It certainly does not mean that prime matter has some positive power by which it actively receives or seeks out form. That is why Avicenna expresses astonishment at Aristotle's suggestion that the matter, so to speak, yearns for the form, as the female (allegedly) yearns for the male:

> For how is it possible that the hyle could move to the form? The incident form [*al-ṣūra al-ṭāri'a*] comes to it because its existent form ceases [*min sabab yabṭul ṣūratuha al-mawjūda*], not because it [the hyle] acquires it [the incident form] by its motion.[30]

Matter is "adapted to every thing," rather, by virtue of its own indeterminate nature, which does not exclude whatever determination might attach to it. Neither the genus nor the "differentia" of prime matter, therefore, implies any distinction of form and matter in it. "The substance of hyle, and its being hyle in actu, is not any other than its being a substance adapted [for form]."[31]

What remains to be explained is the relationship between this wholly indeterminate metaphysical prime matter and the physical prime matter which was needed to solve the paradox of change. It might be supposed that they are different: that the ultimate substrate of all physical change, which is therefore prime matter in the physical sense, has some determinate characteristics — i.e., is metaphysically composite. Aristotle, however, proves that this is not so, by means of his distinction between generation and corruption, on the one hand, and alteration, on the other. The distinction is supposed to be, roughly speaking, that in alteration some thing changes from one state to another, whereas generation is the coming into being of a thing which was not previously there at all. The "thing" that remains in alteration, but comes into being and passes away in generation and corruption, is the subject of accidental qualities — i.e., it is a physical substance.[32]

According to Aristotle, some of his predecessors denied that such a distinction can be drawn — a position he regards as evidently false.[33] Others, however — in particular, Empedocles — tried to explain the difference in terms of mixture and separation. Substances, they said, are composed, in different proportions, of the four elements. When the right mixture comes into being, a substance is generated; when the mixture again changes, that substance is corrupted. Alteration, on the other hand, is a change in qualities which occurs while the underlying mixture of elements remains unchanged. To this theory Aristotle objects that, among other things, it will not serve to explain the generation and corruption of the four elements themselves.[34] He takes it to be evident that these four elements are distinct types of sensible substance, and that they can be transformed completely one into the other — which process of transformation must therefore be one of generation and corruption.[35] But what, then, is the constant substrate in which this transformation takes place— what, that is, is the physical matter common to the four elements?

Whatever matter is common to these four must be common to all physical things, since, as Aristotle agrees, all physical things are composed of those elements. But whatever matter is common to all physical things must remain constant through all physical changes: when one physical thing changes to another, that common matter will remain. A physical matter which remains throughout all physical change is, however, just what we above called "physical prime matter." So the physical matter common to the elements is physical prime matter. But it must also be metaphysical prime matter. For suppose that it is not — i.e., suppose that it is not, in itself, wholly undetermined, but is rather determined by some essential (positive) predicate. Then it would have to be composed of metaphysical prime matter and some determining form — i.e., it would be a composite substance.[36] There would therefore, in every physical change, be some composite substance which remained actually present and numerically the same both before and after the change took place; the predicates which changed would be in this substance as their subject, i.e. as accidents. But that just means that such changes would never truly be generation or corruption — i.e., never the coming-into-being or passing-out-of-being of substance: we would, in other words, land back at the (supposedly) absurd conclusion that there is only alteration. The only way out of this is to assume that the substrate of generation and corruption has no determinate nature of its own, so that there is no determinate thing — no "subject," strictly speaking — that remains the same when the elements are transformed one into another. What is prime matter in the physical sense, in other words, must also be metaphysically so.

Body

Aristotle defines body in several places, and all the definitions point in a single direction: that it is a species of continuous quantity. First, there is the subdivision of quantity in the *Categories*:

> Of quantum, some is discrete, some continuous. . . . Discrete [quantity] is as, [for example], number and speech [*logos*], whereas continuous [quantity] is line, surface, body, and furthermore, besides these, time and place.[37]

The definition in the *De caelo* is also quite clear:

> Continuous, then, is that which is divisible into [parts] which are always divisible, and body is that which is divisible in all ways [*pantêi*]. Of magnitudes, that which is divisible in one [direction] is a line; in two, a surface; in three, a body.[38]

A "magnitude" is simply a continuous quantity whose parts have position.[39] Both of these passages therefore lead to the same conclusion: that body is three-dimensional magnitude, i.e. three-dimensional continuous spatial quantity.

There is a slight subtlety about this definition, however, which we must now consider. Every actual three-dimensional magnitude — i.e, every body, in the sense we are considering — is a finite solid. That is: every actual body has a determinate length, width and depth, or, more generally, determinate limits, in the form of a surface or surfaces that completely enclose it. For short, we can speak of these limits as the body's determinate dimensions.[40] One might therefore suppose that body could be defined as three-dimensional finitude. But this would leave over something else that all bodies have in common: three-dimensional extendedness, in abstraction from the finitude of that extension. If one were to define body as that which has three-dimensional limit, i.e. determinate dimension, then this "indeterminate dimension" would remain ontologically unaccounted for.[41]

Aristotle, however, does not mention limit in his definitions of body, and both Simplicius and Avicenna argue that this is no oversight. An infinite corporeal substance, they contend — a "body" without limit, and hence without any determinate dimensions or figure whatsoever — is perfectly conceivable, even though such a thing could never actually exist.[42] Therefore body as three-dimensional magnitude or measure cannot simply be identified with limitedness:

> If someone wanted to seek the form of magnitude . . . they would not find the surfaces and the containing external limit, for these are a limit of form, but not form, and a surface, but not the solid [*stereon*]. . . . the form of continuous magnitude as such is not the surface, but the nature which spreads through all of it.[43]

Similarly:

> As for continuous quantities, they are measures [*maqādir*] of continuous [things]. . . . And this measure [*miqdār*] is the continuous thing's being such that it is measured [*yumsaḥ*] by so much so many times, or [such that] the measurement [*masḥ*] does not

> terminate [*lā yantahī*], if it [i.e., the continuous thing] is imagined to be infinite [*ghayr mutanāhin*].[44]

On this way of looking at things, body qua continuous quantity is to be identified with, rather than distinguished from, indeterminate triple dimension; the figure and limits, if any, are an accident of body so construed.[45]

There is one other point to be made about body before we continue. Every physical substance, recall, is either one of the four elements, or in some way composed of them.[46] Given that such substances are essentially corporeal, it is therefore not surprising that Aristotle defines the elements as the four fundamental types of body, which differ from one another in their possession of the four fundamental tangible qualities:

> Since, then, we are searching for the principles [i.e., here, elements] of sensible, that is tangible, body, and the tangible is that of which touch is the sense, it is manifest that not all contrarieties make species and principles of body, but only those according to touch.[47]

If the elements are all bodies, however, and differ from one another only in quality, then it is natural to assume, given Aristotle's definitions of body, that they agree with one another in quantity: i.e., that "common" or "absolute" body is "qualitiless body," in the sense of body as pure quantity. True, Aristotle says that there is no such thing as "common body,"[48] and Plotinus, for one, takes this to imply that the very idea of "qualitiless body" is unintelligible: if something is body, then it has qualities.[49] But such an interpretation is hardly necessary. What Aristotle objects to is the idea of qualitiless body existing separately, i.e. being found in actuality without its qualities.[50] This does not mean that qualitiless body is a conceptual absurdity; merely that it can be considered only by abstraction from the qualities with which it always, in reality, exists.

It remains to be established what is the relationship between such qualitiless (i.e., purely quantitative) body, prime matter, and the substantial form of material substance.

Qualitiless Body, Matter, and Substantial Form

If qualitiless body is what all the elements have in common, then it must apparently remain constant as one element is transformed into another. But that would mean that, at least in a physical sense, qualitiless body is prime matter. Simplicius reports that some philsophers, including the Stoics, have attributed just this theory to Plato and Aristotle, and based on just this argument:

> For both Aristotle and Plato, first introducing, based on change, the matter of [things] that change, want the qualities of the elements to be hot, cold, dry, and damp. But these, having body as common subject, change around in it [*peri auto*], so that body would be prime matter.[51]

That qualitiless body does not exist separately, far from being a problem for this theory, is a distinct advantage. Aristotle's doctrine of prime matter is precisely "that there is some matter of sensible bodies, but that it is not separate, but always with contrariety, out of which are generated the so-called elements."[52] There are other problems with the theory, however — problems so serious, indeed, that Avicenna never seriously considers it. Simplicius discusses it at some length, but only, as he says, because it has been put forward by his distinguished colleagues and predecessors.

If we thought of corporeity qua (qualitiless) three-dimensional quantity in terms of *determinate* dimensions (or, in general, in terms of determinate limit and figure), then the theory would not be tenable even with respect to the physical role of matter. For we know that substantial change brings not only changes in quality, but also in quantity. When air, for example, is generated from water, the resulting substance has greater bulk or volume. Aristotle argues, on this basis, that "there is the same matter of great and of small body."[53] This means, as Plotinus points out, that the physical formlessness of matter must extend, not just to quality, but to determinate quantity as well. If not, then the "giver of form" (*ho morphên didous*)

> will be enslaved to its magnitude, and will make it, not so large

> as it wills, but so much as the matter wants. . . . And if [matter] had magnitude, it would necessarily also have figure, so that it would be even more unworkable [*dusergos*].[54]

Simplicius turns this argument to the purpose of showing that matter is not qualitiless body:

> But if matter is body, it will have a certain proper magnitude, and the demiurge will no longer produce all of the forms according to his own will, nor will nature [do so] according to the demiurgic logos in it, but, rather, they will necessarily be enslaved to the magnitude of the matter. But, moreover, if it has magnitude, then it also has figure by its own definition [*logos*]. This, then, is absurd . . . because matter will be unsuitable [*dusergos*] for receiving every figure, being ruled by one certain figure.[55]

This physical argument does not really apply, however, to qualitiless body as Avicenna and Simplicius themselves understand it — i.e., to what I have called "indeterminate dimension." Determinate volume may not be conserved when one substance is corrupted and another is generated, but the simple characteristic of three-dimensional extendedness certainly is. Couldn't body in this latter sense be identified with prime matter?

The problem is that prime matter must be not just physically, but also metaphysically, formless. Even, therefore, if there is some quality or other character which all physical things have in common, that quality or character cannot be identified with prime matter. As Plotinus puts it:

> But if the subject is some quality, existing [*ousa*] in common in each of the elements . . . then if the quality is determinate, how is it matter? But if it is indeterminate, then it is not a quality.[56]

It follows that body, if it has any determinate characteristic whatsoever per se, cannot be identified with matter:

> And neither is corporeity [attached] to [*peri*] it [i.e., matter]. [For] if corporeity is a logos, it [i.e., corporeity] is other than it [i.e., matter]. It itself [i.e., matter] is therefore [something] else.[57]

The indeterminateness of indeterminate dimension, however, is not absolute but relative. To say that something is three-dimensionally extended is not to specify its precise limits or figure, but it is to predicate *something* of it — i.e., to determine it in some way. Simplicius can therefore use several variations of the above metaphysical argument to show that matter is not qualitiless body, even in the indeterminate sense:

> Body is constituted from genus and differentia, for it is triply dimensional substance. But such [a thing] is form, but not matter. And furthermore, body is divided off against the incorporeal qualities, but matter is similarly related to everything. And furthermore, body is determined by three dimensions [*diastaseis*], whereas matter is completely indeterminate.[58]

Qualitiless body is therefore not to be identified with matter. It remains possible, however, that qualitiless corporeity is a generic substantial form — one which all physical substances have in common. In that case all such substances would be essentially corporeal because, and in the sense that, they are all essentially three-dimensional magnitudes. Here again, however, if we take three-dimensional magnitude in the *determinate* sense, then we can dispose of the suggestion rather easily. When water is heated, for example, it expands, and a lump of wax can change its figure arbitrarily, yet neither is corrupted by such a change: their determinate limits and figures are evidently not essential to them.[59] This shows that determinate magnitude is an accident in at least some corporeal substances. Even, therefore, if there are other corporeal substances that are essentially of a certain size and shape, so that some substantial forms are indeed (among other things) species of determinate magnitude, still determinate magnitude cannot be the generic substantial form of all corporeal substances. If there is some sense in which three-dimensional magnitude is such a generic substantial form, then it must be in the sense of indeterminate dimension.

Neither Simplicius nor Avicenna can accept this view, but it is somewhat easier to see why in Avicenna's case. This is because he and Simplicius disagree about a fundamental issue which has troubled nearly all interpreters of Aristotle, regarding the differentiae of substance. It seems that they are qualities: not just because certain qualities are said to differentiate certain substances (e.g., the four elements), but because Aristotle actually states in a blanket way that differentiae are qualities.[60] Yet a quality is a kind of accident. True, Plotinus suggests that sensible substances are nothing but bundles of accidental qualities. But that theory is in outright disagreement with Aristotle, and leads to the radical conclusion that there are not really any sensible substances at all — i.e., that sensible substance is merely phenomenal:

> And one ought not to object if we make the sensible substance out of non-substances: for neither is the whole a true substance, but that which imitates true [substance] . . . a shadow upon that which is itself a shadow, a picture and an appearing [*phainesthai*].[61]

This radical line of thought stops with Plotinus (at least, within the main line of the Aristotelian/Neoplatonic tradition) until, fourteen hundred years later, it is again taken up by Leibniz and Kant. Later Neoplatonists and Aristotelians, beginning with Plotinus' own student Porphyry, abandon the Plotinian theory of sensible substance, and of the sensible categories in general, and return to Aristotle's. They must therefore explain why Aristotle says that the differentiae of substance are qualities, without allowing that those differentiae are merely accidents. There are two solutions, one of which is adopted (following Porphyry) by Simplicius, the other by Avicenna.

Porphyry's solution takes off from something that Plotinus says in the course of describing his own theory. As Plotinus explains:

> [When I say that an accident can be part of a sensible substance,] I do not mean that there, being with the others, it is substance, completing [*sumplêroun*] one bulk of such-and-such quantity and quality, while elsewhere, not completing, it is quality. Rather, neither there is each [individual quality] substance, but the whole [composed] out of all [of them] is a substance.[62]

Porphyry takes up the rejected position, that the very same quality, depending on its context, can be either accidental or substantial. This is the theory of "substantial quality" (*poiotês ousiôdês*):

> Substantial [qualities] are those qualities that are complementa-

> tive [*sumplêrôtikai*] of substances. Those are complementative, which, in passing away, destroy [their] subjects; those that, coming to be and passing away, do not destroy [their subjects], are not substantial. Such as, [for example,] that heat pertains to hot water, and pertains also to fire. But it does not pertain substantially to water . . . whereas it pertains substantially to fire.[63]

It is true, then, that the differentiae of substance are qualities, but only in the sense that the same characteristics, e.g. heat, which serve to differentiate substance, turn up elsewhere as members of the accidental category of quality.

Avicenna is well aware of this theory, and firmly rules it out:

> Many of those who have claimed to be knowledgeable have allowed that there be some thing [*shay' min al-'ashyā'*] which is substance and accident simultaneously, in relation to two things, and say that heat is an accident in bodies other that fire [*fī ghayr jism al-nār*], but in fire, in general, it is not an accident, but . . . its existence in it is the existence of substance. And this is a great error.[64]

He therefore concludes that the term "quality" is just completely equivocal. There is a sense of "quality," sure enough, in which the differentiae of substance (and of everything else) are qualities, but "quality" in that sense is not the name of any genus whatsoever, and in particular does not at all correspond to the *category* of quality, all the members of which fall under it as their true (highest) genus.[65] If the elements and other substances are sometimes described as differentiated by accidental qualities such as heat and cold, that is merely a shorthand way of referring to their true essential characteristics. The true differentiae are not qualities but the powers to produce them:

> The form of water, for example, is a power which constitutes the matter of water as a species, and that [form of water] is not sensible, but from it issue [*taṣdur*] sensible effects, such as sensible cold and weight [and dampness]. . . . And these [qualities of] cold and dampness are accidents which are concomitant to this nature when there is no impediment.[66]

Now, on Avicenna's view, it is perfectly easy to see that three-dimensional magnitude, even in the indeterminate sense, cannot be substantial. For we have already established that it belongs to the genus of quantity — i.e., that it is a kind of accident. It cannot be confused with anything substantial:

> The corporeal form which is the substantial form [of body], is that in which no body exceeds another. . . . And it is the form of a substance. . . . But the thing which is singled out and subject to mensuration [*al-muʿayyan al-muʿarraḍ li-l-taqdīr*] in the three dimensions — determinate or indeterminate mensuration — is the accident that is to be classified as quantity [*alladhī min bāb al-kamm*].[67]

According to the Porphyrean view adopted by Simplicius, however, the issue is not quite so simple. If there can be substantial quality, then why can't there be substantial quantity? Philoponus proposes exactly that.[68] But Simplicius does not, and for good reason. It is, first of all, textually difficult: Aristotle says explicitly that "quantum is not substance."[69] Then, too, there is this question: in what circumstances is (indeterminate) three-dimensional magnitude *not* substantial? Such an accidental indeterminate magnitude would have to inhere in a substance as its subject, and the substance in question would have to be a corporeal substance (for surely no *incorporeal* substance possesses such a magnitude). But, on the "substantial quantity" view proposed by Philoponus, every corporeal substance is *essentially* a three-dimensional magnitude (a substantial quantity). Our hypothetical *accidental* three-dimensional indeterminate magnitude is thus superfluous: presumably there is no room for the exact same quantity to be both substantial and accidental in the exact same substance. Recall, however, that "substantial qualities" are only so-called because the same thing — e.g. heat — which is in some cases a differentia of substance falls, in other cases, under the category of quality, i.e. is a quality strictly speaking. If indeterminate three-dimensional magnitude is *always* substantial, why is it called "quantity" at all? Even if these problems could be explained away, however, there is a more serious one which cannot be avoided. For, as we will see in the next section, Simplicius has arguments which rule out any such thing as substantial corporeity, however it may be defined.

Simplicius: Corporeity as a Privative Characteristic of Matter

The key to understanding Simplicius on this question is clearly to be found in the following passage from the *Physics* commentary:

> Perhaps, then, one ought to posit body in two ways: in one way, existent [*huphestôs*] according to form and logos and determined by three dimensions, and in another way as remission and extension and indeterminateness of the incorporeal and impartible and intelligible nature, this latter not being formally [*eidêtikôs*] determined by three dimensions, but rather remitted and released out in every way [*pantêi*], and emanating out in every direction [*pantakhothen*] from being to non-being. And one must perhaps posit matter as such dimension, but not as the corporeal form, which has already measured and defined the infinity and indeterminateness of such dimension, and has halted its fleeing out from being.[70]

Unfortunately, the passage is less than completely clear. Simplicius mentions: (a) body which is "existent according to form and logos"; (b) body which is "remission and extension and indeterminateness"; (c) "corporeal form." How many things are being distinguished here, and which is to be identified with matter, and why?

Wolfson sees the passage as asserting

> that the matter immediately underlying the four elements is not identical with the first matter of Aristotle, that the former is extended but the latter is inextended and that between these two matters there is a corporeal form which endows the first matter with extension.[71]

He understands it, therefore, to distinguish between two things: on the one hand, true prime matter, which does not in itself possess any form of corporeity, and on the other hand a substantial form, called "corporeal form," the composition of which with prime matter is three-dimensional extended substance. This latter composite is supposed to be a kind of "second matter" which serves as subject for the specific substantial forms of the elements. There are several points to make about this reading.

First of all, Simplicius says here that there are two kinds of body; he says elsewhere, in this same connection, that there are two kinds of quantum, two kinds of magnitude, or two kinds of dimension. He does not, however, say that there are two kinds of matter. On the contrary: throughout his extended discussion of matter and corporeity (pp. 227–32), he consistently uses *hulê* to refer to prime matter only. Even where he does, elsewhere, make use of the concept of intermediate or proximate "matters," the lowest such matters — the second matters, so to speak — turn out to be the four elements.[72] A view according to which something like pure extension, or "qualitiless body," mediates, as a kind of second matter, between prime matter and the elemental forms, is indeed found in Philoponus.[73] But Philoponus claims that his view is original: "That unchangeable body is the second subject," he says, "has been demonstrated by us in the *Miscellaneous Theorems*."[74] Simplicius does not, here or elsewhere, suggest any such thing — and we will see, in a moment, why he could not possibly do so.

First, however, let me continue with my analysis of Wolfson's reading. He asserts that prime matter, according to Simplicius, is "inextended." This is obviously at odds with the passage as I have cited it, inasmuch as Simplicius expressly describes matter as "extension" (*ektasis*).[75] The problem results from a difference between Wolfson's translation and my own: where I have, for *hôs paresin kai ektasin kai aoristian tês asômatou kai ameristou kai noêtês phuseôs*, "as remission and extension and indeterminateness of the incorporeal and impartible and intelligible nature," he has "as characterized by intensions and remissions, and an indefiniteness of an incorporeal, impartible, and intelligible nature." Wolfson's translation seems difficult, however, and would perhaps require some emendation of the text. As it is, he must read *hôs* to mean "as characterized by" (rather than "as"), take *paresin* and *ektasin* as if they were plural, take *ektasis* to mean "intension" (rather than "extension"), ignore what appears to be the coordination of *aoristian* with *paresin* and *ektasin*, and take "*tês asômatou . . . phuseôs*" to mean "of an incorporeal . . . nature" (i.e., as equivalent to something like "*asômaton . . . phusei*"). Despite the great a priori weight of Wolfson's immense learning and scholarship, I therefore feel compelled to stick with my own translation — and that, in turn, requires that we abandon Wolfson's interpretation of the passage.

If Wolfson's reading has proven untenable, then it it tempting instead to follow Sorabji, who proposes to take at face value the identification of matter with "extension" or "dimension." The prime matter of, for example, a table, would be "the *extension* of the table, but with its particular feet and inches ignored."[76] He proposes, in other words, to identify prime matter with what we above called "indeterminate dimension." Aside from the obvious advantages which in general accrue to taking things at face value, he sees three further advantages in this interpretation: it helps make sense of a difficult passage in *Metaph.* 7.3; it results in a view about matter which may usefully be applied to the interpretation of quantum field theory; and it avoids the "embarrassment" of making prime matter into a Lockean "something, I know not what": "for extension is something perfectly familiar."[77]

We cannot, unfortunately, know exactly how Simplicius understood the passage in the *Metaphysics*.[78] Although, moreover, it would be nice if Simplicius could help us out with the interpretation of modern physics, we cannot in all fairness expect him to do so. As for the third advantage, it is also, from a certain point of view, a disadvantage, as Sorabji admits. For while it is true that many modern interpreters find the indeterminateness and unknowability of prime matter embarassing, nothing could be less true of Simplicius himself.[79] On the contrary, as we have seen, it is for him a *sine qua non* of any correct theory that it leave matter thus indeterminate and unknowable. What *would* be embarrassing would be, after insisting through pages of argument on this indeterminateness and unknowability, suddenly to conclude that matter was, after all, "something perfectly familiar." And if he *did* mean to say that, why not just say that matter is the *aoriston diastêma*? What is the point of all that mysterious talk about remission and emanation out away into non-being?

Both Wolfson's and Sorabji's interpretations, furthermore, are ruled out by more fundamental considerations. Wolfson suggests that the "matter" common to the elements is really a composite of prime matter and substantial form. Sorabji does not say this, but in truth his view must ultimately come down to the same thing, since, as we have already seen, corporeity — even in the indeterminate sense — cannot actually be identified with prime matter. So what they are both really suggesting is that there is some substantial form common to all physical things. And that, according to Simplicius, is impossible.

Recall that Aristotle's distinction between generation and alteration rests on the fact that metaphysical prime matter — the ultimate, indeterminate subject of all predication — is a substrate of physical change, i.e. of opposite determinate forms which change one into another. It seems, however, that there is no opposite of body, with which it might alternate. One might even wonder how there could possibly be such an opposite, given that *every* physical substance is corporeal. Philoponus, in any case, does not know of any: that is why he refers to his secondary subject not just as "qualitiless" but as "unchangeable."[80] Every transformation of one element into another, on this view, would be a mere change in state of the underlying corporeal substance.

> But how can these [conclusions] be harmonized with Aristotle and Plato, who want the matter to be a certain subject of opposites? In fact they refer to ultimate body the [things] said by others about matter. For there is no opposite of body. And thus not only celestial body, but also sublunar, will be ungenerable and incorruptible.[81]

In other words: all of Aristotle's hard work in proving the possibility of true generation would be in vain; it would turn out that all changes are mere alterations of a single underlying substance.

We have arrived at the following situation. All physical substances are bodies. But they are not so because of some substantial form which all have in common. It seems to follow that physical substances are not essentially corporeal, and that body is not, as such, a true genus of substance. Simplicius does not say this, however: he says that body is a substance,[82] and identifies it as "enmattered [dimension] along with qualities and physical resistances [*antitupiai*]."[83] He even makes a clear distinction between body as quantity and as substance:

> Body, insofar as it is triply dimensioned and is of a nature to be measured [*metreisthai pephuken*], exists as quantity [*poson huparkhei*]; insofar, however, as it is a subject, and, remaining numerically one and the same, susceptible of opposites — according to this, it is substance.[84]

How can body be a kind of substance, as opposed to a kind of quantity, if there is no substantial form of corporeity?

The clue to the solution of this difficulty is found in the argument which Simplicius uses, finally, to show that "body" must, at least in some sense of the word, refer to matter:

> That which exists [*to huparkhon*] in common in all physical and sensible [things] as such must itself be matter. . . . But what is common to all of them is extension in volume and dimension [*diastasis*].[85]

Matter, in other words, is "body" (and "volume" and "dimension") in the sense that it is what all corporeal substances have in common, in virtue of which each of them, taken individually, is a body. Matter therefore corresponds to what we might normally think of as the *form* of body: the form of ox, for example, is something that all individual oxen have in common, in virtue of which they are called oxen.

The parallel can be carried farther. Just as the form of human is something essential to each human as such, materiality is essential to each corporeal substance. And just as the form of ox, though it is called "ox" (or even "the ox"), is something quite different from the individual oxen, because each individual ox has not only form but also matter, so prime matter, even though it is called "body," is quite different from individual bodies, because each individual body must have not only matter but also a form: a "corporeal form," "which has already measured and defined the infinity and indeterminateness" of the matter. This form, which each body must have, is not the accidental, quantitative form of three-dimensional magnitude: it is a full substantial form, composed of substantial qualities. "As the form which determines the matter one must take the whole [form], along with the qualities."[86] Quantitative form comes to matter only subsequent to this: "quale, the character [*charaktêr*] itself, according to which [a being] is said to be one, coexists [*sunuphistatai*] with being before quantum."[87] Since bodies are of different species, these corporeal forms differ. There is no one substantial form that all corporeal substances have in common. The common essential characteristic of all corporeal substances, by virtue of which they belong to a single genus, is not a form at all, but simply matter.[88]

This seems paradoxical. If prime matter is completely indeterminate, "defined" only negatively, by its complete privation of all form, then how can it serve to distinguish between one kind of substances and another? Doesn't such a distinction amount exactly to a difference in form? The answer is that, in Neoplatonic metaphysics, there is another way, besides formal differentiation, in which two kinds of things can differ from each other. Forms themselves can subsist in different ways — can be of different degrees or ranks of being, or in other words different degrees of closeness to the One. Matter indeed distinguishes the low-ranking corporeal substances from the incorporeal substances of the intelligible world, but not because materiality is some positive differentia: it is rather a defect in the way in which such substances have form. It is, as Simplicius says, the "deviation" (*parallaxis*) of sensible form away from absolute unity, its "turning away from There and being carried down towards nonbeing."[89] An incorporeal substance, which is to say an incorporeal form, is *unique*, i.e. does not have more than one instance, and is *impartible*, i.e. is not potentially many; corporeal substance lacks both these kinds of unity. This double lack of unity, therefore, is prime matter.

Now since prime matter in itself is nothing more or less than these kinds of disunity (though it is possible to describe it with other privative predicates, as well), it is in itself disunity without limit — i.e., "the infinite."[90] Corporeal substance, considered with respect to its matter alone, therefore "tends" toward infinity, and in two ways: it tends towards infinite "dispersion" (*diaspasmos*), i.e. towards utter lack of uniqueness, and towards infinite "extension" (*ektasis*) or "outpouring" (*ekkhusis*), i.e. towards utter lack of impartibility. Substantial forms, moreover, do not directly halt this tendency towards the infinite: measuring and unification requires the accidents of quantity. Thus the double nature of quantity (continuous and discrete) follows from the double nature of the infinite disunity which must be measured:

> That which is removed [*to apostan*] . . . from the one and partless, and which tends to decay [*hupenekhthênai*] towards infinity and indeterminateness — this required a measure, according to which it became quantum. . . . But, being double, it required a double quantity, according both to the discrete and to the continuous.[91]

The discrete quantity in question is aggregate multitude, or number, and the continuous quantity is spatial magnitude, or dimension.[92]

It is also possible, however, to use the terms "multitude" and "magnitude" analogously, to refer to the respective tendencies towards nonbeing which make these quantitative forms necessary:

> Number halted the dispersion of discrete multitude towards infinity, bringing about separation [*diakrisis*] by means of determinate forms, and the magnitudal [*megethikon*] measure determined the indeterminate outflowing of dimensioned quantum.[93]

It is in this way that matter comes to be spoken of as indeterminate quantum, or indeterminate magnitude.[94] It is also in this abstract sense that Simplicius uses the phrase "indeterminate dimension," or, synonymously, "material dimension": not for the accident of continuous quantity in abstraction from its finitude, but for prime matter as pure indeterminateness, "conceived of [*theôroumenon*] privatively according to abstraction from the limit and the other accidents of which it is susceptible."[95] What *we* have called "indeterminate dimension" (and what Philoponus, Avicenna and Averroes all call by that name), Simplicius calls "the form of body," "the form of magnitude" or "the dimension of magnitude." It is "a certain quantity," "magnitude as magnitude of the [substance] composite out of matter and form."[96] He distinguishes between it and "material dimension," which "is not a measured quantity or a form, since it does not participate in the form which corresponds to quantum and to magnitude [*ei mê metaskhêi tou kata to poson kai to megethos eidous*], but is an indeterminate pouring-out [*khusis*]."[97]

True, the accidental, quantitative "form of magnitude," is common to all physical substances, just as much as they are all material. This commonality does not, however, imply that anything determinate is conserved under all physical change. An indeterminate *substantial* magnitude of the kind proposed by Wolfson and Philoponus would put an end to the distinction between generation and alteration, because it would have to be generated from an opposite, which it does not possess. But accidents do not survive the corruption of their subject. When one corporeal substance is corrupted and another generated in its stead, the accidental form of magnitude does not just change its limits, but is completely annihilated and replaced with a new one:

> When what comes to be is a substance, the change also comes about with respect to [*peri*][98] the material deviation, which always remains. For accidents change with respect to substances, but substances with respect to what is called by the Pythagoreans "quantum," either according to privation or according to the deviation from being. For when air is generated from water, not just the qualities change, but also the formal quantity: for the quantity on each side is different [*allo gar hekaterôthi megethos*], and the lesser is not a part of the greater, but each is a distinct form.[99]

This works, however, only because the two quantities are accidents, whereas it is the *substances* that are generated and corrupted. The substantial qualities perish into, or come to be out of, their opposites; the accompanying accidents of quantity simply replace one another.

So far, we understand how matter can be called (indeterminate) "magnitude," "quantity," or "dimension." But this is not a complete answer to our problem, because we want to know how matter can be called "body." "Body" as a kind of quantity is distinguished from other spatial magnitudes by its three-dimensionality. But three-dimensionality is, or so it would seem, just the kind of positive differentia that matter cannot have. Simplicius alludes to this in one of his arguments. Plato, he claims, does not think of matter as "qualitiless body": "According to him, body is the triply dimensioned; for that is what 'also has depth' signifies. But such a [thing] has consubstantial [*sunousiômenon*] number and shape."[100] In stating his own theory, moreover, he emphasizes the distinction between the triple determinateness of formal (quantitative) body, and the indeterminate release out "in every way" (*pantêi*) that is material body. If there were nothing distinctively three-dimensional about matter, however, then, although we might indeed be justified in calling it a kind of magnitude, there would be no reason to call it "body" in particular. What is it about matter that makes it corporeal rather than planar or linear?

The answer lies in Aristotle's demonstration, at the beginning of the *De caelo*, that three is the maximum number of spatial dimensions. "Demonstration" is perhaps too strong a word, since this is one of the least clear and least convincing passages in which Aristotle discusses so fundamental a point — ultimately he must rely on Pythagorean number mysticism. The details of the argument are not important to us here, however; it is enough to know the conclusion: that more than three dimensions are impossible, and hence that "in three ways" (*trikhêi*) is equivalent to "in every way" (*pantêi*).[101] By speaking of body qua matter as "remission and extension and indeterminateness of the incorporeal and impartible and intelligible nature . . . remitted and released out in every way [*pantêi*]," and contrasting it with the three-dimensionality of body qua accident of quantity, Simplicius is suggesting that, while the latter possesses threeness as a positive character, the extension of matter is *trikhêi* insofar as, and only insofar as, it is *pantêi*. Matter, in other words, is the completely indeterminate tendency towards infinite extension, and because it is *completely* indeterminate, it requires every possible spatial determination — i.e., all three of them.

We are now in a position to give the correct interpretation of the long passage with which I began this section (*In Ph.* 1.7, 230,21–29). Simplicius describes not two, but *three* different things: (a) "body" as "existent according to form and logos and determined by three dimensions"; (b) "body" as "remission and extension and indeterminateness of the incorporeal and impartible and intelligible nature," which is not "formally determined by three dimensions," but rather "remitted and released out in every way [*pantêi*], and emanating out in every direction from being to non-being"; and (c) "corporeal form" which "has already measured and defined the infinity and indeterminateness of such dimension." We can now see that (a) is the accident of three-dimensional continuous quantity, in abstraction from its limits. This is what other commentators call "indeterminate dimension"; Simplicius calls it "the form of body" or "the form of magntitude." But (c), "corporeal form," is not to be identified with (a) (as both Wolfson and Sorabji want to do): it is rather, like "sensible form" and "material form," a general name for any substantial form, insofar as it is the form of a body, i.e. is a substantial form in matter. As for (b), it is prime matter, regarded as the tendency to infinite extension, which is *trikhêi* because it is *pantêi*. This is what Simplicius himself calls "indeterminate dimension."

Thus Simplicius is able to solve the dilemma of the essential corporeity of material substance. Material substances are essentially material in that their form or essence is such as to subsist in prime matter; they have no other essential character in common. But matter, although it possesses no positive property of its own, is that in virtue of which every composite substance stands in need of three-dimensional quantity. Matter is that in virtue of which corporeal substances are bodies, and in that way can itself be called "body." Material substances are essentially corporeal, in other words, because corporeity, in the relevant sense, just *is* materiality: it is the defectiveness in being of corporeal substances, in virtue of which they tend to flow out indeterminately into infinite extension and non-being.

Avicenna: Substantial Corporeity as Continuity

Avicenna, it will be recalled, faces the same problem that we have just seen Simplicius solve. He agrees that prime matter is pure potentiality, completely without any positive determination; and he agrees that all material substances are essentially corporeal. But whereas Simplicius solved this problem by explaining how corporeity, in the relevant sense, is a characteristic of matter — i.e., not really a positive characteristic at all — Avicenna argues that corporeity is the first substantial form in matter: a form which all material substances share.

Talk of substances which differ in species sharing a single substantial form, or of one substantial form being prior to another one in matter, gives the impression that the prior, generic substantial form is supposed to serve as subject for the posterior, specific one. I indicated above that Simplicius probably does not hold such a view, and that Avicenna, in any case, certainly does not. If a substantial form were in another substantial form as its subject, then it would be an accident.[102] But as (according to Avicenna) the same thing can never be both substance and accident, it follows that substantial form is never in any subject whatsoever, but always in prime matter.[103] This leaves two other ways in which corporeity might be thought of as prior to other forms: it might have either the priority of a part to a whole, or that of a universal to a particular.

As it turns out, both of these alternatives are correct, though in different ways. Avicenna distinguishes, in general, between two ways in which a more universal concept can be taken in relation to more particular ones. We might, for example, take "animal" to mean anything which is a body and which possesses faculties of nutrition and sense, together with whatever other essential properties it has. In that case we are taking animal as a genus. If, on the other hand, "animal" is taken to mean that which has *only* corporeity, nutrition, and sense, so that any other properties are external to its essence, then animal is not a genus but a "matter": "it might be matter and subject to the human, and its form would be the rational soul."[104] "Subject," however, cannot be meant here in its primary sense. The rational soul is a substance, hence not in a subject; moreover, Avicenna elsewhere insists that the human soul, at least, is not strictly speaking a form of the body at all.[105] In reality this kind of "animal" is a substantial form which enters into individual humans, oxen, and so forth, as a part.

Avicenna similarly distinguishes between "body which is matter" and "body which is genus," and here again we cannot take the idea of body as "matter" to mean that body is, in a strict or primary sense, the *subject* in which other forms inhere. Body which is not a genus ("body which is matter") is really "a part of the substance composite of body and of forms which are posterior to corporeity."[106] It is a substantial form, albeit a "generic" rather than a specific form.[107] It is what Avicenna calls "corporeal form" or "the form of corporeity": "the corporeity which is as form, and not that which is as genus."[108] As a generic form, it cannot be found in reality without further specification: i.e., there is no "absolute body" in the external world (just as there is no "absolute animal").[109] Such an absolute body is nevertheless conceivable — unlike, say an absolute number (i.e., a number which is not any specific number), or an absolute measure (i.e., a magnitude which has no specific dimensionality).[110] It should therefore be possible to explain what substantial corporeity is in itself, without reference to the specific forms which all actual bodies must have. Avicenna's task is to give such an explanation, and then to show, based on that explanation, that the partial or generic form of corporeity is conceptually inseparable from materiality: not, that is, from prime matter itself (which is rather essentially formless), but from the "need" (*ḥāja*) for matter. He must show, in other words, that all and only substantial forms having corporeity as a part or genus are inconceivable except as forms subsisting in matter.

He offers, first of all, the following traditional "description": that "body is a substance which is long and wide and deep."[111] But this, as he points out, and as we have already seen, cannot be taken as referring to body as quantitative — i.e., to either the determinate or to the indeterminate dimensions. The description of body as three-dimensional must rather mean that corporeity is a substantial form by virtue of which certain substances are susceptible to such accidents.

> [T]he dimensions which are posited [*al-mafrūḍa*] in it between its limits, and its limits as well, and its shape and position, are things which are not consituitive of it, but which follow upon its substance.[112]

That is why the above "description" of body is merely a description, and not a proper definition: a definition, as opposed to a description, must be in terms of essential attributes.[113] A true definition of substantial corporeity would have to name the essential characteristic by virtue of which substances receive their accidental three-dimensional quantity.

Avicenna says, in some places, that the characteristic in question is continuity (*ittiṣāl*). "True corporeity is the form of continuity, which receives the [kind of] positing of three dimensions which we have mentioned";[114] "corporeity cannot be conceived [*mutaḥaṣṣila*] in our souls except as matter and continuity merely."[115] In other places, however, he is more cautious, asserting only that corporeity "is either continuity itself, or a nature to which continuity is concomitant, such that it does not exist except that continuity is concomitant to it."[116]

To understand both the identification and the hesitancy about it, we need to look into the various meanings of the ambiguous word "continuity."[117]

Officially, Avicenna recognizes three basic meanings of this word. (1) A thing can be called continuous to something else if the two share a common limit or extremum.[118] (2) More loosely, a thing can be called continuous to something else if the two are attached, possibly just by contact, in such a way that motion in one of them is necessarily accompanied by motion in the other.[119] (3) A thing can be called continuous absolutely, without reference to anything else, if it is one in actu, but divisible into continuous parts — i.e., partible in such a way that the potential parts, at least before the division, share a common limit or extremum, or are continuous to each other, in other words, in the first sense.[120] Of these three definitions, the two relative ones are not suitable as differentiae of substance. Sense (3) is the only one that might work. There are, however, two problems with a straightforward identification of corporeity and that kind of continuity, i.e., divisibility.

The first problem arises from Avicenna's theory of mixture. The main difficulty about mixtures is that the composite substance is uniform, and uniformly unlike its component elements, but can be analyzed back into them. The elements must be somehow absent, and yet somehow still present, when the mixture is complete. Aristotle's solution is as follows:

> Since, of beings, some are in potentia, others in actu, the components [*mikhthenta*] can in a way both be and not be, that which is generated out of them being in actu different [from each], but each of them still being in potentia just as it was before they were mixed.[121]

It sounds as if the elemental substances have been completely replaced by the mixture, so that they are not actually present in it at all, though still potentially so. There are, however, many problems with this view, if it is taken literally.[122] To avoid these, Avicenna proposes that the "potency" (*dunamis* = *quwwa*) in this passage refers to the substantial forms of the elements — which, recall, are not actual qualities (i.e., not qualities in actu) but a power ("potency") which naturally produces such qualities, in the absence of any impediment.[123] Composite bodies consist of very many actual small substances: simple (i.e., elemental) bodies, which are their largest homoeidetic parts.[124] Each of these simple bodies would naturally produce the qualities characteristic of the element in question (e.g., heat, in the case of fire), were it not for the reciprocal action of one upon one another. This reciprocal action is just the kind of "impediment" which prevents the natural qualities from being produced: because of it, all the simple bodies in the mixture instead take on a single, intermediate quality, and that intermediate quality is therefore uniform throughout the mixed body.[125] The mixture itself is this intermediate quality — i.e., it is an accident. In some cases, however, this accident of mixture is such as to dispose the matter of the components to receive a new, additional substantial form or entelechy from the "giver of forms" (*wāhib al-ṣuwar*).[126]

As a reading of Aristotle, this is clearly a stretch, but that is not our concern here. The problem from our present point of view is that bodies composite in this way cannot be strictly speaking continuous: they have parts not just in potentia, but in actu.[127] The parts are united by cohesion.[128] They are continuous to each other, that is, in our sense (2), but they do not make up a continuous unity in sense (3):

> In general, the unity in these [coherent things] is weaker, and goes out of unity by continuity into unity by aggregation [*ijtimāʿiyya*]. Unity by continuity is more suitable [*awlā*] than aggregation to the meaning [*maʿnā*] of "unity," and that is because there is in unity by continuity no multiplicity in actu, but there is in unity by aggregation a multiplicity in actu.[129]

Hence Avicenna says that "the true continuous subject is a simple body."[130]

One response to this problem would be to say that composite bodies are not really bodies in the same sense that simple ones are — i.e., that corporeal form belongs, strictly speaking, only to simple bodies. There are a few places where Avicenna comes close to saying this: he says in one place, for example, that "a single body has no part in actu," implying (on his theory) that a composite is in some sense not a single body.[131] But ultimately this solution is not acceptable, because body qua genus is supposed to be the genus to which all material substances, including minerals, plants, and animals, belong, and body qua substantial form is supposed to be that "part" of such substances in which they are all alike, and by which they are related to their common genus.[132] We will therefore have to admit that the "continuity" which is identified with corporeity is not exactly of type (3). Since, however, the other two types of continuity on Avicenna's list are relative, rather than absolute, the meaning of "continuity" in question must be one that is not mentioned on the official list.

The second problem will ultimately force us to admit the same thing. Avicenna often says or implies that substances are not per se divisible. He says, for example, that a single simple body does not receive multplicity by virtue of its own nature: "its multiplication is in a nature which has unity adapted to multiplicity only because of [something] other than itself."[133] This "something," as he elsewhere makes clear, is nothing other than the accident of continuous quantity:

> Sensible body is not partitioned except insofar as there is dimension in it, and that dimension is divided into that into which it is divided. And it [i.e., sensible body] has a part insofar as it possesses that measure, not insofar as it is body absolutely, or substantial body.[134]

But if continuity is a kind of partibility or divisibility, and divisibility is accidental to body, then continuity itself must be an accident in body. And in fact, when Avicenna discusses the ontological status of continuity, he says that it can be a differentia of quantity, or an accident concomitant to magnitude, but does not mention it as a differentia of substance.[135]

These statements cannot be taken completely literally, however, or, in any case, they cannot apply to divisibility and continuity in all senses of these words. It is not just that the conclusion (that corporeity is not continuity) contradicts Avicenna's own statements elsewhere: on that point he is a times hesitant, as we saw above. The real problem is that, if divisibility is a mere concomitant to corporeal substance, then such substance can be conceived without it — can be conceived, that is, as in itself either having or lacking divisibility. This, however, as we are about to see in some detail, would lead to absurd consequences. As we are also about to see, moreover, true physical division (in reality, as opposed to in thought) requires matter — i.e., must take place in a substrate. But this substrate, ultimately, is prime matter, and so what is ultimately physically divisible must be a substance, not an accident. Avicenna hints at this immediately after one of the passages just cited:

> But if someone says: "If partition cannot be except because of things to the nature [*sha'n*] of which reception of partition belongs, and reception and aptitude are only in matter, then the aptitude for partition is because of matter, not because of quantity," . . . you know that partition with which there is motion and separation in place is different from partition in which there is only a mere singling out [*ta'yīn*] of the part.[136]

We can concede, then, that a simple body receives *conceptual* division in actu only by virtue of the accident of continuous quantity which inheres in it. A *physical* division of this same body, however, after which division the original corporeal substance would no longer exist, must be possible, not by virtue of any accident, but directly through the substantial corporeal form itself. Continuity, in the sense in which we originally defined it, requires the first of these, rather than the second: it involves the possibility of positing two parts within the whole by means of a posited limit which is common to both. Whether this single shared limit is *merely* posited, so that the body remains continuous (in sense [3]), and the two parts remain continuous (in sense [1]) to each other, or whether the single limit instead becomes two in the instant of partition, so that the parts become physically divided, is not relevant.[137] But the most general account of continuity is that "what is one by continuity is that which is one in actu in some respect, and in which there is also multiplicity in some respect."[138] Even though it does not show up on the list of particular senses, the physical, substantial kind of divisibility also deserves to be called "continuity" according to this general account. And any corporeal substance at all, whether simple or composite, insofar as it is unified by some material substantial form, deserves to be called "continuous" in this way.

The doubt of the *Najāh*, about whether corporeity is continuity itself or is merely a nature which implies continuity, can therefore be resolved by saying that both are true. "Continuity" is slightly more equivocal than Avicenna lets on in his official discussion. In one sense, it is a differentia of quantity, and in fact serves to mark out the genus of which quantitative corporeity (i.e., three-dimensional continuous magnitude) is a species. In another sense, however, it is a differentia of substance, or the form corresponding to that differentia, and in that sense is to be identified with substantial corporeity. But substantial corporeity implies quantitative corporeity, and so the first kind of continuity is a concomitant of the second.

Avicenna: Corporeity and Materiality

Let us proceed with the assumption that corporeity is this kind of substantial divisibility-in-unity.

The first thing to notice is that this definition neatly solves the problem which plagued Simplicius: that there is apparently no opposite of body, so that, if corporeity were some substantial form, then, since generation is from opposites, body as such would be incorruptible. If corporeity is continuity, in the sense of divisibility, then it does indeed have an opposite: namely, actual division. Bodies as such are therefore corruptible, not because they may somehow become non-bodies, but simply because they are potentially divided.[139] This, moreover, is already enough to show that corporeal form is essentially material, i.e. that it "needs" matter. The argument is just an adaptation of Plato and Aristotle's general proof that generation and corruption require physical matter as a subject. Opposite cannot receive opposite.

> If [corporeal form] is continuity itself, and a body is continuous, and then becomes divided [*yanfaṣil*], then there is of necessity a thing which is potentially both. For continuity itself, insofar as it is continuity, does not receive division; for that which receives continuity is not absent in the presence of division [*lā yuʿadim ʿind al-infiṣāl*], whereas continuity is absent in the presence of division. . . . So it is manifest that there is a substance which is not corporeal form, and that it is that [substance] that division and continuity both befall.[140]

Since what is continuous is by definition susceptible to division, it follows that every corporeal substance is by definition material.

It remains only to show that every material substance is essentially corporeal: i.e., that substantial form in matter cannot be conceived except as including corporeal form. This direction of proof presents a far more difficult problem, for reasons which should already be familiar. Prime matter, recall, has no positive essence of its own: it is pure potentiality. From this it follows, indeed, that prime matter cannot be found in actu without any substantial form whatsoever.[141] But why must it always have this particular form, which we have identified with continuity? How can that be, unless matter has some positive character of its own, by which it demands one kind of form rather than another?

Avicenna's solution rests on two things: first, an equivalence between the metaphysical potential to receive corporeal form and the physical potential to gain or lose it through change, and, second, the role of place in individuation. Let us examine each of these points in turn.

The first point may seem problematic. Pure potentiality does mean that matter, as such, is "adapted" to any material form. But it does not mean that matter can lose any particular form and gain any other material form in its stead. Consider the case of the celestial bodies. Like all other bodies, they must have the form of corporeity, and they must therefore be material. But they are also supposed to be ungenerated and incorruptible. Some material forms, apparently, are such that matter is capable of receiving them, but not capable of gaining or losing them through change.

One response to this argument would be to maintain that the celestial "bodies" are not bodies. We showed that bodies are material by showing that they are all potentially divisible, which followed in turn from our definition of them as continuous. But the celestial bodies cannot be (physically) divided. It seems to follow, therefore, not that celestial bodies combine materiality and incorruptibility, but that they are not material, and hence not really bodies at all. Averroes, based on these or similar considerations, reaches just that conclusion: that celestial "bodies" are not bodies, or at any rate that celestial and sublunar bodies are equivocally so called, and that the two do not share a common matter.[142] This view faces both textual and conceptual problems, however.[143] Avicenna, in any case, is not even aware of anyone who holds it: he regards the conclusion that "body" is equivocal, or in other words that body is not a true genus, as an evident absurdity.[144] His solution is different. All body as such, he explains, is divisible and hence corruptible, but

> it is possible for corporeity to be conjoined with a thing which makes that body existent [*qā'im*] as [belonging to] a species which does not receive division [*qisma*] or continuity [i.e., coalescence] with something other than itself. And this is what we say about the celestial sphere [*al-falak*].[145]

The same argument, moreover, which establishes that celestial and sublunar bodies share a common form, also serves to show that they have a common matter:

> But perhaps we should posit that the nature of the subject which belongs to the form of that which is not corrupted and the subject of the form which is corrupted are one nature, in itself suitable to receive any form, while it has happened to that which is not corrupted that it is conjoined to a form which has no opposite.[146]

This form which has no opposite, and which prevents celestial body from dividing or coalescing, and hence exempts celestial material substance from generation and corruption, is the form of aether — the element whose natural motion is circular.[147]

From the details of this solution, however, it is already clear why the existence of ingenerable and incorruptible material forms will pose no difficulty for arguments about corporeity. For corporeity itself, obviously, is not such a form: no body is ingenerable or incorruptible by virtue of its corporeity alone. That will be enough to make Avicenna's arguments go through.

As to the second point, about place and individuation: the key issue is what it takes for a material substance to be "designated." Avicenna defines "designation" (*ishāra*) as "a sensible or intellectual reference [*dalāla*] to a thing in itself [*bi-ʿaynihi*] which it does not have in common with any other thing, even if it [i.e., that other thing] is of its species."[148] The talk of sensible or intelligible reference may make it sound like the need for designation is purely subjective — i.e., something which we need in order mentally to refer to an individual, but which is not necessary for an individual to exist. Avicenna, however, thinks that an individual falling under a species can be conceived of only as something which is "designatable" (*ʾilayhi al-ishāra*).[149] Whatever the reasons for this — and there is no room to go into them here — it makes designation, or rather the possibility thereof, into an objective metaphysical necessity.

Now designation as we have just defined it is a matter of distinguishing something from everything else. There are several ways in which such a distinction can come about. In the case of things which exist in a subject (i.e., of accidents), there can be a distinction between otherwise identical things by way of the different subjects in which they inhere. This allows for a kind of designation per accidens, by means of the designation of their subjects, which, ultimately, must be substances.[150] As for substances themselves, they can differ by possessing different substantial forms — i.e., by belonging to different species. As Avicenna indicates in his very definition of designation, however, this will not always be sufficient: there are sensible substances of the same species which are nevertheless distinct. The distinction in such cases must be by means of accidents:

> an individual [*shakhṣ*] can only become a individual in that there are conjoined, to the nature of the species, accidental properties [*khawāṣṣ = idia*] . . . and a designated matter is [thereby] singled out for it [i.e., for the specific form].[151]

Not just any accidents, however, will serve this purpose. True, it might happen to be the case that there has only ever been, and will only ever be, one person of a particular color, or one person who is the son of so-and-so, is tall, and is a philosopher. But designation requires not only that the designated thing be unique, but that this uniqueness be known a priori to the designator.[152] The individuating accidents must therefore be such that no two individuals of the same species could *possibly* share them. The accidents which fulfill this condition are place and time:

> The multiplication of things is either [1] with respect to their quiddity and form, or with respect to their relation to [2a] the *ʿunṣur*[153] and matter, which is multiplied by the multiplication in it of the places that, in a certain respect, contain all matter, and

> [2b] the times which are proper to each one of them in its inception, and [2c] the causes that divide them.[154]

Two things of the same species which come into being at the same time must therefore be in place, or must at least (as in the case of rational souls) have some relation to things which are in place.

With these two points in mind, and recalling our identification of corporeity and continuity, we are ready to follow Avicenna's proof that prime matter cannot exist without corporeal form. The proof is by reductio ad absurdum. Assume that the prime matter can exist without corporeal form — i.e., that it can exist with some substantial form that is not corporeal. There are two possibilities: either corporeity is not the first form in matter, so that the proximate matter of body is already a composite, or prime matter itself can take on (at least) two different forms, one corporeal and the other not.[155]

To take the first case first: assume that there is some composite substance (i.e., prime matter together with its hypothetical pre-corporeal form) which can be either corporeal or incorporeal. Even though there are ingenerable corporeal substances, they are not so by virtue of their corporeity alone, nor can they be so by virtue of their pre-corporeal form (since even sublunar bodies must share it). We can assume, therefore, for the sake of argument, that some incorporeal pre-body becomes a body — i.e., that an incorporeal substance which possesses the pre-corporeal form comes to have corporeal form as well. Call this substance *A*.

Now *A*, first of all, cannot, while it is incorporeal, have any position or location (*ḥayyiz*).[156] For *A*, when it is incorporeal, is not continuous, i.e. not divisible; but an indivisible thing which has position is a point, and a point is a limit, not a substance.[157] The question is, then, whether it is conceivable that *A*, having no position, could become a body.[158] When it *is* a body, it will be in place: it will have three-dimensional continuous extension, and, since an infinite body, though conceivable, is physically impossible, it will have a limiting surface, which in turn will be surrounded by the surfaces of other bodies — i.e., by a place.[159] Now, place individuates because no body can be in more than one place at the same time; it is *necessary* for individuation because neither the substantial forms of a body, nor any of its other accidents, uniquely determine what place it will occupy, so that otherwise identical things can always exist in different places.[160] So *A*, once it becomes a body, must be in some particular place, but nothing about *A* qua body can determine which place that will be. *A* cannot therefore simply acquire a place in the instant in which it becomes corporeal.[161] *A* must already have been located *before* the change occurred:

> The measure must have found it with a location proper to it [*mukhtaṣṣan bi-ḥayyiz*]: otherwise one location would not be more suitable for it [*ʾawlā bihi*] than another. So the measure found it [already] where it [i.e., the measure] became conjoined to it. So it doubtless found it in the location which it was in, and that substance [i.e., the pre-corporeal A] was located....But it was posited as not located at all. This is a contradiction.[162]

Another argument which is based on continuity alone (i.e., without reference to place) works in the same direction. We are supposed to imagine that *A*, before the change, has a form by which it is one, but not by continuity; in other words, by which it is one and indivisible; in other words, by which it is not many either in actu or in potentia. After becoming a body, however, it can be divided. Therefore its original pre-corporeal form must have left it, contrary to what was assumed.[163]

These arguments eliminate the possibility that there is some pre-corporeal form common to both corporeal and incorporeal things. It remains possible, however, that prime matter is directly receptive of two inconsistent forms: one corporeal, the other not. In that case, we may no longer assume that an incorporeal substance becomes corporeal, since such a process would now have to involve the loss of the incorporeal form by corruption, and we have no reason to think that that is possible. We *may*, however, assume that some body becomes incorporeal. For corporeal form itself is not one of those forms which, when conjoined with matter, makes the resulting composite incorruptible. If it is possible for matter to exist without corporeal form, then it is possible for it to lose it.[164]

Avicenna argues as follows.[165] Consider a corporeal substance — call it *B*. As corporeal, it is continuous, i.e. divisible. Imagine that it is divided into two parts — call them B_1 and B_2. Since we are assuming that matter can lose corporeal form, we can imagine any of these three bodies (*B*,

B_1, or B_2) becoming incorporeal, in the sense that its corporeal form is lost and replaced by an incorporeal one. Call the resulting incorporeal (but material) substances C, C_1, and C_2. C is in a sense the sum of C_1 and C_2: all the matter that is in C is, or rather would be, in one of its "pieces." Yet it is impossible to say how C might differ from one of them, say C_1. Certainly they cannot differ in place — Avicenna does not even bother to mention this, presumably because it is so obvious, in light of the previous discussion. He does mention another obvious point: that they do not differ in "measure," i.e. in the accident of continuous quantity. They might conceivably differ in substantial form or in quality. But we are considering B and B_1 purely as bodies (that is: we cannot assume that *they* are quantitatively or substantially different), so if the loss of corporeity in B results in a certain form or quality in C, the loss of corporeity in B_1 must have the same result in C_1. If, similarly, we were to assume that B was annihilated by the loss of corporeal form (i.e., that there is no C at all), then the same would have to be true of B_1. Nor, finally, can we say that C is literally the union of C_1 and C_2. For it is not literally possible for two different substances to be united. Their *matter* can be united, but they themselves are then no longer present; they are replaced by some third substance, and this third substance must, in some way or other, be different from each of them. But this lands us back with our original problem: that we could not explain the difference between C and C_1. If, however, C and C_1 are in every way identical, then the matter of C_1 itself is identical to the matter of C_1 together with with the matter of C_2: "the nature [*ḥukm*] of some of the subject [i.e., prime matter] and the nature of all of it is one in every respect."[166] But this is impossible.[167]

We can sum up all of these arguments up by noting that they all depend on the distinctive nature of corporeal form. In assuming that corporeity could, in one way or another, alternate with incorporeity in matter, we were thinking of corporeity as being similar to other forms, in that its opposite would either be simply it absence (i.e., simply its not being conjoined to some other form, which latter form will remain after it is gone), or would be some other form inconsistent with it. But if corporeity is continuity, then its true opposite is division, and division purely as such means division into parts which are of the same nature as the whole. That is why corporeity is the form that requires measure and position (because it is by measure and position that the parts differ from the whole and from each other). It is also why matter, if it can ever have corporeal form at all, must always have it: body as such is a kind of substance, the only kind, whose corruption is necessarily accompanied by its own generation. Hence material substances are essentially corporeal.

> In general, every thing for which it is possible, at any time at all, to become two, has among its essential characteristics [*fī ṭibā*ʿ *dhātihi*] an aptitude for division, from which it can never part . . . and this aptitude is impossible except by conjunction of measure with its essence.[168]

Conclusion: Avicenna and Simplicius

Simplicius and Avicenna face the same difficult problems, and both reach interpretatively and conceptually radical solutions. The interpretative radicalness is reflected in that their discussions of this issue are unusually disengaged from Aristotle's text. The main discussion in Simplicius is in the commentary on *Ph.* 1.7 — a chapter in which Aristotle does not mention body at all — and begins on its own, without reference to any particular textual segment; Avicenna's main discussion of corporeity at *Sh. Il.*, 2.2–3 is likewise, and unlike most other chapter-length parts of the *Shifā*ʾ, not easily associated with any one locus in Aristotle. Both Avicenna and Simplicius, moreover, introduce terminology — "corporeal form," "indeterminate dimensions," "deviation" — which is not Aristotelian (or even Plotinian). The conceptual radicalness can be summed up by saying that both of these solutions reduce corporeity, in the relevant sense, to something extremely abstract. Both refuse to identify it with any of the familiar and easily picturable properties of bodies (extension, volume, surface, three-dimensionality, rigidity, resistance, inertia, weight). This resort to a high degree of conceptual abstraction, and to a high degree of interpretative independence, reflects both the extreme difficulty of the metaphysical problems and the extreme pressure to achieve systematically maintainable solutions where such fundamental issues are at stake.

The two solutions agree to a great extent in detail. The abstract property with which both Simplicius and Avicenna wish to identify corporeity is divisibility or partibility: the potency or aptitude by which a material substance, one in actu, is at the same time potentially many. The difference between them is subtle. Avicenna thinks of corporeity, roughly speaking, as the kind of unity (ultimately: substantial unity) which possesses such divisibility. He therefore identifies corporeity with a certain substantial form. Simplicius, on the other hand, thinks of corporeity as the privation by which an enmattered substantial form "deviates" from its intelligible archetype — i.e., by which it deviates from true unity and true being. He therefore identifies corporeity with matter. Both solutions are relatively tenable within their own systematic contexts; neither, probably, could survive transplantation to the other system. Simplicius' solution relies ultimately on a full-blown Neoplatonic theory of emanation that Avicenna does not share, while Avicenna's is dependent on his non-Neoplatonic views about essential and accidental properties, and about the coexistence of multiple substantial forms in a single composite substance.

Notes

1. Every Aristotelian science has some genus as its subject matter: see *An. Po.* 1.28, 87a38; *Metaph.* 4.2, 1003b19-20 and 6.1, 1025b7-9; cf. *Najāh*, 2.1, 135,2-4.

   I cite Plato's and Aristotle's works from the Oxford Classical Texts editions, except *De generatione et corruptione*, ed. Harold H. Joachim (Oxford, 1922). In addition to standard abbreviations for the titles of these works, I also use the following. *CAG* = *Commentaria in Aristotelem Graeca*; *Enn.* = *Enneads*, cited from *Plotini Opera*, ed. Paul Henry and Hans-Rudolf Schwyzer, 3 vols., Oxford Classical Texts (1964-83); *Najāh* = *Kitāb al-najāh*, ed. Majid Fakhri (Beirut, 1985); *Sh. M.* = *al-Shifāʾ: al-Manṭiq*, *Sh. Ṭ.* = *al-Shifāʾ: al-Ṭabīʿiyyāt*, *Sh. Il.* = *al-Shifāʾ: al-Ilāhiyyāt*, all ed. Ibrahim Madkour et al. (Cairo, 1950-). In the case of the *Tabīʿiyyāt* and the *Manṭiq*, I cite the part (*fān*) by a short version of its name, e.g. *Samāʿ* = *al-Samāʿ al-ṭabīʿī*, *Samāʾ* = *al-Samāʾ wa-l-ʿalām*. *Ḥudūd* = *Kitāb al-ḥudūd*, ed. A. Goichon (Cairo, 1963), cited by the definition number and the paragraph number in Goichon's edition. *DN* = *Ilāhiyyāt: Dānish-nāma-yi ʿAlāʾī*, ed. M. Muʿīn (Moʻen) (Tehran, 1952) (tr. by P. Morewedge as *The* Metaphysica *of Avicenna [ibn Sīna]* [New York, 1973]).

2. It is true that Neoplatonists, including Simplicius, believe that there is also a kind of "matter" in the intelligible realm. But this is matter in quite a different sense — so different that such Neoplatonists regularly make the same assertion that I have just made, namely that only physical or sensible substances are material. Unfortunately I will not be able to discuss the difficult topic of "intelligible matter" here.
3. See *Cat.* 1, 1a6-12; *Top.* 1.5, 101b38; *Metaph.* 7.5, 1031a11-12.
4. See *Najāh*, 1, 46,4-6. I am not aware of such a definition of "essential" in Simplicius, and Avicenna, indeed, rejects the definitions of his (unnamed) predecessors as unclear (*Sh. M.*, *Madkhal*, 1.6, 33,9). I believe that Simplicius' arguments implicitly require something similar, however.
5. See *Tim.* 49e7-51b6, *Ph.* 1.6, 188a21-26 and 1.7, 190b29-35. Plato does not use the Aristotelian term *hulê*, but Aristotle (e.g. at *Ph.* 4.2, 209b11-12 and 210a1-2; *Cael.* 3.8, 306b16-20; *GC* 2.1, 329a14-24) consistently compares his own matter to Plato's *tithênê* or *dekhomenê phusis*.
6. See *Metaph.* 7.3, 1029a20-23 (quoted below), and see also *Tim.* 49e1-7.
7. *Metaph.* 1.7, 989b18-19. Cf. *Metaph.* 4.5, 1010a1-4; 7.11, 1037a27; 9.7, 1049b1-2.
8. Of course it is controversial among modern interpreters whether Aristotle believed in such a thing as physical, let alone metaphysical, prime matter. Such questions are irrelevant for our purposes, as I have already explained.
9. *Metaph.* 7.3, 1029a20-23.
10. For Aristotle, see *Metaph.* 7.3, 1029a25-26 and *Ph.* 1.7, 190b24-7; for Plotinus, see *Enn.* 2.4.15 and 2.4.14.12-22.
11. *Metaph.* 7.10, 1036a9.
12. *Ph.* 1.7, 191a7-8.
13. *Tim.* 52b2.
14. *In Ph.*, ed. Hermann Diels, *CAG* 9 (1882), 1.7, 226,25-7.
15. See, e.g., *De An.* 2.1, 412a6-9; *Metaph.* 7.10 1035a2; 7.13, 1038b1-6; 8.1, 1042a26-31 and 2, 1042b9-10.
16. See *Ph.* 1.7, 191a7-12; *Cael.* 2.13, 293b15-16; *Metaph.* 3.4, 999b12-14 and 7.3, 1029a23-24 and 27-28. At *Metaph.* 9.7, 1049a34-36, the distinction is between "substance" and "material substance," where "material" (*hulikê*) evidently refers not to something which possesses matter, but to matter itself.
17. See, e.g., St. Thomas Aquinas, *In Metaph.*, ed. M. R. Cathala (Turin, 1926), 5.10 (n. 905), and see, in support of this interpretation, *Ph.* 1.9, 192a6; *Metaph.* 8.1, 1042a27-8 and 12.3, 1070a9-13; *Cat.* 5, 3b10; *Metaph.* 7.3,

1029a28-30.

18. See St. Thomas, *In Metaph.* 7.2 (n. 1276) and ibid. (n. 1289): "that which is the ultimate subject is, speaking per se, neither a 'quid,' that is, a substance, nor a quantity, nor anything else that is in any genus of beings."
19. See, e.g., *Sh. Il.*, 2.1, 60,12 and 2.2, 67,16-17; *Sh. Ṭ.*, *Samāʿ*, 1.2, 14,4; *Najāh*, 3.1, 244,8-10. Simplicius is more ambiguous on this point: see *In Cat.*, ed. Karl Kalbfleisch, *CAG* 8 (1907), 5, 80,17-20; *In Ph.* 1.9, 246,24-7. See also Plotinus, *Enn.* 6.1.3.1-5 and 6.3.4. I should reiterate here what I said in my opening paragraph: it is not my purpose in this paper to determine Aristotle's true opinion about anything. Those who feel certain that the Thomistic view, or one like it, is the correct interpretation of Aristotle, are urged to suspend disbelief long enough to understand Simplicius and Avicenna.
20. *Sh. Il.*, 2.2, 67,14-15. In general I use "aptitude" to translate *istiʿdād* (and hence "adapted" to translated *mustaʿidd*). There are three reasons for preferring this to the perhaps more conventional translation "disposition" (or "predisposition"): (1) the medieval Latin translation has, in all the passages I cite, *aptitudo* for *istʿidād* (and *aptus* or *adaptus* for *mustaʿidd*); (2) *istiʿdād* apparently translates the Greek *epitêdeiotês* (a term which does not occur in Aristotle, but which becomes common in the later tradition), whereas *dispositio* must be reserved for *diathesis* = *ḥāl*; (3) to be *mustaʿidd* = *epitêdeios* for something is to be fit or suitable for it, *not* to be (in the ordinary English sense) predisposed to it. The last point is particularly important for our purposes, since prime matter is indeed adapted (i.e., suitable) to receive all substantial forms, but is not predisposed to receive any of them.
21. A proper "definition" (*horismos* = *ḥadd*) must be in terms of genus and differentia, and substance, as a highest genus, does not have either of these; therefore it has only a "description" (*hupographê* = *rasm*). See Porphyry, *In Cat.*, ed. Adolf Busse, *CAG* 4, pt. 1 (1887), 2, 72,34-73,2; Simplicius, *In Cat.* 5, 81,19-20; *Sh. M.*, *Madkhal*, 1.9, 49,3-7; *Sh. Ṭ.*, *Samāʿ*, 1.2, 14,16.
22. *Cat.* 5, 1b12-13. A so-called secondary substance *is* "said of a subject," though not "in a subject." But matter, when it is said to be a substance, is said to be one in the primary sense: see *Metaph.* 7.3, 1028b33-9b3.
23. *In Cat.*, ed. Adolf Busse, *CAG* 4, pt. 4 (1895), 2, 25,20-26,3. Cf. different (and less interesting) solutions to this problem in Dexippus, *In Cat.*, ed. Adolf Busse, *CAG* 4, pt. 2 (1888), 2, 44,4-19 and Simplicius *In Cat.* 5, 81,15-32.
24. *Sh. Ṭ.*, *Samāʿ*, 1.2, 14,15-15,1; see also *Najāh*, 3.1, 237,10-18; *Ḥudūd*, 7, 31. Simplicius reports a similar view, in the name of Porphyry, at *In Cat.* 5, 78,25-29 (and see also, more sketchily, *Enn.* 6.3.4.29-31). At *In Ph.* 1.9,

246,32-3, Simplicius himself says that prime matter is "somehow a subject, even though it is taken as a part of the [composite] of both [matter and form], which is not so of that which is most properly a subject [*hoper tôi kuriôs hupokeimenôi oukh huparkhei*]." This implies a conclusion even more extreme than Avicenna's: that not only prime matter, but also substantial form, is not properly speaking a subject.

Note that because accidents, by definition, are not substances, they are things which do exist in a subject — i.e., things which do not exist (directly) in prime matter. Hence accidents require prime matter for their existence only if and because their substantial subjects do. It is not, therefore, correct to say, as Allan Bäck does, that matter is the "state of receptivity" by which a substantial quiddity "is able to have other [accidental] quiddities attached to it" ("Ibn Sina on the individuation of perceptible substance", *Proceedings of the PMR Conference* 14 [1989], 30). Prime matter is required for the quiddities of *material* substances to become connected to accidents, but that is just because such quiddities, i.e. substantial forms, cannot exist in reality without matter: in general, the "state of receptivity" in question is not matter but simply existence (in reality). It is true that, according to Avicenna, accidents *which are not concomitants of the substantial form* can be found in a substance only if its specific nature, i.e. substantial form, "is attached to matter" (*Sh. Il.*, 5.2, 208,2-3). That, as he goes on to explain, is because only material substances require external conditions to come into or remain in existence: something must be "prepared" or "disposed" (*muhayya'*) by accidents to receive their form (208,3-6). Such things have non-concomitant accidents, in other words, only because they always come into being from, or remain in being on the basis of, something which itself already had them. Later on we will see a special and fundamental case of this rule, namely that whatever comes into being in place comes to be from something which is already in place; we will then be in a position better to understand the role of accidents and of matter in individuation.

25. *Sh. Il.*, 2.1, 59,1-2. That "in a subject" means "in, not as a part" is from Aristotle, *Cat.* 2, 1a24-25. But the real force of Avicenna's definition in the present context derives from the added stipulation that a subject must first be "existent in itself and in its specificity." Plotinus and Porphyry do not explicitly add such a stipulation, but they have apparently read it, for similar reasons, into the word "in": prime matter is not a subject because substantial form is not, the requisite sense, "in" it.

26. *Sh. Il.*, 2.2, 68,1-4. Note that *ʿāmm* and *khāṣṣ* are not related to *jins* ("genus") and *nawʿ* ("species"), so that the translations "general" and "specify" are misleading. A more technically correct translation would be "common" and "make proper," but this would hardly be understandable in English.

See also *Ḥudūd*, 6, 30, where Avicenna says that prime matter "does not have in its essence [or "in itself": *fī dhātihi*] any form proper to it [*ṣūra takhaṣṣahu*] except for potentiality [*ma'nā al-quwwa*]," and cf. Simplicius *In Cat.* 5, 79,7-8.

27. *Sh. Il.*, 2.2, 68,5; cf. *Enn.* 2.4.7.2-4, where Plotinus implies that, as opposed to Anaxagoras' theory that matter has all things within it in actu, the *true* theory is that matter has merely an "aptitude for everything" (*epitêdeiotês pros panta*; in Ficino's translation: *aptitudines ad omnia,* the reason for the plural being unclear). (Here I am reading, with Steinhart, *hulê* for *hudôr* in 2.4.7.3. On Anaxagoras, cf. *Metaph.* 12.2, 1069b20-23.)
28. *In Ph.* 1.7, 227,4-5.
29. *Enn.* 2.4.13.26-28.
30. *Sh. Ṭ.*, *Samā'*, 1.2, 20,20-21,1. The objection to Aristotle is perhaps not quite fair, since he does add that matter is "female" only per accidens (*Ph.* 1.9, 192a23-5).
31. *Sh. Il.*, 2.2, 67,16-17.
32. See *Cat.* 5, 4a10-11; *GC* 1.4, 319b8-18; *Ph.* 1.7, 190a2.
33. For the details of the following argument, see *GC* 1.1, 314b4-315a3; 1.3, 317b1-11; 1.4, 319b6-31. There are alternate ways of understanding these chapters; I have summarized them according to an interpretation which will make sense of the arguments in Simplicius and Avicenna.
34. Aristotle's full critique is even more devastating than this: because Empedocles thinks of sensible qualities as essential to particular elements, it turns out that his theory doesn't really contain alteration at all. But this latter part of Aristotle's argument is ad hominem; we can imagine an Empedocles who believes in accidents, but not in what Aristotle calls generation and corruption.
35. For an attempt to prove, by appeal to extensive empirical evidence, that the four elements indeed change into each other, see *Sh. Ṭ.*, *Kawn/fasād*, 6, 122,8 ff.
36. One might object that it could rather be an accident. But an accident cannot persist by itself through change — it requires a persistent subject, which must ultimately be a composite substance. (Or so it seems. This line of argument was eventually challenged by Kant.) So if there is some accident *a* which persists throughout all physical change, it must be by virtue of some persistent substance *A* in which *a* (directly or indirectly) inheres. But then it is *A*, and not *a*, that should be called physical prime matter.
37. *Cat.* 6, 4b20-25.
38. *Cael.* 1.1, 268a6-8; cf. a very similar definition at *Metaph.* 5.6, 1016b27-8.

39. See, e.g., *Metaph.* 5.13, 1020a7-11.

40. As Avicenna points out, not every body literally has three dimensions, in the sense that there are three preferred directions along which we can measure its length, width and depth. But it is always possible to measure it in any direction you want, and then to measure it in two other directions which are mutually perpendicular and perpendicular to the first. See *Sh. Il.*, 2.2, 61,16-62,2 and 62,14-63,2; *Najāh*, 3.1, 237,23-238,3.

41. The phrase "indeterminate dimension" (*diastêma aoriston*) does not occur in Aristotle or Plotinus, but is widely used by later commentators. See, e.g., Simplicius *In Ph.* 4.2, 537,13; Philoponus *In Ph.*, ed. Girolamo Vitelli, *CAG* 16-17 (1887-8), 4.2, 515,18-19 and 519,21-22. The Arabic equivalent *buʿd ghayr mutaḥaddid* is implied by contrast with Avicenna's constant talk of *al-ʾabʿād al-mutaḥaddida* (= *ta hôrismena diastêmata*); at *Sh. M., Maqūlāt*, 3.4, 114,3-4 he speaks, in a related context, of "undetermined mensuration" (*taqdīr ghayr maḥdūd).* Averroes uses the phrase in his description of Avicenna's views (assuming that the lost Arabic text of the *Sermo de substantia orbis*, c. 1, had *al-ʾabʿād . . .al-ghayr mutaḥaddida* where the Hebrew, ed. and tr. Arthur Hyman [Cambridge, MA and Jerusalem: Medieval Academy of America and Israel Academy of Sciences and Humanities, 1986], Hebrew side, p. 20, ll. 115-16, has *ha-merḥaqim . . . ha-bilti megubbalim* and the Latin, *Aristotelis Opera cum Averrois Commentarius* [Venice: apud Junctas, 1562-74], vol. 9, 4vK, has *dimensionum . . . non terminatarum*). All of the above except Simplicius use the phrase in more or less the sense I have outlined; for Simplicius' more abstract usage, see below.

Note that I translate both *diastêma* and *diastasis* as "dimension," reserving "extension" for *ektasis*, to which it literally corresponds.

42. For Simplicius, see *In Ph.* 4.2, 538,27-8; for Avicenna see *Sh. Il.*, 2.2, 62,4-5; *Najāh* 3.1, 238,5-6; *Sh. M., Maqūlāt*, 3.4, 113,4-5.

43. *In Ph.* 4.2, 538,23-30.

44. *Sh. Il.*, 3.4, 111,4 and 12-13. See also *Sh. M., Maqūlāt*, 3.4, 114,3-4. (In the corresponding context at *Ḥudūd*, 14, 40, the possibility of the measurement's not terminating is left out, which explains why body as quantity is there defined as "determinate.")

45. See *Sh. Ṭ., Samāʿ*, 1.4, 27,14-15; *Sh. Il.*, 2.1, 57,5-6. I am not aware of an explicit statement to this effect in Simplicius (though the phrase "limit of form" seems to imply it), but he does explicitly refer to "infinite" (i.e., the *lack* of limit) as an accident which inheres in a quantity: see *In Ph.* 3.5, 473,2-8 (commenting on the Aristotelian source for this doctrine, *Ph.* 3.5, 204a17-19). Note that both Simplicius and Avicenna, unlike, for example,

St. Thomas, hold that there can be an accident of an accident: for Avicenna's refutation of the opposing view, see *Sh. M.*, *Maqūlāt*, 3.3, 111,9-14.

46. This is true, anyway, if we ignore the celestial bodies and the fifth element, aether. Including them would complicate our discussion considerably, but would not ultimately change its implications as far as Avicenna and Simplicius are concerned.

    Simplicius' doctrine of absolute (substantial) space also causes complications, which I will ignore.

47. *GC* 2.2, 329b7-10. Cf. also *Metaph.* 8.1, 1042a25-26.

48. *GC* 1.5, 320b23: *sôma gar koinon ouden.*

49. *Enn.* 2.4.8.2-3.

50. See *GC* 2.1, 329a8-13.

51. *In Ph.* 1.7, 227,26-30. The sense of *metaballontai peri auto* is they (the qualities) change while it (body) remains; "change around in it" is the closest I could come to rendering this literally in English.

    Some Aristotelian passages that could be read in this light are *GC* 1.5, 321a9-15; *Ph.* 3.6, 207a21-2; *Ph.* 4.7, 214a13-16 (and cf. *GC* 1.5, 321a6-7). Plato (*Tim.* 52a8, 52b4) calls the common subject of the elements *khôra* ("place" — though not the technical Aristotelian term *topos*), which could be construed as a kind of qualitiless volume or extension.

52. *GC* 2.1, 329a24-6; cf. *Ph.* 4.9, 217a21-25.

53. *Ph.* 4.9, 217a26-7.

54. *Enn.* 2.4.8.14-23.

55. *In Ph.* 1.7, 229,21-7; cf. *Sh. Il.*, 2.3, 77,12-13. Apparently Simplicius is uncertain as to whether Plotinus is using "the giver of forms" to refer to the demiurge or to nature. Avicenna applies the phrase "giver of forms" (*wāhib al-ṣuwar*) to the separate intelligences (see *Sh. Il.*, 9.5, 411,9).

    In general I leave *logos*, in the technical Neoplatonic sense in which it is first used here, untranslated, because it is virtually untranslatable. One possible rendering is "form," but that, of course, must be reserved for *eidos* (and/or *morphê*). Another possibility is something like "immaterial rational principle," but that is very loose.

56. *Enn.* 2.4.13.1-7.

57. *Enn.* 2.4.12.34-5.

58. *In Ph.* 1.7, 230,10-14.

59. *Sh. M.*, *Maqūlāt*, 3.4, 114,5-10; *Sh. Ṭ.*, *Samāʿ*, 1.1, 13,6-10; *Sh. Il.*, 2.2, 64,1-4. The example of wax derives from Aristotle (*Cael.* 3.7, 305b29-30), although it is used there to a somewhat different purpose. It later turns up,

famously, in Descartes (*Meditations* 2, AT 30). See also *Najāh*, 3.1, 238,13-15 (which does not mention wax, however).

60. See, e.g., *Top.* 4.2, 122b16-17 and 6.6, 144a20-21.

61. *Enn.* 6.3.8.30-37; see also 6.3.15.24-38, and the somewhat compressed version of both of these passages at 2.6.1.40-52, and cf. *Ph.* 1.6, 189a33-4: "but how could a substance be [made] out of non-substances, or how could non-substance be prior to substance?" According to Aristotle, the essential characteristics, and hence the differentiae, of substance are certainly not accidents. See *Top.* 6.6, 144a24-7; 1.4, 101b17-19; 1.5, 102b4-5.

    (It is true that in *Enn.* 2.6.2-3, Plotinus appears to reopen this question and even to give a different answer. But in reality the question there is secondary: given that sensible substance is not really substantial but qualitative, how can we distinguish a category of sensible quality? The answer has to do with the status of some qualitative properties as "acts" [*energeiai*] of intelligible productive *logoi.*)

62. *Enn.* 6.3.8.27-30; see also 2.6.1.36-40.

63. Porphyry, *In Cat.* 5, 95,22-7. The expression itself, *poiotês ousiôdês*, is Plotinian: see *Enn.* 6.3.14. The theory which accompanies the expression, however, is not: note how Simplicius specifically attributes it to Porphyry (Simplicius, *In Cat.* 5, 78,21-3), and cf. also the *rejected* attempt to designate some qualities as *ousiôdeis* at *Enn.* 2.6.1.22-9.

    I translate *ousiôdês* here and elsewhere as "substantial" to bring out the connection which Porphyry obviously wants to make between this kind of "quality" and the category of substance. It might also be translated "essential." This is not the place to attempt a complete unraveling of the confusing histories of "substance" and "essence."

64. *Sh. Il.*, 2.1, 58,10-15.

65. See *Sh. M.*, *Maqūlāt*, 1.6, 45,15-17 and 47,17-18.

66. *Sh. Ṭ.*, *Samāʿ*, 1.6, 34,14-35,5. Avicenna expresses this position in many places, including at at *Sh. M.*, *Maqūlāt*, 1.6, 47,5-7 (where one must therefore read *lastu*, rather than *laysat*, and punctuate accordingly). See also *Sh. Ṭ.*, *Kawn/fasād*, 6, 129,15-131,11, and *Najāh*, 3.1, 246,10-247,16.

67. *Sh. M.*, *Maqūlāt*, 3.4, 114,1-4.

68. See Philoponus *In Ph.* 1.2, 38,23-39,2: "If there are three species of magnitude — one, two, and three-dimensional; that is, line, plane, and body — but body is a substance, then magnitude is a substance. Just as, with respect to qualities, some are substantial, such as those that are in the elements . . . so, too, is there substantial quantity." See also *Contra Proclum de aeternitate mundi*, ed. H. Rabe (Leipzig, 1899), 11.5, 424,4-7.

69. *Metaph.* 7.3, 1029a14-15. See also *Metaph.* 11.6, 1063a24-8, and see *Enn.* 6.3.17.10-11.

70. *In Ph.* 1.7, 230,21-29.

71. *Crescas' Critique of Aristotle* (Cambridge, MA, 1929), p. 582.

72. See *In Ph.* 1.7, 225,22-7.

73. Philoponus *In Ph.* 1.7, 156,4-16.

74. Ibid., ll. 16-17. If Philoponus means to suggest that body is literally a subject in which other substantial forms inhere, then Simplicius probably disagrees with him in principle (and Avicenna certainly does). Such a view seems on the face of it inconsistent with the description of substance as "not in a subject." However, it may be that Philoponus means only to say that qualitiless body is the proximate matter of the elemental forms, which leaves open all the various possible understandings of "proximate matter."

For a quite different, apparently older, use of the phrase "second subject," see Porphyry apud Simplicium, *In Cat.* 2, 48,16-21.

75. There is a sense in which extension itself might be called "inextended." But in *that* sense extension will be, not matter, but an incorporeal and supersensible form. See Simplicius *In Ph.* 1.7, 231,27-32 and *Corollarium de loco* 623,14-15.

76. *Matter, Space, and Motion: Theories in Antiquity and Their Sequel* (Ithaca, NY, 1988) (cited hereafter as *MSM*), 6. Sorabji in general translates *diastêma* (my "dimension") as "extension" and *ektasis* (my "extension") as "spreading." This makes little difference to the argument since, as we will see, Simplicius applies both terms to prime matter.

77. Ibid., 8.

78. One of the things that is so difficult about that chapter is that it is by no means clear where Aristotle is expressing his own view and where he is talking about what "seems" to be the case, or even engaged in some kind of reductio.

79. Locke's real concern, by the way, is that, on an Avicennan/Thomistic view, not just prime matter, but sensible substance in general, turns out to be unknowable: we have only relative, not absolute, descriptions of its true differentiae. This, of course, is genuinely embarrassing. The results of Leibniz and Kant's attempts to deal with the problem are well known (see especially *Kritik der reinen Vernunft*, A265-6/B321-2).

80. See also Philoponus *In Ph.* 1.6, 146,4-9.

81. Simplicius, *In Ph.* 1.7, 232,7-11. (Here Simplicius is actually explaining an apparent objection, which he then goes on to answer, to the Neopythagorean view. But the objection also applies to Philoponus, and in that case

Simplicius' answer will not apply.) See also 228,1, and see *Cael.* 1.3, 270a12-22. Note that the problem here does *not* have to do, as Sorabji (*MSM*, 14-15) suggests, with the supposition that celestial and sublunar things share a common prime matter.

82. *In Ph., Corollarium de loco*, 622,21.
83. Ibid., 623,16-17.
84. *In Cat.* 6, 125,13-15.
85. *In Ph.* 1.7, 230,17-20.
86. *In Ph.* 4.2, 538,20-21.
87. *In Cat.* 6, 122,16-17.
88. This, I believe, is how Simplicius wants to understand the Neopythagorean doctrine that a privative "form" of quantum serves as the archetype of prime matter. I see no evidence that he quotes Moderatus (at *In Ph.* 1.7, 231) in order to disagree with him, as Sorabji thinks; on the contrary, he offers the quote as evidence of his own theory's hoary antiquity.
89. *In Ph.* 1.7, 231,20 and 26-7; see also *Corollarium de loco*, 623,10-11.
90. *In Ph.* 4.2, 537,30 (referring to *Ph.* 3.6, 207a21).
91. *In Cat.* 6, 133,31-4.
92. Time — a continuous quantity which is not a magnitude — does not fit easily into this scheme. For Simplicius' attempts to deal with it see *In Cat.* 6, 138,20-22; 32-139,1; *In Ph., Corollarium de loco*, 640,29-30; 641,3-5.
93. *In Ph., Corollarium de loco*, 640,35-641,2.
94. Perhaps matter could also be called "indeterminate number," although Simplicius does not, to my knowledge, ever do so. One would presumably say that the indeterminate number of things which share some material substantial form is the prime matter in which that form exists.
95. *In Ph.* 4.2, 537,13-15. Here "accidents" includes the substantial qualities (which are like accidents of prime matter in that they are predicated of it but not essentially).
96. *In Ph.* 4.2, 537,22-3 and 538,23-4.
97. *In Ph.* 4.2, 537,24-6; see also *Corollarium de loco*, 623,14-19.
98. Here again the sense of *peri* is that one thing (substantial form) changes in another ("material deviation") which remains, and here again my translation ("with respect to") is not very satisfactory.
99. *In Ph.* 1.7, 232,13-21.
100. *In Ph.* 1.7, 228,23-5, referring to *Tim.* 53c6. I take it that this is the force of his argument, since the only number which is *sunousiômenon* to body is the number three, in virtue of which it is three-dimensional.

101. *Cael.* 1.1, 268a24-5.

102. *Sh. M.*, *Maqūlāt*, 1.6, 46,2.

103. Ibid., 46,20-47,1.

104. *Sh. M.*, *Burhān*, 1.10 (100,15-16).

105. *Sh. Ṭ.*, *Nafs*, 5.4, 203,1-2: "the body is not . . . informed by the form of the soul." This is so because the soul is an incorporeal substance (*Sh. Il.*, 2.1, 60,10-13), and an entelechy (*kamāl*) which is essentially separable from that which it perfects (as, in this case, the soul is from the body) "is not in reality [*fī al-ḥaqīqa*] a form of the matter" (*Sh. Ṭ.*, *Nafs*, 1.1, 7,3-4); such an entelechy is rather like the captain of a ship (ibid.; cf. *De An.* 2.1, 413a8-9, and see also *Ph.* 8.4, 254b30-33 and 6.10, 240a8-12 and 17-20; *De An.* 1.3, 405b31-406a8).

Avicenna can still explain Aristotle's explicit statement that the soul *is* the form of the body (*De An.* 2.1, 412a19-21) because he holds that there are other, less strict senses of "form," in which the term can be applied an accident, to a purely immaterial substance, or to a "separate entelechy" (*kamāl mufāraq*) like the soul: see *Ḥudūd*, 5, 29 (where "form," in the sense in which it applies to souls is defined as "a separate incorporeal part through which, together with a corporeal part, a natural species is perfected") and *Sh. Il.*, 6.4, 282,6-12 (where, however, the soul is not explicitly mentioned).

106. *Sh. M.*, *Burhān*, 1.10, 100,8.

107. On the way in which such a form can be called "generic," or a "physical genus," even though, strictly speaking, it is not a genus at all, see *Sh. M.*, *Madkhal*, 1.12, 67,3-7.

108. *Sh. Il.*, 2.2, 69,9-10. Bäck is therefore incorrect to cite this passage as evidence that, according to Avicenna, "corporeity is not the same as body, a genus in the category of substance" ("Individuation", 30). On the contrary: the allusion to the distinction between matter and genus in the *Burhān* shows that the type of corporeity under discussion here must be substantial corporeity, since it is clear there that body as matter and body as genus (like animal as matter and animal as genus) are types of *substance*. The passages *Sh. Il.*, 5.3, 214,1-216,9, 219,11, and 5.9, 249,13 which Bäck cites later as evidence that "on [Avicenna's] account, corporeity...is not essential to the substantial quiddity in itself but only to its material existence" ("Individuation", 31) also concern this same ditinction between matter and genus. Recall also *Sh. M.*, *Maqūlāt*, 3.4, 114,2-3: "the form of corporeity which is its substantial form is that by which no body exceeds any other."

109. See *Sh. Ṭ.*, *Samāʿ*, 1.1, 8,13-9,1.

110. *Sh. Il.*, 2.2, 70,12-14.

111. *Sh. Il.*, 2.2, 61,6-7. He refers to this expression as a "description" a few pages later (63,4). Cf. *Najāh*, 3.1, 238,6-8; *Sh. M.*, *Maqūlāt*, 3.4, 113,9-11 and *Burhān*, 1.10, 99,16.

112. *Sh. Il.*, 2.2, 63,14-15.

113. See *Sh. M.*, *Madkhal*, 1.9, 49,3-7.

114. *Sh. Il.*, 2.2, 64,6-7.

115. *Sh. Il.*, 2.2, 70,2-3.

116. *Najāh*, 3.1, 238,27-239,1. Moses Narboni (in his commentary to Algazali's *Maqāṣid al-Falāsifa*, cited in Wolfson, *Crescas*, 584) says that Avicennan corporeity is "neither continuity nor a nature to which continuity is essentially concomitant [*ṭevaʿ yeḥuyyav lo ha-devequt be-ʿaẓmuto*]." (Note that my translation differs slightly from Wolfson's, on the previous page.) There is some problem here, but it is hard to say, without examining the manuscripts of Narboni's commentary, whether the problem is with Narboni's text of the *Najāh*, or with his understanding of that text, or with Wolfson's text of Narboni.

117. I leave aside Wolfson's suggestion (*Crescas*, 579) that *ittiṣāl* ought really, in this context, to be translated as "cohesion." He has perhaps been misled by the Hebrew equivalent *devequt*, which literally means "sticking together." We will see below to exactly what extent *ittiṣāl* here corresponds to the usual definitions of *sunekheia* = *continuitas*, and to what extent it does not. But nothing we will see suggests that it should be understood as "cohesion," either in the way Avicenna uses that term or in the way Wolfson defines it (in terms of bulk and rigidity).

118. *Sh. M.*, *Maqūlāt*, 3.4, 116,16-17; *Sh. Ṭ.*, *Samāʿ*, 3.2, 182,2-3; *Sh. Il.*, 3.2, 98,16-17; *Ḥudūd*, 63, 95; cf. *Ph.* 5.3, 227a11-12.

119. *Sh. M.*, *Maqūlāt*, 3.4, 117,12-13; *Sh. Ṭ.*, *Samāʿ*, 3.2, 183,3-4; *Sh. Il.*, 3.2, 99,1-2; *Ḥudūd*, 63, 96; cf. *Metaph.* 5.6, 1016a5-6. Note that it is this relation between two bodies, not any property of body as such, that Avicenna actually calls "cohesion" or "coherence" (*iltiḥām*) (*Sh. Il.*, 3.2, 99,2; cf. *Najāh*, 2.3, 178,7-8).

120. *Sh. M.*, *Maqūlāt*, 3.4, 116,9-14; *Sh. Ṭ.*, *Samāʿ*, 3.2, 183,7-8; *Ḥudūd*, 63, 94; cf. *Cat.* 6, 4b25-5a14. The version of this definition at *Sh. Il.*, 3.2, 98,14-16 (based, apparently, on *Metaph.* 5.6, 1016a9-17) is different and much less satisfactory (it implies, for example, that a body with sharp edges is not continuous). What looks like a further Aristotelian definition of continuity at *Cael.* 1.1, 268a6-7 is dismissed by Avicenna as a mere "description" (*Sh. Ṭ.*, *Samāʿ*, 3.2, 183,9-10).

121. *GC* 1.10, 327b21-6.

122. See *Sh. Ṭ.*, *Kawn/fasād*, 7 for a lengthy refutation of it. It was nevertheless defended again later by St. Thomas (see *Summa theologiae* [Ottawa: Commissio Piana, 1953], 1.76.5 ad 4).

123. *Sh. Ṭ.*, *Kawn/fasād*, 6, 127,11-12.

124. *Sh. Il.*, 6.4, 280,16-17. By "homoeidetic" I mean not having actual parts which differ in (substantial) form, i.e. species. This should not be confused with "homeomerous": according to Avicenna, a homeomerous mixture is *not* homoeidetic, in the sense in which I am using that term.

125. *Sh. Ṭ.*, *Kawn/fasād*, 6, 126,17-127,1.

126. *Sh. Ṭ.*, *ʾAfʿāl/infiʿālāt*, 2.1, 253,5-10; 256,9-14. Some material forms and/or first entelchies of material things — in particular, the various kinds of soul — require not just mixture but also "composition" (*tarkīb* = *sunthesis*), in the strict sense in which this involves a combination of parts which remain qualitatively distinct (see *GC* 1.10, 328a5-15). This does not materially affect the following argument.

127. See *Sh. Ṭ.*, *Samāʿ*, 3.3, 184,7 and 12-14.

128. *Najāh*, 2.3, 178,6-7, and see also *Sh. Il.*, 3.2, 99,3.

129. *Sh. Il.*, 3.2, 99,5-8.

130. *Sh. Il.*, 3.2, 99,11.

131. *Sh. Ṭ.*, *Samāʿ*, 3.3, 197,10, and see *Metaph.* 5.8, 1017b11-12. See also *DN*, c. 7, where Avicenna says that "a body is not composed of parts."

132. See again *Sh. M.*, *Burhān*, 1.10, 100,1-7 and 14-15, *Maqūlāt*, 3.4, 114,2-3, *Madkhal*, 1.12, 67,3-7, and *Sh. Il.*, 5.3, 214,15-215,3, and cf. *Metaph.* 3.3, 999a6-13, *EN* 1.6, 1096a17-23, and *Enn.* 6.1.25.16-21.

133. *Sh. Il.*, 3.2, 100,18-101,1.

134. *Sh. M.*, *Maqūlāt*, 3.4, 118,5-7.

135. *Sh. M.*, *Maqūlāt*, 3.4, 116,6-8; *Ḥudūd*, 63, 94-6.

136. *Sh. M.*, *Maqūlāt*, 3.4, 118,10-16.

137. "Division [*qisma*] is either by separation of continuity, or by an accident by the change of which one part is distinguished from another . . . or by imagination and positing" (*Sh. Ṭ.*, *Samāʿ*, 3.3, 184,13-14).

138. *Sh. Il.*, 3.2, 98,12-13.

139. A body can also be corrupted by coalescing with another. Division, however, is corruption of body per se (because continuity is the positive characteristic); coalescence is corruption per accidens (and per se generation). Avicenna focuses mostly on division, as opposed to coalescence, and so will we.

140. *Najāh*, 3.1, 239,1-8; cf. *Sh. Il.* 2.2, 66,15-67,7. Cf. *DN*, c. 5, 15,5-10. Note that Morewedge's translation is somewhat misleading. The passage reads, more or less:

> Now continuity is the contrary of division [*gusistagī*=Ar. *infiṣāl*] and no contrary is receptive of its contrary. For that which is receptive of something must be disposed [*ba-jāy bud*] to receive that other thing; but that which is not [so] disposed cannot receive another thing even if that other thing is [so] disposed. We maintain that a continuous body is receptive of division, and the receptiveness of division is not in continuity; therefore it must be in another thing which is receptive of both, that is, receptive of both division and continuity.

(My thanks to R. Wisnovsky and Wheeler Thackston for their help with the Persian; I have also relied on the French translation *Le livre de science*, tr. M. Achena and H. Masse [Paris, 1955-8], which at least in this case is much more precise.)

141. See *Sh. Il.*, 2.3, 72,4-7.

142. *Sermo de substantia orbis*, c. 3, Hebrew pp. 41-2, ll. 103-4; Latin 10rB. See also *Tafsīr* (*Long Commentary*) on the *Metaphysics*, ed. Maurice Bouyges, 2nd edition (Beirut, 1967), *yā*ʾ (= *I*), comm. 26, 1387,9-1388,2. Note, however, that the most explicit part of this passage is not present the Arabic and Hebrew manuscripts; Bouyges introduces it from the Latin. The passage dates, at least, to an early stage of the Latin tradition, since St. Thomas evidently has it in his text (see *Scripta super libros Sententiarum*, ed. R. P. Mandonnet, 4 vols. [Paris: P. Lethielleux, 1929], 1.19.5.2 ad 1).

143. The main textual problem has to do with the opening of the *De caelo*, where Aristotle discusses body in general, including both celestial and sublunar body. The main conceptual problem has to do with the way in which celestial and sublunar bodies can share the same space — i.e, can contain one another. Averroes' view does, however, lead to a more natural reading of *Metaph.* 12.1, 1069a30-36.

144. *Sh. M.*, *Maqūlāt*, 3.1, 92,1-3. Cf. Philoponus *In Ph.* 1.2, 39,9-10.

145. *Sh. Il.*, 2.2, 66,11-12. Avicenna appears to use *infiṣāl*, *inqisām*, and (in this sense) *qisma* interchangeably. I translate them all as "division," reserving "partition" for *tajazzu*ʾ, *tajziʾa*, etc.

146. *Sh. Ṭ.*, *Samā*ʿ, 1.3, 22,4-7 (reading *mā lā yafsud* for *mā yafsud* in line 7).

147. See *Cael.* 1.3, 270a12-22; *Sh. Ṭ.*, *Samā*ʾ, 4.

148. *Sh. M.*, *Maqūlāt*, 3.3, 103,15-16. There is no direct Greek equivalent for *ishāra*, as Goichon notes (*Vocabulaires comparés d'Aristote et d'Ibn Sina*

[Paris, 1939], s.v. *šwr*). But it is used to translate phrases involving the expression *tode ti*. See, e.g., *Cat.* 5, 3b10, where *tode ti* is translated as *maqṣūd ilayhi bi-l-ishāra* (*Manṭiq Arisṭū* [= *Organon*], tr. Isḥāq ibn Ḥunain, ed. ʿAbd al-Raḥmān Badawī [Cairo, 1948-52]). This translation is quoted verbatim at *Sh. M., Maqūlāt*, 3.3, 103,15.

149. See especially *Sh. M., Madkhal*, 1.12, 65,19-66,11 and 70,9-20.

150. *Sh. M., Maqūlāt*, 3.3, 103,16-17.

151. *Sh. M., Madkhal*, 1.12, 70,9-10.

152. *Sh. M., Madkhal*, 1.12, 70,17-18.

153. *ʿUnṣur* (which means literally something like "origin") is a name for matter (i.e., "*ʿunṣur* and matter," like "quiddity and form," says the same thing twice). It might perhaps in this context be translated as "principle," even though that word should normally be reserved for *mabdaʾ* (which is the standard translation of *arkhê*): as Avicenna explains, "because composition begins [*yabtadiʾ*] with [matter], . . .it is called *ʿunṣur*" (*Sh. Ṭ., Samāʿ*, 1.2, 15,3-4). Another possible translation would be "element," but this seems inadvisable in light of the fact that another name for matter is *isṭaqis* = *stoikheion* (*Sh. Ṭ., Samāʿ*, 1.2, 14,1 and 15,2).

The equivalent for Avicenna of Philoponus' distinction between primary and secondary subject seems to be a distinction between primary and secondary *ʿunṣur* (though he does not use the terms "primary" and "secondary" in this connection): see *Ḥudūd*, 9, 33.

154. *Sh. Ṭ., Nafs*, 5.3, 198,13-15; see also *Sh. Ṭ., Samāʿ*, 2.5, 112,2-3.

I am not completely sure what Avicenna means by (2c), "the causes that divide them" (*al-ʿilal al-qāsima ʾiyāhā*), but I suspect he is referring to the explanation of *how* things come to be at a particular place and time — namely, by virtue of some cause which is itself local and temporal. See *Sh. Il.* 2.3, 73,15-74,2.

155. I am departing somewhat from the way in which Avicenna presents the first case. He assumes without proof, at *Sh. Il.*, 2.3, 72,4-7, that "corporeal matter" is "ultimate matter" (*al-mādda al-ʾakhīra*) — i.e., prime matter. He then goes on to assume, for the sake of argument, that this matter might not be purely receptive, but might have "a proper constituted existence" (*wujūd khāṣṣ mutaqawwim*) (*Sh. Il.*, 2.3, 74,13-14, although such an assumption is really already in place on the previous two pages). Matter without form, however, obviously cannot have such a proper existence, while, on the other hand, it is by no means self-evident that corporeal matter and prime matter can be identified. I therefore think it best to understand the argument as I have represented it.

156. Throughout this argument Avicenna uses *ḥayyiz* rather than the regular

equivalent for *topos*, which is *makān*. Both of these are rendered into Latin as *locus*. If a distinction is to made between the two, it is that *ḥayyiz* involves the idea of position (*waḍʿ* = *thesis*) in the order of the universe in general. Where Aristotle says that each simple body has a natural place, for example, Avicenna says that each body has a natural *ḥayyiz*. (This may tend to support Goichon's contention that *ḥayyiz* translates *khôra*: see *Cael.* 4.5, 312b3.) *Ḥayyiz* in this sense serves to emphasize the role of place in individuation. *Ḥayyiz* is also, or at least can be, more general than *makān*, in that it includes the position of things such as points, which are not in place (*Sh. Ṭ.*, *Samāʿ*, 4.11, 308,11).

157. *Sh. Il.*, 2.3, 72,8-12; *Najāh*, 3.1, 240,1-5. Limits (such as points, lines, and surfaces) cannot be substances: see *Metaph.* 3.5, 1002a4-b11, and see also 11.2, 1060b12-19 and 14.3, 1090b8-13. For Avicenna's arguments on this issue see *Najāh*, 3.1, 140,5-13; cf. also *Sh. Ṭ.*, *Nafs*, 5.3, 187,11-188,17.

158. Avicenna considers two cases, one in which *A* becomes a body instantaneously, another in which it becomes a body gradually. But this distinction seems to me superfluous.

159. This is the standard Aristotelian definition of place: the surface which is the limit of the containing body (*Sh. Ṭ.*, *Samāʿ*, 2.9, 137,8-9 = *Ph.* 4.4, 212a6). One might imagine a case in which there are at first no bodies at all, but only the pre-body *A*, and in which *A* then becomes a single body which fills the entire universe. Such a body which would be finite, but not in place. It is likely, however, that Avicenna thinks such a scenario can be ruled out a priori out on other grounds. It certainly does not correspond to any possible past or future of *our* universe, since the celestial bodies, which are ingenerable and incorruptible, are distinct from each other and from all sublunar bodies.

160. This is true for all sublunar bodies, at any rate. But since we are imagining our body as the product of generation, it must be sublunar.

161. *Sh. Il.*, 2.3, 73,4-9.

162. *Sh. Il.*, 2.3, 72,15-73,3. Note that Avicenna is implicitly appealing here to a principle of sufficient reason (i.e., he would not allow the kind of thing modern physicists call "spontaneous symmetry breaking" — which may or may not be a real feature of modern physics, depending on one's interpretation of quantum mechanics).

It might be objected that a place could be proper to *A* not because *A* itself was in it, but because *A* was related to some located thing (as for example the rational soul is related to its body). But if *A* is related to place only through some external thing *C*, then we can *conceive* of *C*'s being removed from the picture, even though that may, in any particular case, be impossible (as for example no rational soul can come into existence without the simultaneous generation of a human body). Then consider the precorporeal *A* becoming corporeal with no *C* at all: the argument goes through as before.

163. *Sh. Il.*, 2.3, 75,3-6.

164. Of course, the *real* way in which matter "loses" corporeal form — i.e, division — does not result in its becoming incorporeal. See below for more discussion of this point.

165. For this argument, see *Sh. Il.*, 2.3, 75,12-77,4; cf. another version at *DN*, c. 8.

166. *Sh. Il.*, 2.3, 77,1-2.

167. One might object that C_1 and C differ by their respective relations to B and B_1, which are different bodies: this would be similar to the way in which human rational souls are individuated. I am not completely certain how Avicenna would respond to this, but I think that the difference between the two cases is as follows. If B is in fact divided, then B and B_1 must differ in time, and, at the instant of division, in place and quantity as well. But C results from B only in a case where B is *not* divided, so nothing prevents us from adjusting the details such that the B from which C comes about is intrinsically indistinguishable from the B_1 which gives rise to C_1. The only difference between B and B_1 which cannot, without changing the example, be imagined away, is one of relation: B_1 is related to B in a way that B itself is not. Avicenna must take it as obvious that this kind of purely relational difference-without-distinction between B and B_1 is not sufficient to create a difference between C and C_1. (Note that the relational difference between B and B_1 is not paralleled by a relational difference between C and C_1, unless we assume that counterfactual possibles can be terms of actual relations.) A parallel case involving human bodies cannot be constructed: if we imagine one human body as possessing the same intrinsic characteristics as another one, then we are simply imagining the same human body twice. It is *divisibility* which creates the possibility of a purely relational difference between B and B_1. (A human being cannot be divided into two human beings: it is one of the proofs of the immateriality of the intellect that the subject of abstracted form cannot be divisible.)

168. *Sh. Il.*, 2.3, 77,5-8.

Avicenna at the ARCE*

DAVID C. REISMAN

Introduction.[1]

During a period of research in Cairo in 1993-4 sponsored by the Fulbright Organization, I was asked by the director of the American Research Center in Egypt to retrieve a number of cardboard boxes filled with photostats of manuscripts from the ARCE storehouse and compile a brief list of their contents. The collection, some 200 photostats of manuscripts from around the world, can be generally divided into medieval Arabic philosophical works (including medical works) and medieval Arabic literature (including historical writings). The vast majority of the philosophical manuscripts are of Ibn Sīnā's works. The collection appears to have formed part of the estate of Charles Kuentz, at one time the Director of the Institut Français d'Archéologie Orientale in Cairo, and was purchased by the ARCE around 1978.[2] It is reasonable to surmise that the majority of the photostats, particularly those still enclosed in their original brown wrappers, were collected by Kuentz; indeed the interests

* I would like to thank Hammam Fawzy Hassan, Ian Whitney, and Solaiman Gomaʿa Abdallah of the ARCE library for their hospitality during the summer of 1999. Funding for my research during the summer of 1999 was provided by the United states Information Agency and managed by the American Research Center in Egypt. Dimitri Gutas, Felizitas Opwis, and Everett Rowson kindly corrected earlier versions of this catalogue.

Kuentz displayed in his publications on Ibn Sīnā coincide with the emphases found in that part of the photostat collection related to Ibn Sīnā's works.[3] There are also indications that some of the older material was acquired from the library of Max Meyerhof. A number of these older photostats remain in their envelopes, addressed to Max Meyerhof, from his colleague Helmut Ritter, then living in Bebek, Istanbul. They contain copies of medieval Arabic medical manuscripts from libraries in Istanbul.[4] The earliest date found amongst this set of photostats is on one of Max Meyerhof's prescription pads, from his Cairo clinic in Sharia Bab El Sharky: 191-. The last digit of the date has been left blank, presumably so that the prescription pads would remain valid through the years 1910-1919. The latest date for this set is found on a printed card made by Max Meyerhof, bearing the date 1928. The questions of the provenance of the non-Ibn Sīnā photostats, and whether or not any part of the photostat collection as a whole was once in the posessesion of Paul Kraus, remain to be solved.[5]

In 1994, I completed a rough author and title list, on index cards, organized according to shelf numbers I had assigned the wrappers containing the photostats. I made a brief report to the director of the ARCE about the great significance of this collection, and deposited the photostats and the index cards in the ARCE library. In 1997, having begun dissertation research into the transmission and reception of Ibn Sīnā's *Kitāb al-Mubāḥathāt*, I recalled this important if neglected collection and applied for a research grant from the ARCE for the summer of 1999. My intention was to catalogue the photostats of Ibn Sīnā manuscripts and make use of any relevant manuscripts for my dissertation research. In my absence, the Head Librarian of the ARCE library had assigned new shelf numbers to the wrappers and compiled a very general handwritten list of author and title. These new numbers are used in the following catalogue. In most cases, this new list amounted to only a rough identification of the manuscripts as *majmūʿa*s on a particular topic (medicine, philosophy, etc.) with the name of the author who had composed the majority of the treatises in a given *majmūʿa*. Clearly, if the collection were to be used by researchers, a more detailed inventory had to be undertaken.

An evaluation of the worth of a collection of Ibn Sīnā's works such as the one found at the ARCE must be based on a number of considerations. The main weakness of the collection is to be located in the fact that a number of the exemplars of a given work are incomplete, largely because loose pages of the photostats were separated from their groups. Another problem is that in some cases the photostats are of poor quality, which makes them unreadable and hence unusable. However, if we evaluate the collection within the larger context of Ibn Sīnā studies as a whole, it becomes very significant. The chief obstacle facing the study of Ibn Sīnā's philosophical and medical works at present is the decided absence of definitive critical editions for the majority of his works. The very fact that so many exemplars of such a wide variety of his works are gathered in one place will hopefully be an incentive to overcoming this obstacle.[6] Within this context, the strengths of the ARCE collection, understood in terms of the number and variety of exemplars of a given work, are the result of the scholarly interests of the original collector(s). Ibn Sīnā's poem on the soul, *al-Qaṣīda al-ʿayniyya*, is found in no fewer than fifteen exemplars, with multiple commentaries. The *Mabdaʾ wa-al-maʿād* is found in eighteen exemplars, more than half of the manuscripts listed by Mahdavī for this work. Ibn Sīnā's *al-Urjūza fī al-ṭibb* (M15a) is found in twenty-eight exemplars, with numerous commentaries, including the very important one by Ibn Rushd. Needless to say, there are no substantive codicological studies of any of these three works, and none of them have been published in a completely critical edition.[7] Ibn Sīnā's major works, such as the *Qānūn fī al-ṭibb*, the *Shifāʾ*, the *Najāt*, *al-Ḥikma al-mashriqiyya*, *al-Mubāḥathāt*, are not represented extensively in the ARCE collection, but nearly all of the minor treatises, poems, and letters are present in abundance. There is an especial emphasis on the medical works, which have received little scholarly attention to date. Clearly, there is enough material in the ARCE collection to occupy generations of scholars.

My research interests have limited this undertaking to a detailed inventory of the photostats of Ibn Sīnā manuscripts in the collection. While a number of works by other authors regularly appear in the codices of Ibn Sīnā's works, I have concentrated my attention on providing a thorough description of the Master's works, with an addendum for exemplars of Bahmanyār's *al-Taḥṣīl* also present in the collection. The numbers in **bold** are the new shelf numbers assigned to the wrappers of photostats.

For each number, I have provided provenance information (where ascertainable), shelf number, folio numbers, titles of the works, and references to the standard bibliographies of Ibn Sīnā's works. I have limited references to library catalogues, since that information can be obtained from Yaḥyā Mahdavī's bibliography. The publication record of a given work is indicated by reference to J Janssens' survey of the published works of Ibn Sīnā where applicable.[8] Not all of the folio numbers of the codices are readily discernible from the photostats. Where there is doubt about precise foliation, I have omitted such indication. There are numbers handwritten in pencil on the reverse of all of the photostats. Occasionally, these numbers coincide with the folio numbers of the manuscript, and so I have been able to foliate those manuscripts according to the handwritten numbers (the use of these numbers here is indicated by the lack of recto/verso notation).

In the contents lists to some of the more important *majmūʿa*s of Ibn Sīnā's treatises, I have included treatises actually missing from the photostats. The purpose of these additions is to correct minor errors made by Mahdavī and other bibliographers.[9] It is also hoped that an arrangement of the manuscripts of Ibn Sīnā's works which provides the contents in the order they appear in the codices will eventually aid in identifying and plotting the textual transmission of those works.

The collection has suffered in varying degrees from the vagaries of time. Their physical condition on the whole is stable, but will require preservation efforts in the near future if the collection is to be accessible to scholars. Mold and mildew have attacked a relatively few number of the photostats. In some cases, photostat pages have become separated from their groups and lost, leaving us with incomplete copies of the manuscripts.

3. Ahmet III 3268, ff. 61-110r. *Al-Mabdaʾ wa-al-maʿād.* M106. J, p. 20. The colophon states that the scribe, Muḥammad ibn ʿĪsā ibn ʿAlī ibn Habbāj al-Ṭabīb completed his copy in Dhū al-Qaʿda 580/February-March 1185. See another photostat of this exemplar at **48**.

5. Cairo, Dār al-Kutub, 397 falsafa. *Kitāb al-Nafs ʿalā ṭarīq al-dalīl wa-al-burhān.* M121. J, p. 14 (*Aḥwāl al-nafs*).

6. Kılıç Ali Paşa 1027, ff. 70r-73v. *Al-Qaṣīda al-ʿayniyya*, with an anonymous commentary. Colophon is dated Muḥarram 876/June-July 1471. M99 does not list this exemplar. J, p. 54.

7. Ragıp Paşa 1482. Two of the treatises of this codex are found in this wrapper. There are two ownership notes on the title page. One is by Sālim ibn al-Ḥājj Yaḥyā al-Bāsī (?), dated 27 Ramaḍān 1304/19 June 1887. The other states that Muḥammad Baram al-Rābiʿ purchased the manuscript from ʿUthmān al-Najjār. Only the last two digits, 89, of the date of purchase are legible.

1-69v. Madyan ibn ʿAbd al-Raḥmān al-Ṭabīb [al-Qawṣūnī] (d. 1034/1634). *Al-Qawl al-anīs wa-al-durr al-nafīs ʿalā manẓūmat al-Shaykh al-Raʾīs*. A commentary on Ibn Sīnā's *al-Urjūza fī al-ṭibb*. M17 *apud* Anawati. The title states that the work was composed in the Dār al-Shifāʾ in Cairo; the colophon indicates that the work was completed in 1010/1601-2.

70r-77r. Madyan ibn ʿAbd al-Raḥmān al-Ṭabīb [al-Qawṣūnī]. *Hādhā muntahā al-ghāyāt fī taʿrīf al-layla* [title page has *taʿrīf al-yawm wa-al-layla*]. The author of this work states in his introduction that he is copying the last part of his book entitled *Qāmūs al-aṭibbāʾ wa-nāmūs al-ābāʾ* (GAL II, 364, S II, 492, does not list this extract). He completed his copy in the middle of Muḥarram 1030/Nov.-Dec. 1620.

8. Rampur Reza 2955, ff. 1-65, via Maʿhad al-Makhṭūṭāt. *Al-Mabdaʾ wa-al-maʿād*. M106.

9. Leiden cod. or. 983. *Al-Urjūza fī al-ṭibb*. M15a. J, p. 37. Colophon: Muḥammad ibn al-Ḥājj Zakarīyāʾ completed his copy on 18 Muḥarram 961/24 December 1553.

12. Escurial 863.

2-41. *Al-Urjūza fī al-ṭibb*. M15a.

42r-47r. [Different, later hand] *Al-Urjūza fī al-mujarrabāt*. MS not listed in M20.

13. Şehid Ali Paşa 2106. *Al-Urjūza fī al-ṭibb*. MS not listed in M15a. One ownership note f. 1r, dated 1181/1767-7.

15. Université Saint-Joseph, Or. 288.

4v-19r. *Al-Urjūza fī al-ṭibb* [*fī al-fuṣūl al-arbaʿa*]. Incomplete (lacking folios 1v-4r). M17j. J, p. 56.

19r-35v. Ibn Rushd. *Sharḥ al-Urjūza fī al-ṭibb*. Incomplete (lacking folios 36r-76). M15a, *shurūḥ*.

16. Vehbi 1407. Folios 1-26?[10] *Al-Urjūza fī al-ṭibb*. There appears to have been some shuffling of folios in the manuscript. Ibn Sīnā's *Urjūza* is interrupted at f. 14v by a page of Persian poetry, followed by a medical treatise attributed to Naṣīr al-Dīn al-Ṭūsī (which is described as *ṣaghīr al-ḥajm kathīr al-fawāʾid*), entitled *Kitāb al-Albāb al-nāhiyya wa-tarākīb al-sulṭāniyya*.[11] Ibn Sīnā's *Urjūza* then resumes. M15a does not list this manuscript.

18, **28**, **59**, **115**, **116**, **119**, **208**. Ahmet III 3447. F. E. Karatay provided palaeographical details and a contents list of this codex in his 1966 catalogue of the Arabic manuscripts of the Topkapı Saray Museum.[12] The codex has been dated to 866/1462. A number of errors in the contents lists made by Mahdavī and Karatay are corrected here.

1v-5r. *Tafāsīr*:

Sūrat al-Ikhlāṣ. M50a.

Al-Muʿawwidhatayn (*Sūrat al-Falaq*; *Sūrat al-Nās*). M50b1-2.

Qawluhū thumma stawā ilā al-samāʾ. M50d **116**

13v-18v. *Risāla fī al-ṣalāt*. M85. **116**

20v-26v. *Manāqib al-Shaykh al-Raʾīs*. Autobiography/Biography Complex, Longer Bibliography only.[13] 116

27v-34v. *Asbāb ḥudūth al-ḥurūf*. M25. **116**

35v-39r. *Risāla fī ʿilm al-iksīr* (= *Amr mastūr al-ṣanʿa*, M33). **116**

40v-48v. *Risāla fī al-ʿishq*. M90. **116**

49v-51v. *Risāla fī al-akhlāq*. Two copies. M13. **116**

52v-59v. Pseudo-Ibn Sīnā (Fārābī?). *Risāla fī al-taṣawwuf* (= *Al-Firdaws*. M192; J, pp. 69-70). **116**

60v-61v. *Al-Muʿāwada* [addressed to al-Shaykh al-Fāḍil]. M4j.[14] **116**

62v-64r. *Risāla fī al-malā'ika*. M113. **116**
64v-82v. *Al-Aḍḥawiyya*. M30. J, p. 63. **116**
83v-105r. *'Uyūn al-ḥikma*. M93. J, pp. 46-7. **116**
106v-122v. *Risāla fī al-ṭibb* (= *Fuṣūl ṭibbiyya*. M97.) **116**
123v-125r. *Sabab ijābat al-du'ā'* [addressed to Abū Sa'īd]. M4d. **59, 116**
123v-137r. *Masā'il Ḥunayn*. M110. **116**. Two more copies in **59**, one of which is incomplete.
137v-141r. *Risāla ilā ba'ḍ al-mutakallimīn* (= *Al-Wus'a*). M129. J, p. 52. **116, 59**
141v-148r. Pseudo-Ibn Sīnā (Ikhwān al-ṣafā'). *Tashrīḥ al-a'ḍā'*. M150 **116, 59**
148v-150r. *Al-'Ahd*. M92. **59, 116** (poor quality photostats), **18**.
150v-153r. *Al-'Arūs*. M89. **18**
153v-164v. *Risāla fī al-nihāya wa-al-lānihāya* (= *Al-Ḥukūma fī ḥujaj al-muthbitīn [anna] li-al-māḍī mabda'an zamaniyyan*; M64. J, pp. 52-3). **18**
165r-174v. *Ibṭāl aḥkām al-nujūm*. M2. **18, 28**
175v-178r. *Risāla fī ḥadd al-jism*. M56. **208**
179v-188r. *Risālat al-Qadar*. M100. **18**
188v-190v. *Ḥuṣūl 'ilm wa-ḥikma* [addressed to Abū Sa'īd in title; in text: *fulān*]. M4w. **208**
191v-198r. *Al-Birr wa-al-ithm*. M40. **208**
198v-204v. *Risāla fī 'illat qiyām al-arḍ fī wasṭ al-samā'*. M91. J, p. 60. **18**
205v-212v. *Risāla fī al-siyāsa*. M82. J, p. 72. **18, 28**
213v-214v. *Risāla fī intifā' 'ammā nusiba ilayhi min mu'āraḍat al-Qur'ān*. M34.[15] **208**
215v-216r. *Risāla ilā 'Alā' al-Dīn ibn Kākūyah*. M79 does not list this copy. J, p. 73.[16] **208**
216v. Pseudo-Ibn Sīnā. *Al-Irshād* (Quote from 'Ayn al-Quḍāt's *al-Tamhīdāt*). M4z.[17] **208**
216v-217r. *Min aqwāl al-Shaykh al-Ra'īs*. M103. **208**
217v-218r. *Risāla ilā Abī Ṭāhir ibn Ḥassūl*. M79j.[18] **208**
218v. *Risāla ilā al-Shaykh Abī al-Faḍl ibn Maḥmūd*. M79h.[19] **208**
220v. *Anwā' al-qaḍāyā*. M37. **208**

220v. *Qāla al-Shaykh al-Raʾīs*. The following lines were overlooked by Mahdavī and Karatay: *qāla l-shaykhu l-raʾīsu qaddasa llāhu rūḥahū l-shayʾu lladhī bi-l-fiʿli huwa l-mawjūdu fī l-āni wa-l-shayʾu lladhī bi-l-quwwati huwa l-shayʾu l-ātā fī l-zamāni l-mustaqbali mithālu l-awwali quʿūdu l-qāʿidi wa-qiyāmu l-qāʾimi wa-mithālu l-thānī qiyāmu l-qāʿidi wa-quʿūdu l-qaʾimi*. **208**

221v. *Risāla ilā al-Shaykh Abī al-Qāsim ibn Abī al-Faḍl*. M79w. **208**

222v-249v. *Risāla fī al-nafs ʿalā ṭarīq al-dalīl wa-al-burhān*. M121. **18**

250v-272v. *Al-Adwiya al-qalbiyya*. M14. J, pp. 35-7. **18**

273v-275r. *Ḥuṣūl ʿilm wa-ḥikma* [addressed to Ibn Zayla]. M4w. **208**

275v-283v. *Risāla fī jawhar al-ajrām al-samāwiyya*. M53. **18**

284v-286r. *Dustūr ṭibbī*. M73. **208**

[omit 286v-288v. *Al-Khuṭba al-sharīfa* (= *Al-Khuṭba al-tawḥīdiyya*, M70)]

289v-298v. *Kitāb al-Ḥudūd*. M57. **18**

299r-v. *Nuskhat ruqʿa ilā Abī Jaʿfar al-Qāshānī*. M79b.[20] **208**

299v-300r. *Nuskhat ruqʿa ilā Abī Ṭāhir ibn Ḥassūl*. M79j. **208**

299v. *Al-Qaṣīda al-ʿayniyya*. M99. **28**, incomplete. **208**, complete.

300v-304r. *Al-Hindibāʾ*. M131. **18**, complete. **28**, incomplete.

304v-308r. *Al-Risāla al-Nayrūziyya*. M127. **18**

308v-314v. *Aqsām al-ʿulūm*. M32. J, p. 45. **18**

315v-326v. *Fuṣūl min al-ḥikma* [Passages from *al-Taʿlīqāt*]. M196. **208**

328v-371v. *Al-Taʿlīqāt*. M49b. J, pp. 24-5. **18**

372v-396r. *Al-Mubāḥathāt*. This exemplar contains MIVb, MVa, and part of *al-Najāt*, here entitled *Risāla fī al-ṭabīʿiyyāt*.[21] M105, M118. **18**

396v-404v. *Al-Ilāhiyyāt* from *al-Shifāʾ* (ed. Cairo, pp. 3.4-23.16). M84, 11. **18**

404v-408r. Pseudo-Ibn Sīnā. *Al-Mufāraqāt*. M228. **208**

408r-413v *Al-Ajwiba ʿan al-masāʾil al-ʿashr* (a). M6a. **18**

414v-419r. *Al-Fayḍ al-ilāhī* (= *Al-Afʿāl wa-al-infiʿālāt*, M97, J, p. 62). **18**

[Omit 419v-462r. Pseudo-Ibn Sīnā (Afḍal al-Din al-Kāshī). *Risāla fī al-manṭiq*. M188.]

462v-472v. *Taḥṣīl al-saʿāda*. M43. Incomplete. **18**
472v-474r. [*Al-Mabdaʾ wa-al-maʿād*]. M106, *dhayl*. **18**
475v. *Risāla fī al-nafs*. M123. **18**
478v-479r. Pseudo-Ibn Sīnā. *Masāʾil ʿan aḥwāl al-rūḥ*. M135. J, p. 55. **18, 119**
[Omit. 480v-512v. *Al-Mūjaz fī al-manṭiq*. M114.]
567v-569r. *Al-Ajwiba ʿan al-masāʾil*. M11. **18**
569v-574r. *Al-Ajwiba ʿan al-masāʾil al-ʿashr* (a). M6a. **119**
574v-579v. Pseudo-Ibn Sīnā (Abū al-Faraj ibn al-Ṭayyib). *Al-Quwā al-arbaʿa*. M205. **208**
580v-583v. *Al-Radd ʿalā kitāb Abī al-Faraj ibn al-Ṭayyib*. M76. **208**
584v-585r. *Risāla fī al-ḥuzn*. M59. **119**
586v-591r. *Masʾala ṭibbiyya* (= *Risāla fī al-bāh*, M39). **208**
592v-595r. *Risāla fī al-faṣd*. M95. **208**
596v-598v. *Risāla fī tadbīr al-musāfir*. M45. J, p. 72. **208**
599v-601v. *Risāla marmūza/Risālat al-Ṭuyūr* (= *Al-Ṭayr*. M88). **119**
602v-609v. *Ḥayy ibn Yaqẓān*. M65. **119**
610v-612v. *Al-Urjūza fī al-waṣāyā*. M21. **119**
613v-618r. *Al-Urjūza fī ʿilm al-manṭiq*. M22. J, p. 48. **208**
619v-624v. *Al-Jumāna al-ilāhiyya*. M51. **119**
[Omit: 625v-649v. *Dafʿ al-maḍarr*. M75]
650v-654v. Pseudo-Ibn Sīnā. *Risāla fī ʿilm al-nafs*. M238. **115**
655v-695v. [Hand change] *Dānishnāmah-yi ʿAlāʾī*. M73. **115**
696v-708v. *Tarjamah dar māhiyyat al-nafs* (= *Al-Nafs ʿalā ṭarīq al-dalīl wa-al-burhān*. M121, *tarjama*). **115**
709v-736r. *Al-Ajwiba ʿan masāʾil Abī Rayḥān al-Bīrūnī*. M5. **115**
736v-741v. *Tarjamah-yi Risāla fī al-nafs wa-aḥwālihā*. M121, *tarjama* 1. **115**

25, **52**, **181**. Istanbul University 1458. *Majmūʿa* of Ibn Sīnā treatises. The scribe of this collection, Muṣṭafā Bahjat, indicates in four colophons (ff. 22r, 31v, 52r, 162v) that he made his copy in the course of 1236/1821.
2v-9r. *Al-Tafāsīr*. M50, J, pp. 64-5. **181**
Sūrat al-Ikhlāṣ. M50a.
Al-Muʿawwidhatayn (*Sūrat al-Falaq*, *Sūrat al-Nās*). M50b.

Āyāt al-Nūr. M50h.
Sūrat al-Aʿlā. M50j.

9r-11r. *Ḥayy ibn Yaqẓān*. M65. J, p. 66. **181**

11v-12v. *Al-Ḥāshiya ʿalā tilka al-risāla* [i.e. *Ḥayy*]. Mahdavī (M65, *shurūḥ* 1) argues that this is the commentary by Ibn Zayla, but there is no indication of this in the manuscript; compare the next entry. **181**

12v-22r. Ibn Zayla. *Sharḥ Ḥayy ibn Yaqẓān*. M65, *shurūḥ* 1. Colophon states that the scribe, Muṣṭafā Bahjat, the *raʾīs al-aṭibbāʾ* in the *dawla al-ʿulyā* (Ottoman Empire?) completed his copy at the beginning of Jumād al-akhir (*sic*) 1236/March 1821. **52**, **181**

22v-24r. *Salāmān wa-Absāl*. M204. J, p. 70. **181**

24r-29v. Anonymous. *Risāla fī ḥaqīqat al-rūḥ li-wāḥid min akābir* (*sic*). The work is divided into two sections: the first in 10 *baḥth*s concerns the *rūḥ*; the second in 6 *baḥth*s is entitled *bayān ḥālāt al-rūḥ wa-bayān al-nafs wa-al-ʿaql wa-al-farq baynahumā*.

Incipit. (after the *basmala*): *wa-baʿdu fa-hādhihī risālatun mushtamilatun ʿalā fawāʾida jalīlatin min bayāni māhiyyati l-rūḥi wa-l-ḥayāti wa-l-nafsi wa-l-ʿaqli wa-aqsāmihā wa-tawābiʿihā wa-hiya murattabatun ʿalā faṣlayni wa-sittata ʿashara baḥthan.* **181**

29r-31v. Al-Dawwānī (d. 907/1501). *Risāla fī ḥaqīqat al-nafs*. See M238, GAL, S II, 308. Colophon by same scribe with same date. **181**

32-45v. *Risāla fī ḥaqīqat al-nafs* (= *Al-Nafs ʿalā ṭarīq al-dalīl wa-al-burhān*, M121). **181**

45v-46v. *Waṣāyā* of Fakhr al-Dīn al-Rāzī. (*Waṣiyya*; see GAL, I, 668, no. 15, which does not list this copy). **181**

46v-47v. Scribe adds additions to the *waṣiyya* and biographical notes on Fakhr al-Dīn al-Rāzī from Ibn Abī Uṣaybiʿa. **181**

47v-48r. *Waṣiyya* of Suhrawardī al-maqtūl. **181**

48r-v. *Al-ʿAhd*. M92. J, p. 69. **181**

48v-50r. *Asbāb ḥudūth al-ḥurūf*. M25. J, p. 49. **181**

50r-52r. *Risāla fī al-muʿjizāt* (= *Al-Afʿāl wa-al-infiʿālāt*, M97, J, p. 62).

Colophon dated end of Rajab 1236/March 1821, by Muṣṭafā Bahjat. **181**

52v-54v. *Ithbāt al-nubuwwa*. M3. J, p. 71.[22] **181**

54v-55r. *Sabab ijābat al-duʿāʾ*. M4d; J, p. 65. **181**

55r-v. *Risāla fī ajwibat baʿḍ al-asʾila*. M, p. 216. **181**

55v-56v. Anonymous. *Risāla fī al-mawʿiẓa al-laṭīfa wa-al-naṣāʾiḥ al-sharīfa manqūlun ʿan Hirmis al-Harāmisa wa-huwa Idrīs al-nabī*. **181**

56v-62. Al-Dawwānī. *Al-Risāla al-Khalkhāliyya*. GAL, S II, 308, no. 42 does not list this exemplar. **181**

62v-65v. Persian Pseudo-Ibn Sīnā. *Risāla fī ḥaqāʾiq al-insāniyya* (*sic*). M150. **181**

65v-66v. *Risālat al-ʿArūs*. M89. **181**

66v-68r. Pseudo-Ibn Sīnā. *Risāla fī aqsām al-nufūs wa-aḥwālihā*. Persian. M121, *tarjama*?
Incipit: *faṣl dar aqsām-i nufūs va-ān chahār qism ast*....**181**

68v-71r. *Risālat al-Ṣalāt*. M85. J, p. 67. **181**

71r-v. *Risāla fī al-malāʾika*. M113. J, p. 64. **181**

71v-75r. *Risāla fī manāqib al-shaykh*. Autobiography/Biography Complex; contains the Longer Bibliography, but not the Shorter Bibliography. J, pp. 41-3. **181**

75v-79r. *Ibṭāl aḥkām al-nujūm*. M2.[23] Complete copy in **52**; incomplete copy in **181**

83r-87v. *Risāla fī al-ʿishq*. M90. J, p. 68-9. **181**

88r-92r. Al-Ghazālī. *Risāla fī maʿrifat al-nafs*.[24] **181**

92r-96v. Al-Dawwānī. *Tafsīr Kāfirūn*. GAL, S II, 307. Colophon dated beginning of Rajab 1236/April 1821 by Muṣṭafā Bahjat. **181**

96v-100r. Al-Ghazālī. *Risāla sharīfa*. Persian.[25] **181**

Pseudo-Ibn Sīnā (Miskawayh). *Risāla fī ḥaqīqat al-mawt* (= *Dafʿ al-ghamm min al-mawt*; extract of Miskawayh's *Tahdhīb al-akhlāq*; M168, J, p. 67). **25**

Sirr al-qadar. M4ḥ. J, p. 61. **25**

Risāla fī al-ḥuzn. M59. J, p. 66. **25**

Risāla fī al-akhlāq. M13. J, p. 71. **25, 181**

Al-Birr wa-al-ithm. M40. J, pp. 14-15. **25, 181**

161r-162v. *Risāla fī ṣanʿat al-mastūr* (= *Amr mastūr al-ṣanʿa*, M33). Persian translation. Colophon dated 1232/1821. **25**
187r-189r. *Risāla fī al-akhlāq*. M13. **25**
231v-232v. *Risālat al-Ṭayr*. M88. J, p. 68. **25**
232v-233v. ʿAlī ibn Shāhik. *Sharḥ Risālat al-Ṭayr*. M88, *shurūḥ* 1. **52**
233v-238r. *Al-Qaḍāʾ wa-al-qadar*. M100. J, pp. 62-3. **25**
238r-v. *Al-Muʿāwada* [addressed to al-Jūzjānī]. M4j. **25**
243v-247v. Pseudo-Ibn Sīnā (Fārābī?). *Risālat al-Firdaws*. M192. J, pp. 69-70. **25**
248r-257r. *Al-Risāla al-Aḍḥawiyya*. M30. **25**
271r-275v. *Risāla fī al-ḥujaj al-ʿashr*. M43. J, p. 53. **25**
283v-285v. *Al-Ajwiba ʿan al-masāʾil al-ʿashr* (a). M6a. J, p. 44. **25**
285v-289v. *Al-Ḥudūd*. M57. J, p. 46. **25**
289v-292r. *Risāla fī asbāb ḥudūth al-ḥurūf*. M25. **25**

28. See **18**.

29, **48**. Ahmet III 3268
27r-33r. Al-Sharīf Bashīr ibn Naṣr al-Hāshimī al-Baghdādī. *Sharḥ Risālat al-Ṭayr*. M88, *sharḥ* 2. **29**
33v-37v. *Ḥayy ibn Yaqẓān*. M65. **29**
37v-41v. Muḥammad ibn Muḥammad ibn Ṣāliḥ ibn al-Habbāriyya. Verse rendition of *Ḥayy ibn Yaqẓān*. M65, *naẓm*. **29**
41v-60v. Ibn Zayla. *Sharḥ Ḥayy ibn Yaqẓān*. M65, *shurūḥ* 1. **29**
61r-110r. *Al-Mabdaʾ wa-al-maʿād*. M106. Colophon dated 580/1184-5.[26] **48**. See another photostat of this exemplar at **3**.

31. Ayasofya 4853, ff. 40-44v. *Al-Jumal min al-adilla al-muḥaqqaqa li-baqāʾ al-nafs al-nāṭiqa*. M52.

32. Serez 3807 (3824), ff. 60v-67v. *Sharḥ al-Qaṣīda al-ʿayniyya*. A93, *shurūḥ*, and M99, *shurūḥ* 13, list this manuscript as a commentary by ʿAbd al-Jawwād ibn al-Qayyim Saʿīd al-Khūnjī (al-Khvānjī), but this name appears nowhere in the manuscript. The introduction mentions two names: Abū ʿAbd Allāh Ḥusayn ibn Jamāl ibn al-Ḥusayn al-Anbarī *thumma* al-Qahshānī, identified as the *shaykh* of the author, and Zakarīyā' ibn Muḥammad ibn ʿUbayd Allāh al-Nasafī, identified as the *shaykh* of al-Qahshānī.

33. Laleli 1630, ff. 1-185r. Mūsā ibn Ibrāhīm ibn Mūsā ibn Muḥammad al-Mutaṭabbib. *Al-Jawhar al-nafīs fī Sharḥ Urjūzat al-Shaykh al-Ra'īs*. A 114, M15a, *shurūḥ*. The scribe Aḥmad ibn ʿAlā' al-Dīn al-Tarjumān, who made his copy in 1042/1632-3, indicates that his copy is a fourth-generation copy of the author's holograph composed in 780/1378-9: *wa-fī ākhiri aṣli l-aṣli l-manqūli mina l-manqūli minhu bi-khaṭṭi mu'allifihī mā sūratun: tamma l-sharḥu bi-ʿawni llāhi taʿālā ʿalā yadi mu'allifihī l-faqīri ilā llāhi Mūsā ibni Ibrāhīm ibni Muḥammad al-mutaṭabbibi sanata sabʿīna wa-thamāni mi'atin.*
There are some additional minor works in the codex:
185v-186r. Anonymous. A short untitled tract on the creation of Adam (cites Qur'ān, *ḥadīth*, Galen, various *ḥadīth* experts)
186r-191r. Anonymous. Incipit: *Fawā'id al-makhlūqāt taḥta falaki l-qamri wa-kalāmunā fī khalqi jasadi l-insān....*
192r. [Different hand]. *Faṣl al-Falūnīyā al-rūmī al-ṭarsūs nuqilat* (*sic*) *min Kitāb al-Qānūn li-Abī ʿAlī ibn Sīnā* (edition Beirut: ʿIzz al-Dīn, 1987, 5:2298-9).

36. British Museum Add. 16, 659. The colophon to *al-Aḍḥawiyya* at 34v dates this codex to 1182/1768-9 and the colophon at 101r suggests that it was copied in a Catholic environment. Another colophon at 548r is dated 1091/1680, but this may be the colophon of the archetype used for the codex.
[Missing:
4v-5r. Longer Bibliography of the Biography Complex.[27]
5v-7v. Autobiography.
8v-13r. *Risāla fī al-ʿishq*. M90.
13v-15v. *Ḥayy ibn Yaqẓān*. M65.
16v-24v. Ibn Zayla. *Sharḥ Ḥayy ibn Yaqẓān*. M65, *shurūḥ* 1.
25v-34v. *Al-Aḍḥawiyya*. M30. Colophon dated 1182/1768-9.
35r-101r. *Al-Najāt*. M118.2. The colophon states that many of the "things" Ibn Sīnā says in the *Najāt* contradict "our Catholic faith", but that it is permissible to copy it for the benefit to be

had from other "things" in it and especially for those who want to learn the Arabic language.

101v-140r. Persian translation of *al-Ishārāt wa-al-tanbīhāt*. M26, *tarjama* b]

141-200v. *Al-Taʿlīqāt*. M49b.

201v-228v. *Al-Mubāḥathāt*. Entitled in the codex *al-Taḥṣīlāt*, which appears to be the title Bahmanyār gave this earliest recension of what is now known as *al-Mubāḥathāt*. The scribe indicates in *nuskha* marginal variants that this copy derives ultimately from Bahmanyār's holograph, but his copy indicates that one of the immediate archetypes was severely damaged.[28]

228v-235r. Pseudo-Ibn Sīnā (Miskawayh). *Risālat Ḥikmat al-mawt*. Persian translation of pseudo-Ibn Sīnā. M161.

235v-258r. Ibn Ṭufayl. *Ḥayy ibn Yaqẓān*. GAL, I, 460, S I, 831-2.

259v-342v. *Ḥikmat-i ʿAlāʾī* (= *Dānishnāmah-yi ʿAlāʾī*, M73, J, pp. 15-17).

342v-345r. *Aqsām al-ʿulūm*. M32.

346v-368v. Extract of al-Shahrastānī's section on Ibn Sīnā from *Kitāb al-Milal wa-al-nihal*.[29]

368v-369v. Pseudo-Ibn Sīnā (Theophrastus). *Asbāb al-raʿd wa-al-barq*. M26. J, p. 52.

369v-370r. *Sirr al-qadar* [the questioner here is identified simply as *baʿḍ al-nās*]. M4ḥ.

370v-373r. *Al-Fayḍ al-ilāhī* (= *Al-Afʿāl wa-al-infiʿālāt*, M97, J, p. 62).

373r-381v. *Al-Risāla al-Miʿrājiyya* (= *Miʿrājnāmah*, M227; J, p. 73).

381v-402r. *Tarjamah-yi Risālah-yi al-maʿād*. Persian translation. M121, *tarjama* 2.

403v-410r. *Tarjamah-yi Risālah-yi al-nafs*. Persian translation. M121, *tarjama* 1.

410v-411r. *Al-Muʿāwada* [addressed in the title to al-Jūzjānī]. M4j.

414v-413v. *Risāla fī al-Ḥudūd*. M57.

419v-421r. Pseudo-Ibn Sīnā. *Risāla fī ʿilm al-akhlāq*. See M, p. 23.

421v-422v. *Risāla ilā baʿḍ al-mutakallimīn* (= *Al-Wusʿa*. M129).

424v-435r. Ibn Sahlān as-Sāwī. Persian translation of his commentary on *Risālat al-Ṭayr*. M88, *tarjama*.

435v-436v. *Al-Risāla al-Nayrūziyya*. M127.

436v-437v. *Al-Risāla al-Marmūza/Risālat al-Ṭayr*. M88.
438r-v. *Risāla fī al-farq bayna al-ḥarāra al-gharīziyya wa-al-gharība*. M94.
438v-439v. *Risāla fī bayān al-ṣūra al-ma'qūla al-mukhālifa li-al-ḥaqq*. M36, J, p. 53.
440v-449r. *Risālat al-Nafs* (= *Al-Nafs 'alā sunnat al-ikhtiṣār*. M120, J, p. 21).
449v-461r. *Kitāb al-Ma'ād* (= *Al-Nafs 'alā ṭarīq al-dalīl wa-al-burhān*. M121).
461v-491r. *Risālat al-Mabda'* (= *Al-Mabda' wa-al-ma'ād*. M106.)
491v-496r. Pseudo-Ibn Sīnā (Fārābī?). *Al-Firdaws*. M192. J, pp. 69-70.
496v-498v. *Al-Ajwiba 'an al-masā'il al-'ashr* (a). M6.
498v-502v. *Risāla fī fawā'id fī al-ra'y al-muḥaṣṣal* (= *Jawhar al-ajrām al-samāwiyya*. M53, J, p. 53).
502v-509v. *Risāla fī ḥujaj* (= *Al-Ḥukūma fī ḥujaj*.... M64).
510v-514v. *Tafāsīr*:
    510v-512r. *Sūrat al-Ikhlāṣ*. M50a
    512r-513v. *Al-Mu'awwidhatayn* (*Sūrat al-Falaq*; *Sūrat al-Nās*). M50b1-2
    513v-514v. Another copy of the *tafsīr* of *Sūrat al-Ikhlāṣ*. M50a.
514v-515v. *Sabab ijābat al-du'ā'*. M4d.
515v-517v. *Fī asrār al-ṣalāt*. M85.
518v-548r. *Al-Risāla al-Manāmiyya* (= *Ta'bīr al-ru'yā*. M47, J, p. 59). The colophon to this treatise has been crossed out but contains the following information. Ibn Muḥammad Amīn Muḥammad Naṣīr (or Naṣr) al-Lāhijānī al-Shahrastānī (?) al-Kīlānī copied the treatise on Thursday 18 Ṣafar 1091/20 March 1680 for Muḥammad Taqī ibn Muḥammad Ḥusayn al-Kīlānī originally of Dār al-Khilāfa Akbarābād, "one of the regions of Hindūstān". The fact that this colophon was crossed out might suggest that it was the colophon of the archetype used by the scribe of Add. 16, 659, but this cannot be established with certainty.
551-554v. *Kitāb Ḥudūth al-ḥurūf*. M25.
554v-555v. *Al-Khuṭba al-tawḥīdiyya*. M70.

555v. Pseudo-Ibn Sīnā. *Al-Irshād* (Quote from ʿAyn al-Quḍāt's *al-Tamhīdāt*). M4z.
556v-559r. *Al-Urjūza fī al-manṭiq*. M22.
559v-562r. *Īḍāḥ barāhīn mustanbaṭa fī masāʾil ʿawīṣa*. M38.
562r-564v. *Aqsām al-ʿulūm*. M32
565v-572v. *Al-Ajwiba ʿan masāʾil Abī Rayḥān al-Bīrūnī*. M5. J, pp. 51-2.

43, **191**. Escurial 703. Two colophons date this manuscript to 928/1522. There is also an ownership note on the title page stating that one Muḥammad ibn Muḥammad al-Muwaqqit acquired the codex in the middle of Shawwāl 940/April-May 1544 in Istanbul.
71-83. *Kitāb al-Ḥudūd*. M57. **191**
83-178. *Al-Mabdaʾ wa-al-maʿād*. M106. Colophon dated mid-Rajab 928/June 1522. **43**, **191**
180-242. Saʿd al-Dīn al-Masʿūdī. *Sharḥ* on Ibn Sīnā's *al-Khuṭba al-tawḥīdiyya*. M70 *shurūḥ*. Colophon dated Jumādā al-Ūlā 928/March-April 1522; scribe identifies himself as Sirāj al-Munīr Ḥasan ibn Muʾayyadī Muḥammad.[30] **191**
244-246. Anonymous. *Sharḥ al-Arwāḥ* (?), in Persian. **191**

48. See **29**.

52. See **25**.

57. Leiden cod. arab. Leo. 25 (1), 2r-64v. *Al-Urjūza fī al-ṭibb*, here entitled *Kitāb Manẓūmat al-Shaykh al-Raʾīs*. M15a. The scribe has used two archetypes; witness the many *nuskha* marginal notes. He has also added a biography of Ibn Sīnā (ff. 64v-65r) based, as he himself states, on the beginning and end of Ibn Sīnā's biography in a *mukhtaṣar* of Ibn Khallikān's *Wafayāt al-aʿyān*.

58. Contains portions of two manuscripts.
a. Ragıp Paşa 1481?, ff. 1r-17v. Ibn Sīnā. *Al-Urjūza fī al-mujarrabāt*. M20.
b. Unknown provenance. One photostat page bears the stamp of

Maktabat al-Mathaf al-ʿIrāqī, Baghdād and the title page of a manuscript with shelf numbers 462 and 608, and the title *sharḥā* (*sic*) *al-u.ḥ.ūra Ibn Sīnā* (*sic*) *fī al-ṭibb*, along with an ownership note by one al-Shaykh Ṭālib al-Kaḥḥāl Ibn Ukht al-Shaykh Muḥammad al-Asāwī, dated 1304/1886-7. But the work that follows is neither a commentary nor apparently has anything to do with Ibn Sīnā. Folios 1v-58r, one hand change at 21r, but the work continues (note the catchword *fa-innahū*, f. 20v).

Incipit: *al-ḥamdū li-llāhi l-ghanīyi l-ḥamīdi wa-ṣalawātuhū ʿalā nabīhī Muḥammad wa-ālihī wa-ṣaḥabihī ajmaʿīna iʿlam anna l-ṭibba ʿilmun yuʿrafu minhu aḥwālu badani l-insāni.*

Explicit: *...wa-najʿaluhū namūdhajān li-maqāṣidinā thumma yuqāsu ghayruhū ʿalayhi bi-ḥasbi mā ḥaṣala min al-qawānīn in shāʾa llāhu.*

59. See **18**.

61, **63**. Leiden cod. or. 184, Leiden cod. or. 958. Duplicate photostats of both manuscripts.

a. Leiden cod. or. 184. The scribe provides his name and dates of copying in the colophons to two treatises in this codex. At the end of Ibn Sīnā's *On the Construction of Astronomical Instruments* (62r), Vandarīn ibn Rūzbihān tells us that he finished his copy on 17 Rajab 514/12 October 1120 "in his own hand" (*bi-khaṭṭihī*). And he dates his copy of the Ibn Sīnā - al-Bīrūnī correspondence (65v-86v) to 16 Dhū al-Ḥijja 515/25 February 1122, and tells us that he "copied it for himself" (*li-nafsihī*). Ibn Rūzbihān also composed a table of contents for the codex on f. 1r. In addition, there is an ownership note on f. 1r, by one Muṣliḥ ibn Ḥamīd ibn Ḍayf al-Arabshahrī, who tells us that he acquired the codex sometime in the 7th/13th century (only the six of the six hundred is clear). This owner is responsible for the tract in praise of Muḥammad on f. [-1v], and a treatise he has entitled *Qāla baʿḍ al-ḥukamāʾ* on ff. 62v-63r which he copied in 681/1282-3.

1-5. Bahmanyār. *Risāla fī marātib al-mawjūdāt*. A7a.

6v-11. Bahmanyār. *Risāla fī mawḍūʿ al-ʿilm al-maʿrūf bi-mā baʿd al-ṭabīʿa*. A7b. This work consists of a series of extracts from the *Ilāhiyyāt* part of Ibn Sīnā's *al-Shifāʾ*. It was incorporated into the *Mubāḥathāt* (Bīdārfar 799-817[31]) at a date later than the date of this codex, but continued to circulate independently.[32]

12v-20r. Ibn Zayla. *Talkhīs li-ṣifāt wājib al-wujūd*. These passages, concerning God's attributes, were also incorporated into the *Mubāḥathāt* (Bīdārfar 820-824, 829-843). There are also three additional passages at the end of the *talkhīṣ* that appear to be Ibn Zayla's narrative of questions he put to Ibn Sīnā and the latter's responses (Bīdārfar 825-828).

20v-27r. *Al-Ajwiba ʿan al-masāʾil al-ʿashr* (a). M6a.

27v-36v. *Al-Rajaz al-manṭiqī* (= *Al-Urjūza fī ʿilm al-manṭiq*. M22.).

37r-41r. Abū al-Faḍl ibn al-ʿĀmid. *Risāla fī al-ḥumrā al-ḥāditha fī al-jaww*. GAL S II, 1032.

42v-47r. Al-Fārābī. *Fīmā yanbaghī an yuqaddama qabla taʿallum al-falsafa*. GAL I, 235.

47v-48r. *Faṣl min kalām al-Shaykh al-Raʾīs fī fāʾidat al-manṭiq*.
Incipit. *al-ʿilmu ʿalā ḍarbayni taṣawwurun wa-taṣdīqun....*
Explicit: *wa-idhā kāna ka-dhālika fa-lā budda ḥīnaʾidhin min maʿrifati l-manṭiqi tamma l-faṣlu.*

49v-62r. *Al-Ālāt al-raṣadiyya*. M1. J, pp. 59-60.

62v-63r. Anonymous. *Qāla baʿḍ al-ḥukamāʾ*.
Incipit: *ṭuftu l-bilāda wa-ʿāsartu l-ʿibāda wa-jarrabtu l-umūra wa-rakibtu l-aḥwāla....*
Explicit: *...wa-subḥāna man lahū l-khalqu wa-l-amru wa-l-ʿilmu wa-l-qudratu tabāraka llāhu aḥsanu l-khāliqi* (*sic*).

65v-86v. *Al-Ajwiba ʿan masāʾil Abī Rayḥān al-Bīrūnī*. M5.

87r-89r. Ibn al-Haytham. *Jawāb ʿan suʾāl al-sāʾil*. GAL I, 470.

89r. Bahmanyār. *Faṣl*. Note on numbers as the principles of the universe.[33]

89v-94v. *Ḥadd al-jism*. M56.

95r. *Al-Qaṣīda al-ʿayniyya*. M99.

96v-103r. Al-Fārābī. *ʿUyūn al-masāʾil*. M189, GAL I, 211, S I, 377.

b. Leiden cod. or. 958
25r-27v. Bahmanyār. *Risāla fī ithbāt al-mufāraqāt wa-aḥwālihā.* A7h.
27v. Quṭb al-Dīn al-Rāzī. *Risāla mushtamila ʿalā taḥqīq maʿnā al-taṣawwur wa-al-taṣdīq*. GAL II, 209, S II, 293.

62. British Museum Add. 23, 403, parts.
61-106v. Pseudo-Ibn Sīnā (Afḍal al-Din al-Kāshī). *Fī al-ʿilm wa-al-nuṭq*. M188.
172r-177r. *Risāla fī al-bāh.* M39.
191r-193v. Pseudo-Ibn Sīnā. *Risāla fī ithbāt al-ṣāniʿ*. M195. Colophon dated Shaʿbān 1019/Oct.-Nov. 1610, Lahore.
194r-199r. *Risāla fī al-ṣalāt.* M85.
199v-201r. *Risālat al-ʿArūs.* M89.
201r-217v. Pseudo-Ibn Sīnā. *Sharḥ Asmāʾ allāh.* M175.
218r-223v. Pseudo-Ibn Sīnā. *Risāla fī al-ṣalāt ʿalā lisān al-ʿuqalāʾ li-bayān al-ʿaql.* Not listed in M.
224r-225r. Naṣīr al-Dīn al-Ṭūsī. *Fī wujūd al-jawhar* (= *Risāla fī ithbāt al-jawhar al-mufāraq*; GAL, II, 510, S I, 928).
225r-226v. Gregorios Thaumaturgos. *Mukhtaṣar fī qawl al-Ḥakīm Arisṭū fī al-nafs.* J, p. 54.
226v-227r. Miskawayh. *Min Kitāb Tahdhīb al-akhlāq li-Miskawayh.* GAL, I, 343. Incomplete.

63. See **61**.

68, **113**. Leiden Or. 1020, *Majmūʿa* (CCO III, pp. 324-332). The treatise *al-Mabdaʾ wa-al-maʿād* was separated from the remainder of the codex and placed in a separate wrapper. Two ownership notes are found on f. 98r, one in the hand of Muḥammad ibn Muḥammad ibn Aḥmad, another perhaps in the same hand that states the purchase was made in 608/1211-12.
1v-2r. Beginning of *al-Khuṭba al-gharrāʾ* (= *Al-Khuṭba al-tawḥīdiyya*, M70). Incomplete. **113**
3r-39r. *Al-Mabdaʾ wa-al-maʿād.* M106. **68**
39r-57r. *Risāla fī al-nafs* (= *Risāla fī al-nafs ʿalā ṭarīq al-dalīl wa-al-*

burhān, M121). **113**

57r-63v. *Al-Anmāṭ al-thalāth min ākhir Kitāb al-Ishārāt*. Not noted by M. **113**

57v. *Al-Namaṭ al-thāmin fī al-bahja wa-al-saʿāda*;

58r. *Al-Namaṭ al-tāsiʿ fī maqāmāt al-ʿārifīn*;

60v. *Al-Namaṭ al-ʿāshir fī asrār al-āyāt*.

63v-69r. *Risāla fī al-siyāsa*. M82. **113**

69r-71r. *Risāla fī al-akhlāq*. M13. **113**

71v-74r. *Risāla fī ithbāt al-nubuwwāt*. M3.[34] **113**

74r-75v. *Al-Risāla al-Nayrūziyya*. M127. **113**

75v-78r. *Ḥayy ibn Yaqẓān*. M65. **113**

78r-79v. *Al-Ṭayr*. M88. **113**

79v-85v. *Risāla fī al-qadar*. M100. **113**

86r-91v. *Risāla fī anna li-al-māḍī mabdaʾan zamāniyyan*. M64. **113**

91v-98r. *Risāla fī al-radd ʿalā al-munajjimīn* (= *Ibṭāl aḥkām al-nujūm*. M2). **113**

71. Parts of two different manuscripts are found in this wrapper.

a. Beirut (AUB) 610 I13a. *Majmūʿat al-rasāʾil al-ṭibbiyya*. Acquired from ʿĪsā Iskandar al-Maʾlūf al-Lubnānī *wa-awlāduhū* (according to an ownership note). The scribe identifies himself on p. 100 as Jibrāʾīl Mūsā Maydānī. The wrapper also contains an unidentified scholar's notes (Kuentz?).

82-89. Anonymous. *Urjūza fī al-nabḍ wa-al-bawl ismuhā Kifāyat al-murtāḍ fī ʿilmay al-abwāl wa-al-anbāḍ*.

b. Vat. Borg. 87. See also **80**.

27r-28r. Anonymous. *Manẓūma fī al-kuḥl*.

29r-32r. *Urjūzat al-Shaykh al-Raʾīs Abī ʿAlī al-Ḥusayn Ibn Sīnā fī tadbīr al-ṣiḥḥa fī al-fuṣūl al-arbaʿa*. M17 does not list this manuscript.

75[b][35], **101**, **128**, **162**, **221**. Hamidiye 1448

1v-198r. *Al-Najāt*. M118. J, pp. 22-4. **75[b]**

222-296. *Kitāb al-Ishārāt*. M27. J, pp. 18-20. **101**

297-344. *Hādhihī al-Risāla al-ʿAlāʾiyya* (= *Dānishnāmah-yi ʿAlāʾī*. M72). **101**

344-346. Persian pseudo-Ibn Sīnā. *Risāla fī al-ʿazāʾim* (= *Kunūz al-muʿazzimayn*. M210). **101**

346v-353r. *Al-Jumāna al-ilāhiyya*. M51. **128**; another, incomplete copy, **162**

356-364. *Al-Urjūza fī ʿilm al-manṭiq*. M22 does not list this exemplar. **162**

365. *Al-Qaṣīda al-ʿayniyya*. M99. **162**

365. Pseudo-Ibn Sīnā? *Al-Wird al-aʿẓam*. M128. J, p. 71. **162**

366-373. Autobiography/Biography Complex. J, pp. 41-3. **162**

373-379. *Asbāb ḥudūth al-ḥurūf*. M25. **162**

379-385. *Amr mastūr al-ṣanʿa*. Not listed M33. **162**

385-389. *Al-Ajwiba ʿan al-masāʾil al-ʿashr* (a). M 6a. **162**

389-398. *Risāla fī al-ʿishq*. M90. **162**

398-401. *Risāla fī al-akhlāq*. M13. **162**

401-408. *Ḥayy ibn Yaqẓān*. M65. **162**

408-416. Pseudo Ibn Sīnā (Fārābī?). *Risālat al-Firdaws*. M192. J, pp. 69-70. **162**

417-418. *Al-Muʿāwada* [addressed in title to al-Jūzjānī]. M4j. **162**

418r-419. *Ruqʿa* to al-Qāshānī. M79b. **128, 162**

421-438. *Al-Aḍḥawiyya*. M30; incomplete **162**

466-479. *Al-Adwiya al-qalbiyya*. M14; incomplete **162**

480-484. Conclusion of *al-Adwiya al-qalbiyya*. **221**

484v-485v. *Ḥuṣūl ʿilm wa-ḥikma* [addressed to Ibn Zayla]. M4w. **128, 221**

486-491. *Taʿrīf al-raʾy al-muḥaṣṣal...* (= *Jawhar al-ajrām al-samāwiyya*. M53). **221**

491-493. *Dustūr ṭibbī*. M73. **221**

493. *Risāla* (= Parts of *al-Mubāḥathāt* [Badawī 470-478; Bīdārfar 852-860]). M202. **221**

493-4. *Khuṭba fī al-khamr*. M71. **221**

494-496. *Al-Risāla al-Marmūza*/*Risālat al-Ṭuyūr* (= *Al-Ṭayr*. M88). **221**

496-513. *Fuṣūl ṭibbiyya*. M96. **221**

513-515. *Sabab ijābat al-duʿāʾ*. M4d. **221**

515-527. *Masāʾil Ḥunayn*. M110. **221**

527. Pseudo-Ibn Sīnā? *Wird al-ākhir*. Incipit: *allāhuma yā wājiba l-*

dhāt wa-l-huwiyya wa-yā dā'ima l-faḍl.... Not listed in Mahdavī. **221**

527-528. *Al-Khuṭba al-tawḥīdiyya*. M70. **221**

528-536. *Kitāb al-Ḥudūd*. M57. **221**

536. Anonymous. Sayings by Socrates, Plato, Aristotle, Ibn Sīnā on the soul. Not listed by Mahdavī. **221**

536-539. *Al-Hindibā'*. M131. **221**

539-541. *Risāla ilā ba'ḍ al-mutakallimīn* (= *Al-Wus'a*. M129). **221**

549-551. Pseudo-Ibn Sīnā (Miskawayh). *Daf' ghamm al-mawt*. M168. **221**

552-554. *Al-Ṭayr*. M88. **221**

554-?. *Al-'Ahd*. M92, incomplete. **221**

558-568. *Al-Ḥukūma fī ḥujaj al-muthbitīn [anna] li-al-māḍī mabda'an zamāniyyan*. M64, incomplete. **221**

568-578. *Ibṭāl aḥkām al-nujūm*. M2. **221**

578-581. *Risāla fī ḥadd al-jism*. M56. **221**

581-591. *Risāla fī al-qadar*. M100. **221**

591v-592v. *Ḥuṣūl 'ilm wa-ḥikma* [addressed in title to Abū Sa'īd]. M4w. **128**, **221**

593-613. *Risāla fī tadāruk al-khaṭa' al-wāqi' fī al-ṭibb* (= *Daf' al-maḍarr*. M75). **221**

614-620. *Al-Birr wa-al-ithm*. M40. **221**

620-624. *Qiyām al-arḍ fī wasṭ al-samā'*. M91. **221**

624-632. *Al-Siyāsa*. M82. **221**

633v?-644r. *Risāla ilā Abī al-Qāsim ibn Abī al-Faḍl*. Not listed M79w. **128, 221**

634r-634v. *Risāla ilā al-Shaykh Abī al-Faḍl ibn Maḥmūd*. M79h. **128, 221**

634v-635r. *Risāla ilā 'Alā' al-Dīn ibn Kākūyah*. M79d, J, p. 73. **128, 221**

635r-v. *Risāla ilā Abī Ṭāhir ibn Ḥassūl*. M79j. **128**, **221**

636r. Pseudo-Ibn Sīnā. *Al-Irshād* (Quote from 'Ayn al-Quḍāt's *al-Tamhīdāt*). M4z. **221**

636-643. *Tafāsīr*:

Sūrat al-Ikhlāṣ. M50a. **221**

Al-Mu'awwidhatayn (*Sūrat al-Falaq*, *Sūrat al-Nās*). M50b1-2. **221**

*Qawluhū thumma stawā ilā al-samā*ʾ. M50d. **221**
643r-654v. *Al-Risāla al-Nayrūziyya*. M127. **128**, **221**
646-652. *Aqsām al-ʿulūm*. M32. **221**

80. Vatican Borg. arab 87, ff. 2v-50v. *Al-Urjūza fī al-ṭibb*. M15a.

86. Feyzullah 1315. ʿAlī ibn Abī al-Ḥazm al-Qurashī. *Al-Jawhar al-nafīs fī sharḥ Urjūzat al-Raʾīs*. A114 lists this manuscript, but records the author as Mūsā ibn Ibrāhīm ibn Mūsā al-Baghdādī.

87. Āṣafīya 2929 (?), via Maʿhad al-Makhṭūṭāt microfilm 3187. *Al-Mabdaʾ wa-al-maʿād*. M106 does not list this manuscript. Dated al-Rabīʿ al-Awwal 905/October-November 1499.

88. Ahmet III 3125. *Kitāb al-Mabdaʾ wa-al-maʿād*. M106.

92. Ayasofya 2403. *Al-Ḥikma al-Mashriqiyya*. Natural sciences sections; not listed by M63. J, p. 21

94. Provenance unknown. There are two shelf numbers on the title page: 4420, 4276. The work is Ibn Rushd's commentary on Ibn Sīnā's *al-Urjūza fī al-ṭibb*. M15a, *shurūḥ*. A comparison of the incipit of **94** with **95** indicates that while **94** lacks the detailed introduction in which Ibn Rushd explains the context of his decision to comment on Ibn Sīnā's work, the remainder of the text is identical. The pages have been numbered; they total 228. The photostat appears to be incomplete.

95. Ahmet III 1953, ff. 1r-188r. Ibn Rushd. *Sharḥ al-Urjūza fī al-ṭibb*. M15a, *shurūḥ*. The library identification card copied with the photostat attributes the commentary to ʿAbd al-Ḥamīd ibn Hibat Allāh al-Madāʾinī, but the title page and incipit of the work states that the commentary is by Ibn Rushd. Colophon information: copied in 882/1477-8 by Muḥammad Muḥsin (?) who says he is the lowest of the *mawālī mawlā al-mulūk wa-salāṭīn sulṭān al-ghuzāh wa-al-mujāhidīn fātiḥ qusṭanṭīna*.

96. Ragıp Paşa 872, ff. 1-69v. *Al-Mabdaʾ wa-al-maʿād*. M106. Colophon information: scribe is Haṣan ibn Masʿūd ibn ʿAbd Allāh; date of copy is 14 Ramaḍān 625/17 August 1228.

97. Ahmet III 3247, ff. 1r-118v. *Al-Mabdaʾ wa-al-maʿād*. M106.

99. Baghdad Iraq Museum 530. Saʿd al-Dīn al-Masʿūdī. *Sharḥ* of Ibn Sīnā's *al-Khuṭba al-gharrāʾ*. M70 does not list this commentary.

101. See **75[b]**.

111. Leiden Warn. Or. 551, 143 folios. Ibn Rushd's commentary on Ibn Sīnā's *al-Urjūza fī al-ṭibb*. M15a, *shurūḥ*. Colophon: copy completed in Alexandria, 26 Dhū al-Qaʿda 693/18 October 1294.

113. See **68**.

115. See **18**.

116. See **18**.

119. See **18**.

121. Istanbul University A. 4756, ff. 2v-50r. Ibn Tumlūs. *Sharḥ* on Ibn Sīnā's *al-Urjūza fī al-ṭibb*. M15a *shurūḥ*. Incomplete.

122. Istanbul University A.Y. 1566, ff. 176-242v. ʿAbd al-Raʾūf al-Minā wī. Commentary on Ibn Sīnā's *al-Qaṣīda al-ʿayniyya*; incomplete. This commentary begins with a brief biography and bibliography of Ibn Sīnā the sources for which remain to be identified.

126. Esad Efendi 1234, ff. 1v-70r. ʿAbd al-Raʾūf al-Minā wī. Commentary on Ibn Sīnā's *al-Qaṣīda al-ʿayniyya*.

128. See **75[b]**.

130. Paris arabe 2943. De Slane, 1:526

1v-193. Holograph copy by Muḥammad ibn Ismāʿīl al-Ḥanbalī of his *Sharḥ al-Urjūza fī al-ṭibb* (M15a), entitled (according to de Slane) *al-Tawfīq li-al-ṭabīb al-shafīq bi-sharḥ urjūzat al-Shaykh al-Raʾīs imām al-ṭarīq*. Colophon of the first part of the work (f. 131v) states that the author completed his copy in 988/1580-1. Folios 193-203 are taken up by two additional *faṣl*s which the author says he felt compelled to write after completing his commentary: the first concerns the measures or weights (*awzān*) that physicians use; the second consists of brief biographies of authorities that the author cites in his commentary.[36]

132. Esad Efendi 3774, parts.

45v-85v. *Taʿbīr al-ruʾyā*. M47

86v-87v. Unidentified treatise; incipit: *rabbanā waffiqnā li-mudāwāti hādhihī al-qulūbi al-marḍā...*

89v-96v. Pseudo-Ibn Sīnā. *ʿIlm al-firāsa*. M191. Ibn Sīnā's name is nowhere associated with this work in this codex. Colophon dated 973/1565-6; the scribe gives his name simply as Muḥammad.

133. Provenance unknown. *Al-Shifāʾ*. M84. Covers *al-Fann al-awwal min jumlat al-ʿilm al-riyāḍī, Uṣūl al-handasa* (ed. Cairo, 16.9) to the end of *al-Ilāhiyyāt* (ed. Cairo, 455.16).

140. Université Saint-Joseph, Or. 289, ff. 2r-86r. *Al-Urjūza fī al-ṭibb*. M15a. Incomplete.

141. Private Collection? There are photostats of two different manuscripts in this wrapper. The first appears to be from the collection of a lawyer (*muḥāmī*) named ʿAbbās al-Gharāwī. The provenance of the second is unknown.

a. 1-20r. Anonymous. *Nubadh al-kitāb manṣūmat* (*sic*) *al-Qānūnchah*.
Incipit: *al-ḥamdu li-llāhi l-ḥakīmi l-shāfī wa-ḥāfiẓi l-ayyāmi bi-l-alṭāfi*

b. No folio numbers. *Al-Urjūza fī al-ṭibb*. M15.

142. There are photostats of parts of two manuscripts from the John Rylands Library, Manchester, in this wrapper.

a. J. Rylands 453 [486], ff. 1-3. (See Mingana, col. 751.) *Ashʿār al-Shaykh al-Raʾīs... fī al-nafs* (= *Al-Qaṣīda al-ʿayniyya* with commentary. M99. Mingana, following Ahlwardt (no. 5358), suggests that the commentary is by one Abū al-Baqāʾ al-Aḥmadī.

b. J. Rylands 384 [460].[37] (See Mingana, coll. 626-636.)

[1v]-2r. *Al-Risāla al-Nayrūziyya.* M128.

2r-v. *Al-Muʿāwada.* M4j.

3r-4r [...] . *Al-Ḥujaj al-ʿashr.* M43. Incomplete; treatise should conclude at 7r.

9v-13r. *Taʿrīf al-raʾy al-muḥaṣṣal* (= *Jawhar al-ajrām al-samāwiyya.* M53). Incomplete; treatise should conclude at 13r.

13r-18r. *Al-Risāla al-ʿArshiyya* (= *Ḥaqāʾiq ʿilm al-tawḥīd.* M61). J, pp. 61-2.

18r -[...] . *Risāla fī al-ʿishq.* M90. Incomplete; treatise should end at 23r.

23r-24v. Al-Fārābī. *Sharḥ ʿalā risāla li-Zīnūn.* GAL I, 213, S I, 377.

24v-25r [...]. Untitled treatise by Muḥammad ibn Muḥammad ibn Bāqir al-Dāmād al-Ḥusaynī (d. 1041/1631). Incomplete; treatise should end at 26r.

53v-55r. Al-Fārābī. *ʿUyūn al-masāʾil.* M189, GAL I, 211, S I, 377.

56r-84v. *Al-Mabdaʾ wa-al-maʿād.* M106.

84v-85r. *Al-Aḍḥawiyya.* M30. Incomplete.

144. Istanbul University 4390, ff. 20v-99v. *Al-Mabdaʾ wa-al-maʿād.* Colophon dated mid-Rajab 920/beginning of September 1514.

150. Leiden Warn. 46? Title page has: *majmūʿun fī l-handasati wa-fīhi urjūzat Ibn Sīnā fī l-ṭibbi wa-fīhi faḍāʾilu dimashqa wa-fīhi awṣāfu l-ghilmāni l-shām (sic) wa-fīhi mukātabātun ʿarabiyyatun wa-ghayru dhālika min al-qaṣāʾidi wa-l-fawāʾidi wa-l-abyāti wa-l-ashʿāri ʿām* (*sic*). Colophon, f. 45r, is dated 14 Shawwāl 908/12 April 1503, by

one ʿUmar ibn Muḥammad ibn ʿUmar.
2v-18v [f. 3v-4r missing]. Anonymous. *Abwāb fī ṭafyi al-nār* (?)
19r. Anonymous. Short tract on the use of Qur'ān *sūra*s as talismans.
21v-45v. Title states that this is *al-Urjūza fī al-ṭibb* by Ibn Sīnā, but this cannot be correct. First two lines:
al-ḥamdu li-llāhi lladhī barānā//wa-rakiba l-ʿuqūli wa-l-adhhānā
wa-mā bi-l-asmāʿi wa-l-abṣār//yahdī bihā man kāna dhā ʿtibār

154. Bibliotheque Royale (Bibl. Nat.?). *Avicenna Latinus. Libri quinque canonis medicinae Abu Ali principis filii sinae alias corrupté Avicennae.* Romae in Typographia Medicea MDXCIII. Rés. $T^{29}5$, R83, $T^{29}6E$, $T^{29}6H$, $T^{29}6E$, $T^{22}8$, $T^{29}16$, $T^{29}22$, $Td^{60}12$, $Td^{60}14$, $Td^{60}15$, $T^{29}4$, $R82^{(2)}$.

156. Paris Bibl. Nat. 2943?, ff. 203r-251v. *Hādhihī Urjūzat al-Ra'īs. Al-Urjūza fī al-ṭibb.* M15a. Colophon is dated 1186/1772-3.[38]

158. Multiple photostats.

a. Paris Bibl. Nat. 2992, ff. 99r-104r. *Manẓūmat Ibn Sīnā fī al-ṭibb.* M17. (De Slane, 1:533ff.). Incomplete.

b. Paris Bibl. Nat. 3039 (De Slane, 1:540). Colophon (f. 272v) states that the *majmūʿa* was completed on Thursday 23 Dhū al-Qaʿda 1113/10 April 1702 by ʿAbd Allāh ibn al-Marḥūm al-Shaykh Tāj al-ʿārifīn al-Wafā' al-Ṣughrānī (?) al-Shāfiʿī.
1v-27v. Ibn Māsawayh (?). *Kitāb al-Manāfiʿ al-mubayyana fī mā yanfaʿu fī al-arbaʿ al-azmina.*
28v-29r. Extract of Ibn Sīnā's *al-Qānūn*, comprising the *faṣl fī ḍuʿf al-intishār* (ed. Beirut: ʿIzz al-Dīn, 1987, 5:2488-9). Incomplete.
94r-98v. *Urjūza fī waṣāyā Ibuqrāṭ.* M19. Lacks beginning [87-93r].
98v-103v. Ibn Māsawayh (?). Tract on the four seasons, which appears to include the next work as part of the disquisition:
103v-107v. Ibn Sīnā. *Urjūza fī al-ṭibb* (*fī al-fuṣūl al-arbaʿa*). M17j.

107v-109v. Anonymous. *Urjūza fī al-ṭibb balīgha nāfiʿiyya.*

Incipit: *inna l-dawā huwa l-ḥimā ʿinda l-suqm//wa-l-dā yabdū min ṭarīqāti l-tukhm*

Explicit: *thumma l-ṣalātu baʿda l-salāmi// ʿalā nabī dīnuhū l-islāmi*

109v-110r. Ibn Yamūn? *Wa-hādhihī Urjūza tusammā Irtiyāḥ al-arwāḥ fī ādāb al-nikāḥ.*[39] Incomplete.

268v-269r. Ibn Māsawayh. *Ṣifat jawāsīn* (?) *al-mutawakkil.* (Overlooked by De Slane). Neither GAL I, 232, S I, 416, nor GAS 3:234 lists this tract.

269v-272r. Anonymous. *Urjūza.*

Incipit: *al-ḥamdu li-llāhi l-ʿaẓīmi l-shān//dhī l-shāni wa-l-anʿāmi wa-l-insān*

Explicit: *tammat bi-ḥamdi li-llāhi khāliqi l-bashar//fīhi l-dawā li-kulli dā wa-ḍarar*

c. Paris Bibl. Nat. 2943? (see de Slane, 1:535-6).

253-258r. Anonymous. *Kifāyat al-murtāḍ fī ʿilmay al-abwāl wa-al-anbāḍ.* Here attributed to Ibn Sīnā. Colophon dated Dhū al-Qaʿda 1185/February-March 1772.

258r-260v. Anonymous. *Urjūza fī amrāḍ al-ʿayn.*

? Muḥammad ibn Makkī. *Urjūza wajīza fī ʿadad al-ʿurūq al-mafṣūda.* GAL, S II, 1030.

? Muḥammad ibn Makkī. *Urjūza fī jadhb al-khalṭ.* GAL, S II, 1030.[40]

d. Paris Bibl. Nat. 3038, ff. 62r-70r. *Kitāb al-Manẓūma fī al-ṭibb* (= *Al-Urjūza fī al-ṭibb.* M15a.) Incomplete in the manuscript itself.[41]

e. Paris Bibl. Nat.? Suppl. Pers. 139, ff. 9v-12r.

10r-11r. *Qāla al-Shaykh al-Raʾīs Abū ʿAlī.* Unidentified *qaṣīda* of ten lines.

Incipit: *tuwaqqi idhā staṭʿamta idkhāla maṭʿam//ʿalā maṭʿamin min qabli fiʿli l-hawāḍim*

Explicit: *fa-ayyu bihā [?] awṣā l-ḥakīm bayādhiq//akhā l-ʿadli nūshirfān malk l-aʿājim*

10v-11r. *Al-Qaṣīda al-ʿayniyya.* M 99.

f. Paris, Bibl. Nat.? Suppl. Pers. 139. *Risāla min Abī ʿAlī Sīnā* (sic). Incipit: *bi-dānkah bārī subḥanahū wa-taʿālā avval-i ḥayyiz dar*

ʿālam-i ajsād āfarīd....

g. One folio of what appears to be Leiden Gol. 4548 (?) (Bibliothecae Regiae, stamp), f. 67r.

161. Multiple photostats

a. Vatican arab. 1130, 359v-362r. *Al-Qaṣīda al-ʿayniyya.* M99.

b. Istanbul University 1581, ff. 13v-20v. *Al-Qaṣīda al-ʿayniyya.* M99.

c. Istanbul University 4755 (Yıldız 889), ff. 218r-218v. *Al-Qaṣīda al-ʿayniyya.* M99.

162. See **75[b]**.

163. Nuruosmaniye 4894, parts.

200r-201r. *Risāla fī al-arzāq.* M23.

233r-235r. *Al-Urjūza fī al-ṭibb.* Two copies. M15.

252r-253v. *Naṣāʾiḥ ṭibbiyya* (= *Al-Urjūza fī al-waṣāyā*, M21).

595r-596r. *Al-Urjūza fī al-mujarrabāt.* M20.

165. Laleli 3763

21r-29r. ʿAbd al-Jawwād ibn Abī al-Faqīr Saʿīd al-Khvānjī. Holograph copy of his commentary on Ibn Sīnā's *al-Qaṣīda al-ʿayniyya.* One ownership note f. 21r dated 1008/1599-60. M99, *shurūḥ* 13, does not list this manuscript.

166. Şehit Ali Paşa 2786

37r-77r. ʿAbd al-Raʾūf al-Mināwī. *Al-ʿAlq al-nafīs ʿalā Qaṣīdat al-Shaykh al-Raʾīs.* Al-Mināwī's commentary on Ibn Sīnā's *al-Qaṣīda al-ʿayniyya.* M99, *shurūḥ* 9.

167. Escurial 851, ff. 1r-46v. *Al-Urjūza fī al-ṭibb.* M15a.

168. Three photostats are found in this wrapper.

a. Esad Efendi 1239, ff. 62v-85v. Ibn Zayla. *Sharḥ Ḥayy ibn Yaqẓān.* M65, *shurūḥ* 1, does not list this manuscript.

b. Aşır Efendi 441, ff. 18v-19v. Naṣīr al-Dīn al-Ṭūsī. *Taʾwīl Qiṣṣat*

Absāl wa-Salāmān. M204.

c. Yeni Camı 1181

254v-255r. *Al-āthār al-ʿulwiyya*. M24.

255v-256v. Pseudo-Ibn Sīnā. *Ḥudūth al-ajsām*. M155.

171. Istanbul University A.Y. 4755. *Majmūʿa*. Title, folio 1v: *Rasaʾil min taṣānīf al-Shaykh al-Raʾīs Abī ʿAlī raḥimahū allāh taʿālā wa-baʿḍuhū manqūlun min khaṭṭihī*. Some parts are missing from the photostat. I add these in brackets. I have made some minor corrections to Mahdavī's information, particularly with regard to foliation and variant titles.

1v-2r. Beginning of *al-Mūjaz al-ṣaghīr fī al-manṭiq*. M115.

[Missing ff. 3r-44r:

a. End of *al-Mūjaz*.

b. *Urjūza fī ʿilm al-manṭiq*. M22.

c. *Al-Mūjaz fī ʿilm al-manṭiq*. M116.]

44r-83r. Beginning of *ʿUyūn al-ḥikma*. This copy is extremely important as it was collated with a copy made by Bahmanyār; witness the *nuskha* marginal variants introduced as *nuskhat Bahmanyār*.

83v-92r. *Aqsām al-ḥikma*. M32.

92r-102v. *Risāla fī taʿrīf al-raʾy al-muḥaṣṣal*; alternate title in margin in later hand: "This treatise is also known as *Risālat al-Ajrām al-ʿulwiyya*." (= *Jawhar al-ajrām al-samāwiyya*. M53).

103r-125v. *Kitāb al-Nafs lahū al-maʿrūf bi-al-ʿashara fuṣūl*. M120.

125v-169r. *Risāla fī al-nafs ʿalā ṭarīq al-dalīl wa-al-burhān*, with variant marginal title in later hand: *Kitāb al-Maʿād al-aṣghar*.[42] M121.

169v-186r. *Risāla fī al-nafs wa-mā yaṣīru ilayhi* [*sic*] *baʿda mufāraqatihā al-badan*, with variant marginal title in later hand: *Kitāb fī taḥṣīl al-saʿāda yuʿrafu bi-al-ḥujaj al-ʿashr*. M43.

186v-204v. *Kitāb* [then changed to *Risāla*] *fī-mā taqarrara ʿindahū min al-ḥukamāʾ fī ḥujaj al-mashāʾīn [anna] li-al-māḍī mabdaʾan zamāniyyan*. M64.

205r-207r. *Al-Kalima al-ilāhiyya allatī tuʿrafu bi-al-Tasbīḥiyya*. Marginal note in the later hand states: "al-Jūzjānī says in his list that it is *al-Khuṭba al-tawḥīdiyya fī al-ilāhiyyāt*". M70.

207r-214v. *Ḥayy ibn Yaqẓān*. M65.

214v-218r. *Risālatuhū al-Marmūza fī waṣf yūṣiluhū ilā al-ʿilm al-ḥaqq al-maʿrūfa bi-Risālat al-Ṭayr* (= *Al-Ṭayr*. M88).[43]

218r-v. *Al-Qaṣīda al-ʿayniyya* [this title is in a later hand; original hand has simply *wa-qāla ayḍan*]. M99.[44]

219r-250r. *Risālatuhū al-Aḍḥawiyya fī al-maʿād*. M30.

250r. Cryptogram.

[Missing:

250v-260v. *Amr mastūr al-ṣanʿa*. M33

?. *Al-Ishāra ilā ʿilm al-manṭiq*.

264r-266v. *Al-Ajwiba ʿan al-masāʾil al-ʿashr* (b). M7b.]

[...] 267v-277r. *Asbāb ḥudūth al-ḥurūf*. Lacks beginning only. Colophon of this work says that it was written for Abū Manṣūr al-Jabbān[45] and was copied on 10 Ramaḍān 588/19 September 1192.

277v-283r. *Maqālatuhū fī al-akhlāq*. M13. The last line of this treatise states that the discussion has a conclusion (*tamām*) that is mentioned in its proper place; a marginal note in the hand of the scribe states "that is, in *Kitāb al-Mabdaʾ wa-al-maʿād*".

[Missing:

283v-285v. *Khaṭaʾ man qāla inna al-kammiyyata jawharun*. M67.]

285v-292v. Al-Fārābī (here ascribed to Ibn Sīnā). *Kitāb ʿUyūn al-masāʾil lahū*. M189, GAL I, 211, S I, 377. Scribe states that his archetype was copied by one Majd al-Dīn al-Rūdhrawarī (variant note 285v).

292v-305v. *Kitāb al-Ḥudūd al-maʿrūf bi-al-mabāḥith al-ṣadīqiyya*. M57.[46]

306r-307r. [Different hand] *Faṣl wujida bi-khaṭṭihī*. Parts of *al-Mubāḥathāt* (Bīdārfar 712-713, 787, 673-4)

307v. Blank

308r-317v. *Sīrat al-Shaykh...wa-fihrist kutubihī*; Autobiography/ Biography Complex. Longer Bibliography only. J, pp. 41-3.

318r-322r. *Maqāla fī al-hindibāʾ lahū*. M131.

322v. Illegible piece in different hand

323r-324v. Passages from *al-Mubāḥathāt* (Bīdārfar 591-3, 882, and Badawī 276 [cf. Bīdārfar 694-695]) and elsewhere (unidentified), introduced as "what I copied from the hand of Manṣūr ibn Muslim ibn ʿAlī known as Ibn Abī al-Kharajayn." This Ibn Abī al-Kharajayn appears to have made his copy from Ibn Sīnā's holographs.[47]

324v. Question from Abū Ṭālib al-ʿAlawī to Ibn Sīnā with his response. Not listed by Mahdavī.

325r. Galen. Extract of *Adwār al-ḥummayāt*.

325v. Illegible piece.

172. Leiden 186 Gol. 129 folios. Ibn Rushd. *Sharḥ* on Ibn Sīnā's *al-Urjūza fī al-ṭibb*. M15a , *shurūḥ*, does not list this MS.

175. Two photostats

a. Paris Bibl. Nat. 2562.

226v-284v. Anonymous. Unidentified medical work. Incomplete at beginning.

289r-292v. *Al-Urjūza fī al-ṭibb* (*fī al-fuṣūl al-arbaʿa*). M17j.

292v-293v. Anonymous. Three brief tracts on *bāh*, one of which is ascribed to ʿAli.

294r. Dāwūd al-Anṭākī. *Ṣifat maʿjūn*. GAL II, 364, S II, 491-2 does not list this work.

b. Paris Bibl. Nat. 2661

61v-62r. *Al-Urjūza fī al-mujarrabāt*. M20. Colophon dated 28 Dhū al-Ḥijja 1039/29 July 1630. There appear to be more lines to the poem than the twelve Mahdavī describes.

179. Photostats of two manuscripts

a. Nuruosmaniye 4894. These pages have been cut into fragments.

i. Beginning of *Manṭiq al-mūjaz* (*sic*). M114.

ii. Beginning of *Risāla fī al-nafs wa-baqāʾihā wa-maʿādihā* (= *Risāla fī al-nafs ʿalā ṭarīq al-dalīl wa-al-burhān*. M121).

iii. Conclusion of *al-Nukat fī al-manṭiq*. M125.

iv. *Hādhihī fawāʾid wa-nukat*. Parts of *al-Mubāḥathāt*, *al-Taʿlīqāt*, and other works. M200.

v. Conclusion of *al-Ishārāt wa-al-tanbīhāt*. M27.
vi. Pseudo-Ibn Sīnā. *Risālat Manāfiʿ al-aʿḍāʾ*. M229.
vii. *Risāla fī ibṭāl aḥkām al-nujūm*. M2.

b. Serez 4009[48]
49r-50v. *Asbāb al-āthār al-ʿulwiyya*. M24.
? *Risāla fī ḥaqīqat kayfiyyat al-ṣalāt* (= *Al-Ṣalāt*. M85).

181. See **25**.

182. Feyzullah 1213, ff. 1v-90r. *Al-Mabdaʾ wa-al-maʿād*. M106.

183. Ahmet III 3225, 1r-115r. *Al-Mabdaʾ wa-al-maʿād*. M106.

184-5. These two numbers are found in one wrapper.
184. Ahmet III 1584, ff. 2v-65v. *Al-Mabdaʾ wa-al-maʿād*. M106.
185. Patna 2590, ff. 178v-213r, via Maʿhad al-Makhṭūṭāt microfilm 3138. *Al-Mabdaʾ wa-al-maʿād*. M106. 12th/18th century. *Taʿlīq*. 135 x 205 cm.

190[a].[49] Cairo, Dār al-Kutub, *Ṭibb* 32, via Maʿhad al-Makhṭūṭāt microfilm 436. Anonymous. *Al-Jawhar al-nafīs bi-sharḥ manẓūmat al-Raʾīs*. A commentary on Ibn Sīnā's *al-Urjūza fī al-ṭibb*. M15a. Colophon states that the scribe, Yūsuf ibn Muḥammad ibn Yūsuf, known as Ibn al-Wakīl, completed his copy in 1093/1681-2.

190[b], **199**. These two entries belong together as the end of 190 is found at beginning of photostat 199; both entries come from codex Vehbi 1488; no folio numbers available.
190. *Taʿbīr al-ruʾyā*. M47
199. *Al-Qawlanj*. M101. J, p. 57. Incomplete.

191. See **43**.

192. Unknown provenance, folios 50v-104v. Anonymous. A commentary on Ibn Sīnā's *al-Urjūza fī al-ṭibb*. M15a. Incomplete.

193. Unknown provenance. *Al-Urjūza fī al-ṭibb.* M15a. Folios 24v-41r. Lacks beginning. Colophon is dated 1263/1846.

194. There are parts of three different manuscripts in this wrapper, the provenance of none of which is known.

a. This manuscript is dated Dhū al-Qaʿda 1274/June-July 1858 according to a note on the title page.

i. *Urjūza fī ḍurūb al-ḥummayāt li-Ibn Sīnā* (= *Al-Urjūza fī al-ṭibb*, M15a).

ii. *Urjūza fī al-mujarrabāt.* M20.

iii. *Urjūza fī waṣāyā Ibuqrāṭ.* M19. J, p. 56. Incomplete.

b. Anonymous commentary on Ibn Sīnā's *al-Qaṣīda al-ʿayniyya.* First line of commentary: *habaṭat ay nazalat wa-innamā lam yaqul nazalat li-anna l-khiṭaba li-l-nufūsi l-nāṭiqati fī l-qurʾāni bi-mā shtaqqa mina l-hubūṭ....*This is followed by one folio of a work entitled *Risāla li-al-Fārisī.*

c. Five folios of a codex that appears to contain brief extracts of two different commentaries on Ibn Sīnā's *al-Qaṣīda al-ʿayniyya*, and two other unidentified works

i. Beginning of the commentary found also in Serez 3807; see above **32**.

ii. Anonymous. Another commentary. Incipit after *basmala*: *fa-hadhihī ḥāshiyatun li-l-qaṣīdati l-rūḥāniyyati l-mansūbati ilā l-shaykhi l-raʾīs....*

iii. Anonymous. Another commentary that deals only with the final line of the *qaṣīda*. Incipit: *al-ḥamdu li-llāhi l-ʿazīzi l-jabbāri l-ʿalīyi l-qahhār....*

iv. Another commentary which appears to be the beginning of (**b**) above, albeit in another exemplar.[50]

196. Provenance unknown. Folios 4r-110r. Folios 1-3r missing. Mūsā ibn Ibrāhīm ibn Mūsā ibn Muḥammad al-Mutaṭabbib al-Baghdādī. Holograph copy of *Al-Jawhar al-nafīs*, a commentary of Ibn Sīnā's *al-Urjūza fī al-ṭibb.* M15a. In the colophon Mūsā ibn Ibrahīm states that he completed the work in the year 870/1465-6.

199. See **190[b]**.

204. British Museum, Or. 3691.
1r-34v. *Al-Urjūza fī al-ṭibb*. M15; see C. Rieu, p. 543, no. 801, I.

205, **206**. Leiden Or. 912.[51]
50v-236r. Ibn Rushd. *Sharḥ al-Urjūza fī al-ṭibb*. M15a. Inc. Colophon is dated 983/1575-6. There is a hand change at 155r. **205**
238v-248r. Anonymous. A work on *materia medica*, with extensive cryptography at the end. **206**

206. See **205**.

208. See **18**.

221. See **75[b]**.

232. Provenance unknown. *Al-Shifāʾ*. M84. Incomplete. This photostat has suffered considerable mildew and mold damage.

234. Majlis-i Shūrā-yi Millī 7851 (5), ff. 16v-30r, via Maʿhad al-Makhṭūṭāt 307. *Ḥaqāʾiq ʿilm al-tawḥīd*. M61. Includes a handwritten copy of the text by an unidentified scholar (Kuentz?)

236. Şehit Ali Paşa 57, ff. 106v-112r. ʿAbd al-Wāḥid ibn Muḥammad. *Sharḥ al-Qaṣīda al-ʿayniyya*. M99, *shurūḥ* 1. Also in this wrapper:
a. Four copies of *al-Jumāna al-ilāhiyya* (Ham. 1448, Ahmet III 3447, Nur. 3427, Nur. 4894) and a handwritten anonymous copy of Ibn Sīnā's *al-Jumāna al-ilāhiyya*;
b. and folios 84-96 of Arundel Or. 41, 16099, with Max Meyerhof's German translations of chapter and section headings, along with one of his prescription notes.

270. Vienna 344, ff. 21r-26v. Ibn ʿAbd al-Wāḥid. *Sharḥ Qaṣīdat Ibn Sīnā*. Anawati (A93, *al-shurūḥ*), attributed this commentary to al-Jūzjānī, but Mahdavī (M 99, *shurūḥ* 1), questioned that attribution.[52]

271. Provenance unknown. Part of Ibn Sīnā's *al-Taʿlīqāt*. Folios 80v-122r? Fragment covers ed. Badawī 82.9-129.22.

Addendum. Exemplars of Bahmanyār's *al-Taḥṣīl*. See A7.

49. Majlis-i Shūrā-yi Millī 111, 265ff. *Taḥṣīl lubāb al-ḥikma*. Incomplete.

134. Tūnk 134, via Maʿhad al-Makhṭūṭāt microfilm 3017. *Al-Taḥṣīl*. Dated 997/1588-9, 158 folios, 24 x 15 cm.

146. Ahmet III 3287. *Al-Taḥṣīl*. A does not list.

189. Rampur Reza 3887, via Maʿhad al-Makhṭūṭāt microfilm 3063. *Al-Taḥṣīl*. 9th c.; 494pp.; 120 x 180 cm.

Notes

1. Abbreviations used in this article:

A: G. Anawati. *Muʾallafāt Ibn Sīnā*. Cairo: Dār al-Maʿārif, 1950.

Badawī: Ibn Sīnā, *Al-Mubāḥathāt* in *Arisṭū ʿind al-ʿarab*. Edited by A. Badawī. *Dirāsāt Islāmiyya* 5. Cairo: Maktabat al-Nahḍa al-Miṣriyya, 1947, pp. 119-246.

Bīdārfar: Ibn Sīnā. *Kitāb al-Mubāḥathāt*. Edited by M. Bīdārfar. Qum: Intishārāt-i Bīdār, 1992.

CCO: C. Landberg, R. P. A. Dozy, P. de Jong, and M. J. De Goeje. *Catalogus Codicum Orientalium Bibliothecae Academiae Lugduno-Batavae*. Leiden: E.J. Brill, 1883-1851.

De Slane: W. M. de Slane. *Catalogue des manuscrits arabes*. Paris: Imprimerie Nationale, 1883-95.

GAL: C. Brockelmann. *Geschichte der arabischen Litteratur*. Two volumes, Leiden: E. J. Brill, 1943-9; three supplemental volumes, Leiden: E. J. Brill, 1937-1942.

GAS: F. Sezgin. *Geschichte des arabischen Schrifttums*. Leiden: E.J. Brill, 1967-. Vol. 3: *Medizin, Pharmazie, Zoologie*.

J: J. L. Janssens. *An Annotated Bibliography on Ibn Sīnā (1970-1989)*. Leuven: University Press, 1991.

M: Y. Mahdavī. *Fihrist-i nuskhah-hā-yi muṣannafāt-i Ibn Sinā*. Tehran: Dānishgāh-yi Ṭihrān, 1954.

Mingana: A. Mingana. *Catalogue of the Arabic manuscripts in the John Rylands Library.* Manchester: Manchester University Press, 1934.

Rieu: C. Rieu. *Supplement to the catalogue of the Arabic manuscripts in the British museum.* London, 1894.

Voorhoeve: P. Voorhoeve. *Codices Manuscripti VII. Handlist of Arabic Manuscripts in the Library of the University of Leiden and other collections in the Netherlands.* Second Enlarged Edition. The Hague: Leiden University Press, 1980.

2. Email communication (10/4/99) from Paul Walker, who was at the time Director of the ARCE.
3. For example, Kuentz's article on the didactic medical poems of Ibn Sīnā ("Al-Arājīz al-ṭibbiyya mimmā ahmalahū al-ta'rīkh min turāth Ibn Sīnā," *al-Kitāb al-dhahabī li-al-mihrajān al-alfī li-dhikrā Ibn Sīnā/Millénaire d'Avicenne*, Cairo: Jāmiʿat al-Duwal al-ʿArabiyya, al-Idāra al-Thaqāfiyya, 1952, pp. 136-144) must have been written on the basis of the photostats now in the possession of the ARCE, since the misattribution of an *urjūza* to Ibn Sīnā is both found in the photostat of a manuscript containing the *urjūza* and explicitly stated to be by Ibn Sīnā in Kuentz's article (see **158.c** below; cf. "Al-Arājīz," p. 140). Kuentz also published an edition (lacking critical apparatus and any detailed information concerning the provenance of the manuscripts used) of Ibn Sīnā's *Risālat al-ʿArūs*, most likely on the basis of the exemplars found in the ARCE collection in "Risālat al-ʿArūs min mu'allafāt Ibn Sīnā allatī lam tunshar," *al-Kitāb*, 11.4 (Rajab 1371/April 1952), pp. 391-399. There are also indications that Kuentz had granted access to the photostat collection to other memebers of the IFAO. For instance, A.-M. Goichon thanks Kuentz in the introduction to her edition of *Kitāb al-Ḥudūd* (PIFAO, 1963, p. iii) for providing her with copies of four exemplars of the *Kitāb al-Ḥudūd*; however, she does not specify which four copies. There are five copies of the *Kitāb al-Ḥudūd* now in the collection at the ARCE (see below, numbers **18**, **25**, **36**, **191**, **221**), three of which Goichon used for her edition. (I thank Dimitri Gutas for this reference.) Aḥmad Fu'ād al-Ahwānī thanks Kuentz for allowing him use of a photostat of Leiden 1468 held at the IFAO for his edition of *Risāla fī al-nafs al-nāṭiqa* (see M122); see al-Ahwānī's article "ʿIlm al-nafs" in *al-Kitāb*, *op. cit.*, pp. 414-423, reprinted in his *Aḥwāl al-nafs: Risāla fī al-nafs wa-baqā'ihā wa-maʿādihā*, Cairo, 1952, pp. 196-199. This photostat no longer appears to be part of the collection. See also the list of current research projects Kuentz provides in his "al-Arājīz," pp. 143-4, a number of which could have been undertaken with access to the photostat collection. However, most of these projects do not appear to have been completed. Other parts of Kuentz's library are also now found in the ARCE library, for example, a signed copy

of Sulaymān Dunyā's first edition of *Kitāb al-Ishārāt wa-al-tanbīhāt.*

4. The first envelope, with the ARCE shelf number **50**, contains parts of Ayasofya 3711: 64v-68r, *Risāla fī al-awzān wa-al-akyāl* by Ḥunayn ibn Isḥāq (GAS 3:255); 68r-74v, *Risāla fī al-wazn wa-al-kayl* by Qusṭā ibn Lūqā (GAS 3:272); 74v-102r, *Kitāb Sharḥ al-ʿAqqār* by Maimonides (GAL, S I, 894). This last work has been annotated on the photostat by Meyerhof. The second envelope, with the ARCE shelf number **75a** contains a number of parts. Part 1 is a collection of small envelopes containing microfiches of the following manuscripts: Leiden 2701 (2); Leiden 1174; Leiden 1194 (2), (6), (7); Leiden 2697 (2). Part 2 is a microfiche and photostat copy of ʿAbd al-Ghānī al-Nābulusī's poem *Taʿbīr al-manām* (GAL II, 346, S II, 473); provenance unknown. Part 3 is a gratitude card sent by Meyerhof to the Faculty of Philosophy at University of Bonn on the occasion of his acceptance of an honorary doctorate from that university (an event mentioned by J. Schacht in his memorial of Meyerhof, *Osiris* 9, 1943, p. 11); Meyerhof provides his address in Cairo as Sharia Emad el-Din Block J, with the date September 1928. Part 4 is a photostat of treatises from Ayasofya 3725: 73r-79r, *Kitāb Jālīnūs fī al-nawm wa-al-yaqẓa*, translated by Yaḥyā ibn Sayyār (GAS 3:126), with a colophon dated 12 Rabīʿ al-Awwal 457/21 February 1065; 183-192, *Maqālat Jālīnūs fī ajzāʾ al-ṭibb* (GAS 3:112), with a colophon dated 10 Jumādā al-Ūlā 456/30 April 1064; 193v-206v, *Kitāb Jālīnūs fī al-ʿādāt*, translated by Ḥunayn ibn Isḥaq (GAS 3:105), with an anonymous commentary (Meyerhof suggests "Hunain?" in upper margin of f. 206v). The photostat collection at ARCE also contains a copy of MS Osler 7508, which Meyerhof used for his edition of al-Ghāfiqī's *al-Jāmiʿ fī al-ṭibb fī al-adwiya al-mufrada* (*The Abridged Version of "The Book of Simple Drugs" of Ahmad ibn Muhammad al-Ghāfiqī*, Cairo, 1932; re-issued Frankfurt am Main: Institue for the History of Arabic-Islamic Science at the Johann Wolfgang Goethe University, 1996).
5. For the confused history of Paul Kraus's *Nachlass*, which was in the possession of Charles Kuentz during his tenure at the IFAO, see Joel L. Kraemer, "The Death of an Orientalist: Paul Kraus from Prague to Cairo," in *The Jewish Discovery of Islam: Studies in Honor of Bernard Lewis*, edited by Martin Kraemer, Tel Aviv: The Moshe Dayan Center, 1999, pp. 181-223, particularly *Appendix 2: The Kraus Papers and Library*, pp. 208-210. In this regard, it is worth noting that not all of Kraus's books were donated to the Cairo University, as Kraemer states, p. 210; a number of his books, including a signed first edition copy of Louis Massignon's *La Passion d'al-Hallāj* (Paris: Geuthner, 1922), with Kraus's emendations in the margin, can be found in the library of the American University in Cairo.
6. The problems and frustrations that attend the acquisition of copies of man-

uscripts from the libraries of the Middle East unquestionably figure as one of the major factors at the root of this problem.

7. The *Qaṣīda al-ʿayniyya* was of great importance for the generations of philosophers after Ibn Sīnā, judging from the numerous and variegated commentaries to which it was subjected. Of editions, Janssens (p. 54) lists two, by F. Kholeif and A. Milla, neither of which claims to be definitive. If Janssens' information concerning the *Mabdaʾ wa-al-maʿād* (p. 20) is correct, the edition of the work by A. Nūrānī, based it seems on but one manuscript, is in sore need of revision. Finally, while Janssens' review of M. al-Bābā's edition of the *Urjūza fī al-ṭibb* is largely favorable, the exemplars of the work and the numerous commentaries of it found in the ARCE collection will prove valuable for a future critical edition.
8. I have provided occasional references to publications overlooked by Janssens, but these references are not comprehensive.
9. I have done this only for those manuscripts that I have examined *in situ* or on the basis of microfilms in my own collection.
10. There are three sets of folio numbers in the manuscript itself.
11. This exemplar is not listed in GAL I, 512, S I, 932.
12. *Topkapı Sarayı Müzesi Kütüphanesi Arapča yazmalar kataloğu*, Istanbul: Millī Eğitim Bakanlığı Yayınları,1966, 3:618-620.
13. For the terms "Shorter Bibliography" and "Longer Bibliography" in relation to the Autobiography/Biography Complex, see *The Life of Ibn Sīnā*, ed. and transl. by William E. Gohlman, New York, 1974, *Introduction to the Edition, passim.*
14. Mahdavī has included this letter as part of the Ibn Sīnā - Abū Saʿīd ibn Abī al-Khayr correspondence, a collection of letters that has yet to be authenticated or even studied in any detail. This particular letter, which exists in at least two different versions, is alternately entitled *al-Muʿāwada fī amr al-nafs wa-al-fayḍ* and *Mumkin al-wujūd* (the latter title has more bearing on the subject of the letter). It is also alternately addressed to Abū Saʿīd ibn Abī al-Khayr and al-Jūzjānī. However, in this letter Ibn Sīnā addresses his correspondent as ash-Shaykh al-Fāḍil, a title that he elsewhere reserves for Bahmanyār (see for example *al-Mubāḥathāt*, ed. Bīdārfar, pp. 38, 49, 55).
15. A very poor edition of this letter is published in H. Z. Ülken, *İbn Sina risaleleri, 2, Les opuscules d'Ibn Sina*, Istanbul, 1953, pp. 41-3.
16. See the edition in H. Z. Ülken, *op. cit.*, pp. 44-5, based in part on this exemplar; ʿAbd al-Amīr Z. Shams al-Dīn also used this exemplar for his publication of the letter in *al-Madhhab al-tarbawī ʿind Ibn Sīnā*, Beirut: al-Sharika al-ʿĀlamiyya li-al-Kitāb, 1988, pp. 399-400.
17. See ʿAyn al-Quḍāt, *al-Tamhīdāt*, printed in *Muṣannafāt-i ʿAyn al-Quḍāt*

Hamadānī, ed. ʿAfīf ʿUsayrān, Tehran: Tehran University, 1341Sh, pp. 349-50. This quotation became a part of the spurious Ibn Sīnā - Abū Saʿīd Ibn Abī al-Khayr correspondence.

18. H. Z. Ülken, *op. cit.*, p. 46, published this exemplar with his corrections.
19. See H. Z. Ülken, *op. cit.*, p. 47-8.
20. See H. Z. Ülken, *op. cit.*, p. 47.
21. For a complete discussion of this exemplar, see the author's *The Making of the Avicennan Tradition: The Transmission, Contents, and Structure of Ibn Sīnā's Discussions (al-Mubāḥathāt)*, Yale Ph.D. diss., 2001.
22. Now edited by M. Marmura, *Kitāb ithbāt al-nubuwwāt*. Beirut: Dār al-Nahār, 1991, who examined and eliminated this exemplar for his edition.
23. Semi-critical edition of the work, which includes this exemplar, by H. Z. Ülken, *op. cit.*, pp. 49-67.
24. Is this *Maʿrifat ʿunwān al-nafs*? See M. Bouyges, *Essai de chronologie des oeuvres de Al-Ghazali*, p. 170, no. 395.
25. This treatise is not listed in M. Bouyges, *op. cit.*
26. Cf. Mahdavī, p. 330, n. 1.
27. This exemplar agrees with MSS A, J, and N of William E. Gohlman's edition of the Autobiography/Biography Complex, *op. cit.*, pp. 90/91ff.)
28. For a detailed discussion of this exemplar, see Yale dissertation by the author.
29. Al-Shahrastānī, *al-Milal wa-al-nihal*, ed. W. Cureton, London, 1846, 2:348-429; ed. M. S. Kaylānī, Beirut: Dār al-Jīl, 1987, 2:158-231.
30. This colophon may belong to the archetype of Esc. 703; there is a correction to it in the margin.
31. See the notes in Bīdārfar's edition of the *Kitāb al-Mubāḥathāt* to these paragraph numbers for the references to the *Shifāʾ*.
32. Full details are discussed in the above mentioned Yale dissertation.
33. This note was tentatively ascribed to Ibn Sīnā by D. Gutas, "Notes and Texts from Cairo Manuscripts, II: Texts from Avicenna's Library in a Copy by ʿAbd-ar-Razzāq aṣ-Ṣighnāḫī," *Manuscripts of the Middle East* 2 (1987), p. 13. The ascription of the note to Bahmanyār in MS Leiden 184, definitely dated to 515/1122, may very well prove to be correct; the Ṣighnākhī codex is not dated but was likely made sometime in the first half of the 6th/12th century.
34. Marmura, *op. cit.*, used this exemplar (which he refers to by the catalogue number 1464) for his edition.
35. There are two wrappers that bear the number **75**. To distinguish the two, I have added [**a**], and [**b**].

36. De Slane understood this final section to consist of biographies of authorities Ibn Sīnā cites in his *Urjūza*.
37. This is one of the manuscripts Goichon used for her edition of *Kitāb al-ḥudūd*. The copy of the work itself is no longer a part of the photostat. Goichon, *op. cit.*, viii, stated that the *Kitāb al-ḥudūd* falls between folios 2r-7r of the manuscript. Mingana's catalogue, however, provides the folio numbers as 42-47. Did Kuentz separate the work from the photostat of the codex and give it to Goichon?
38. This identification appears to agree with de Slane (1:526) but for the copy date, which de Slane stated to be 1185.
39. GAL S II, 693. I thank Everett Rowson for this reference.
40. The last two entries, by Ibn Makkī, most likely belong to Vat. Borg. 87.
41. De Slane, 1:540, no. 3038.
42. M43 incorrectly associated this variant title with *Risāla fī al-nafs wa-mā yaṣīru ilayhi ba'd al-sa'āda*.
43. M65 incorrectly associated this variant title, i.e. *al-Risāla al-Marmūza*, with *Ḥayy ibn Yaqẓān*.
44. Another copy of this exemplar is found in wrapper **161.c**.
45. Abū Manṣūr al-Jabbān was the philologist who challenged Ibn Sīnā's knowledge of philology at the court of 'Alā' al-Dawla in Iṣfahān, a challenge which, according to al-Jūzjānī (Biography, Gohlman, *op. cit.*, 68-70/69-71), prompted Ibn Sīnā to take up the study of this subject for three years and finally produce a tome with which he exacted his public revenge on Abū Manṣūr. For biblographical information on Abū Manṣūr, see Gohlman, *op. cit.*, 133-4.
46. Note that this variant title does not appear in the Longer Bibliography that the scribe copied earlier in his codex. Does this suggest that the variant title originates with his archetype of the *Kitāb al-Ḥudūd* or is it the work of a later scribe?
47. For these passages, see the Yale dissertation by the author. Ibn Abī al-Kharajayn might be identified as the minor poet and literary scholar Manṣūr ibn al-Muslim ibn 'Alī b. Muḥammad ibn Aḥmad ibn Abī al-Kharajayn, known as al-Dumayk, a native of Aleppo who pursued his career in Damascus 457-510/1060-1117; see Ziriklī 7:304c and the references cited there.
48. I base this identification on the fact that the treatise *Asbāb al-āthār al-'ulwiyya* is found on folios 49r-50v in the photostat and these are the same folios Mahdavī records for Serez 4009; see M24.
49. There are two wrappers that bear the number **190**. To distinguish the two, I have added [**a**], and [**b**].

50. **C.i** and **iv** may be by ʿIzz al-Dīn ʿĀmir ibn ʿĀmir Baṣrī. See M. T. Dānishpāzūh, *Fihrist-i kutub-i khaṭṭī-yi Kitābkhānah-yi Majlis-i Shūrā-yi Islāmī*, vol. 2, Tehran, 1359Sh, p. 211.
51. This identification of the treatise as a commentary on a medical *urjūza* was determined from the lines 236r.7-8: *wa-hunā nqiḍāʾu l-qawli fī sharḥi hādhihī l-Urjūza.* The provenance was determined by a comparison of the copies of the commentaries on Ibn Sīnā's *Urjūza* held at Leiden University with this exemplar. In the catalogues of that collection, Or. 912 agrees with this exemplar both in the copy date (983/1575-6), and folio numbers (248 folios). See Voorhoeve, p. 391, who refers to CCO 1327. CCO, however, does not note the final anonymous treatise.
52. However, Mahdavī states that the Vienna manuscript names the author as ʿAbd al-Wajīd ibn Muḥammad Mudarris Kūtāhiyyah, but this is not evident in the photostat.

Index to Avicenna at the ARCE

Ibn Sīnā

A

Al-Aḍḥawiyya **25, 36, 116, 162, 142, 171**
Al-Adwiya al-qalbiyya **18, 162, 221**
Al-Afʿāl wa-al-infiʿālāt, see *al-Fayḍ al-ilāhī*
Al-ʿAhd **18, 59, 116, 181**
Al-Ajwiba ʿan al-masāʾil **18**
Al-Ajwiba ʿan masāʾil Abī Rayḥān al-Bīrūnī **36, 61, 63**
Al-Ajwiba ʿan al-masāʾil al-ʿashr (a) **18, 25, 36, 61, 63, 119, 162**
Al-Ajwiba ʿan al-masāʾil al-ʿashr (b) **171**
Al-Ālāt al-raṣadiyya **61, 63**
Amr mastūr al-ṣanʿa **162, 171**
    Risāla fī ʿilm al-iksīr **116**
    Risāla fī ṣanʿat al-mastūr, Persian transl. **25**
Anwāʿ al-qaḍāyā **208**
Aqsām al-ʿulūm **18, 62, 171, 221**
Al-ʿArūs **18, 62, 181**
Asbāb al-āthār al-ʿulwiyya **168.c, 179.b**
    Al-āthār al-ʿulwiyya **168**
Asbāb ḥudūth al-ḥurūf **25, 36, 116, 162, 171, 181**
Autobiography **36**
Autobiography/Biography complex **116, 162, 171**
    Longer Bibliography **36**
Avicenna Latinus **154**

B

Al-Birr wa-al-ithm **25, 181, 208, 221**

D

Dafʿ al-maḍarr al-kulliyya ʿan al-abdān al-insāniyya fī tadāruk al-khaṭaʾ al-wāqiʿ fī al-ṭibb **221**
Dānishnāmah-yi ʿAlāʾī
    Hādhihī al-Risāla al-ʿAlāʾiyya **101**
    Ḥikmat-i ʿAlāʾī **36**
Dustūr ṭibbī **208, 221**

F

Faṣl min kalām al-Shaykh al-Raʾīs fī fāʾidat al-manṭiq **61, 63**
Al-Fayḍ al-ilāhī **18, 36**

Risāla fī al-muʿjizāt **181**
Fuṣūl min al-ḥikma (Passages from *al-Taʿlīqāt*) **208**
Fuṣūl ṭibbiyya **221**
Risāla fī al-ṭibb **116**

Ḥ, H

Ḥadd al-jism **61, 63, 208, 221**
Hādhihī fawāʾid wa-nukat, see *al-Mubāḥathāt* and *al-Taʿlīqāt*
Ḥaqāʾiq ʿilm al-tawḥīd see *al-Risāla al-ʿarshiyya*
Ḥayy ibn Yaqẓān **29, 36, 113, 119, 162, 168.a, 171, 181**
Al-Ḥikma al-Mashriqiyya **92**
Al-Hindibāʾ **18, 28, 171, 221**
Kitāb al-Ḥudūd **18, 25, 36, 191, 221,**
Kitāb al-Ḥudūd al-maʿrūf bi-al-mabāḥith al-ṣadīqiyya **171**
Ḥudūth al-ḥurūf, see *Asbāb ḥudūth al-ḥurūf*
Al-Ḥukūma fī ḥujaj al-muthbitīn [anna] li-al-māḍī mabdaʾan zamāniyyan **221**
Risāla fī anna li-al-māḍī mabdaʾan zamāniyyan **113**
Risāla fī ḥujaj **36**
Risāla fī al-nihāya wa-al-lānihāya **18**
Ḥuṣūl ʿilm wa-ḥikma **128, 201, 208**[2]

I

Ibṭāl aḥkām al-nujūm **18, 28, 52, 181, 221**
Risāla fī al-radd ʿalā al-munajjimīn **113**
Īḍāḥ barāhīn mustanbaṭa fī masaʾil ʿawīṣa **36**
Risāla fī ʿilm al-iksīr see *Amr mastūr al-ṣanʿa*
Al-Ishāra ilā ʿilm al-manṭiq **171**
Al-Ishārāt wa-al-tanbīhāt **101, 179.a.v**
Al-Anmāṭ al-thalāth min ākhir Kitāb al-Ishārāt **113**
Persian translation **36**
Ithbāt al-nubuwwa **181**
Risāla fī ithbāt al-nubuwwāt **113**

J

Risāla fī jawhar al-ajrām al-samāwiyya **18**
Risāla fī fawāʾid fī al-raʾy al-muḥaṣṣal **36**
Risāla fī taʿrīf al-raʾy al-muḥaṣṣal **142.b, 221**
Risāla fī taʿrīf al-raʾy al-muḥaṣṣal/Risālat al-ajrām al-ʿulwiyya **171**
Al-Jumal min al-adilla al-muḥaqqaqa li-baqāʾ al-nafs al-nāṭiqa **31**
Al-Jumāna al-ilāhiyya **119, 128, 162, 236.a**

Kh

Khaṭaʾ man qāla inna al-kammiyyata jawharun **171**
Khuṭba fī al-khamr **221**
Al-Khuṭba al-tawḥīdiyya **36, 191, 221**
    Al-Khuṭba al-gharrāʾ **113**
    Al-Kalima al-ilāhiyya **171**

M

Kitāb al-Maʿād, see *Kitāb al-nafs ʿalā ṭarīq al-dalīl wa-al-burhān*
Al-Mabāḥith al-ṣadīqiyya, see *Kitāb al-Ḥudūd*
Al-Mabdaʾ wa-al-maʿād **3, 8, 36, 43, 48, 68, 87, 88, 96, 97, 142.b, 144, 171, 182, 183, 184, 185, 191**
[*Al-Mabdaʾ wa-al-maʿād*] M106, *dhayl* **18**
Manṭiq al-mūjaz **179.a.1**
Kitāb al-Manẓūma fī al-ṭibb, see *Al-Urjūza fī al-ṭibb*
Masʾala ṭibbiyya, see *Risāla fī al-bāh*
Masāʾil Ḥunayn **59, 116, 221**
Min aqwāl al-Shaykh al-Raʾīs **208**
Miʿrājnāmah, see *al-Risāla al-Miʿrājiyya*
Al-Muʿāwada **25, 36, 116, 142.a**
Al-Mubāḥathāt **18**
    Hādhihī fawāʾid wa-nukat **179.a.iv**
    Passages from *al-Mubāḥathāt* **171**
    Risāla **221**
    Al-Taḥṣīlāt **36**
Al-Mūjaz al-ṣaghīr fī al-manṭiq **171**

N

Kitāb al-Nafs ʿalā sunnat al-ikhtiṣār
    Kitāb al-Nafs lahū al-maʿrūf bi-al-ʿashara fuṣūl **171**
    Risālat al-Nafs **36**
Kitāb al-Nafs ʿalā ṭarīq al-dalīl wa-al-burhān **5, 18, 113**
    Kitāb al-Maʿād **36**
    Kitāb al-Maʿād al-aṣghar **171**
    Risāla fī ḥaqīqat al-nafs **181**
    Risāla fī al-nafs wa-baqāʾihā wa-maʿādihā **179.a.ii**
    Tarjamah-yi Risālah-yi al-maʿād **36**
    Tarjamah-yi Risālah-yi al-nafs **36**
Al-Najāt **18, 36, 75[b]**
Naṣāʾiḥ ṭibbiyya, see *al-Urjūza fī al-waṣāyā*
Al-Nukat fī al-manṭiq **179.a.iii**

Q

Al-Qaḍāʾ wa-al-qadar **25**
    Risāla fī al-qadar **18, 113, 221**
Qāla al-Shaykh al-Raʾīs **208**
Al-Qānūn
    Faṣl al-Falūnīyā al-rūmī al-ṭarsūs **33**
    Faṣl fī ḍuʿf al-intishār **158.b**
Al-Qaṣīda al-ʿayniyya **6, 28, 32, 61, 63, 122, 126, 161.a-c, 162, 165, 166, 171, 194.c, 208, 236, 270**
Al-Qawlanj **199**
Qiyām al-arḍ fī wasṭ al-samāʾ **221**
    Risāla fī ʿillat qiyām al-arḍ fī wasṭ al-samāʾ **18**
Question from Abū Ṭālib al-ʿAlawī to Ibn Sīnā with his response **171**

R

Al-Radd ʿalā kitāb Abī al-Faraj ibn al-Ṭayyib **208**
Al-Risāla al-ʿArshiyya (*Ḥaqāʾiq ʿilm al-tawḥīd*) **142.b, 234**
Al-Risāla al-Miʿrājiyya **36**
Al-Risāla al-Nayrūziyya **18, 36, 113, 128, 221, 142.b**
Risāla fī ajwibat baʿḍ al-asʾila **181**
Risāla fī aqsām al-nufūs wa-aḥwālihā (Persian) **181**
Risāla fī bayān al-ṣūra al-maʿqūla al-mukhālifa li-al-ḥaqq **36**
Risāla fī intifāʾ ʿammā nusiba ilayhi min muʿāraḍat al-Qurʾān **208**
Risāla fī al-akhlāq **113, 116, 162, 171, 181**
Risāla fī al-arzāq **163**
Risāla fī al-bāh **62, 208**
Risāla fī al-farq bayna al-ḥarāra al-gharīziyya wa-al-gharība **36**
Risāla fī al-faṣd **208**
Risāla fī al-ḥuzn **25, 119**
Risāla fī al-ḥujaj al-ʿashr **25**
Risāla fī al-ʿishq **36, 116, 142.b, 162, 181**
Risāla fī al-malāʾika **116, 181**
Risāla fī al-muʿjizāt, see *Al-Fayḍ al-ilāhī*
Risāla fī al-nafs wa-mā yaṣīru ilayhi baʿda mufāraqatihā al-badan, see *Taḥṣīl al-saʿāda*/*al-Ḥujaj al-ʿashr*
Risāla fī al-nafs **18**
Risāla fī al-ṣalāt **62, 116, 181**
    Fī asrār al-ṣalāt **36**
Risāla fī al-siyāsa **18, 28, 113, 221**
Risāla fī tadbīr al-musāfir **208**
Risāla fī al-ṭibb, see *Fuṣūl ṭibbiyya*
Risāla ilā Abī Jaʿfar al-Qāshānī **128, 162**

Nuskhat ruqʿa ilā Abī Jaʿfar al-Qāshānī **208**
Risāla ilā Abī al-Qāsim ibn Abī al-Faḍl **128, 208, 221**
Risāla ilā Abī Ṭāhir ibn Ḥassūl **128, 221**
Nuskhat ruqʿa ilā Abī Ṭāhir ibn Ḥassūl **208**[2]
Risāla ilā ʿAlāʾ al-Dīn ibn Kākūyah **128, 208, 221**
Risāla ilā baʿḍ al-mutakallimīn, see *Al-Wusʿa*
Risāla ilā al-Shaykh Abī al-Faḍl ibn Maḥmūd **128, 208, 221**
Risāla min Abī ʿAlī Sīnā **158.f**

S, Sh
Sabab ijābat al-duʿāʾ **36, 59, 116, 181, 221**
Sirr al-qadar **25, 36**
Al-Shifāʾ **133, 232**
Al-Ilāhiyyāt from *al-Shifāʾ* **18**

T
Taʿbīr al-ruʾyā **132, 190[b], 199**
Al-Risāla al-Manāmiyya **36**
Tafāsīr
Āyāt al-Nūr **181**
Al-Muʿawwidhatayn (*Sūrat al-Falaq*, *Sūrat al-Nās*) **36, 116, 181, 221**
Sūrat al-Aʿlā **181**
Sūrat al-Ikhlāṣ **36**[2]**, 116, 181, 221**
Qawluhū thumma stawā ilā al-samāʾ **116, 221**
Taḥṣīl as-saʿāda/al-Ḥujaj al-ʿashr **18, 142.a, 171**
Al-Taʿlīqāt **36, 271**
Fuṣūl min al-ḥikma **208**
Hādhihī fawāʾid wa-nukat **179.a.iv**
Taʿrīf al-raʾy al-muḥaṣṣal, see *Jawhar al-ajrām al-samāwiyya*
Al-Ṭayr **25, 29, 36, 52, 113, 221**[2]
Al-Risāla al-Marmūza **36, 119, 171**

U
Al-Urjūza fī al-manṭiq **36, 162, 208**
Al-Rajaz al-manṭiqī **61, 63**
Urjūza fī ʿilm al-manṭiq **171**
Al-Urjūza fī al-mujarrabāt **12, 58.a, 163, 175, 194.a.ii**
Al-Urjūza fī al-ṭibb (M15a) **7, 9, 12, 13, 15, 16, 33, 57, 58.b, 80, 86, 94, 95, 111, 121, 130, 140, 141.b, 156, 163, 167, 172, 192, 193, 190[a], 150, 204, 205**
Kitāb al-Manẓūma fī al-ṭibb **158.d**
Urjūza fī ḍurūb al-ḥummayāt li-Ibn Sīnā **194.a.i**
Al-Urjūza fī al-ṭibb (M16b)

Manẓūmat Ibn Sīnā fī al-ṭibb **158.a**
Al-Urjūza fī al-ṭibb (*fī al-fuṣūl al-arbaʿa*) **15, 71.b, 158.b, 175.a**
Al-Urjūza fī al-waṣāyā **119**
Naṣāʾiḥ ṭibbiyya **163**
Al-Urjūza fī waṣāyā Ibuqrāṭ **158, 194.a.iii**
ʿUyūn al-ḥikma **116, 171**

W
Al-Wusʿa **36, 59, 116, 221**

Pseudo-Ibn Sīnā

Abū al-Faraj ibn al-Ṭayyib. *Al-Quwā al-arbaʿa* **208**

Afḍal al-Din al-Kāshī.
Fī l-ʿilm wa-al-nuṭq **62**
Risāla fī al-manṭiq **18**

Anonymous
Ḥudūth al-ajsām **168.c**
ʿIlm al-firāsa **132**
Masāʾil ʿan aḥwāl al-rūḥ **18, 119**
Al-Mufāraqāt **208**
Qāla al-Shaykh al-Raʾīs Abū ʿAlī. Unidentified *qaṣīda* **158.e**
Risāla fī al-ʿazāʾim **101**
Risāla fī ḥaqāʾiq al-insāniyya (*sic*) **181**
Risāla fī ʿilm al-akhlāq **36**
Risāla fī ʿilm al-nafs **115**
Risāla fī ithbāt al-ṣāniʿ **62**
Risāla fī al-ṣalāt ʿalā lisān al-ʿuqalāʾ li-bayān al-ʿaql **62**
Risālat Manāfiʿ al-aʿḍāʾ **179.a.vi**
Sharḥ Asmāʾ allāh **62**
Wird al-ākhir **221**
Al-Wird al-aʿẓam **162**

ʿAyn al-Quḍāt al-Hamadhānī. *Al-Irshād* (Quote from *al-Tamhīdāt*) **36, 208, 221**

Fārābī
Al-Firdaws (?) **25, 36, 162**
Risāla fī al-taṣawwuf (?) **116**

ʿUyūn al-masāʾil **171**

Ikhwān al-ṣafāʾ. *Tashrīḥ al-aʿḍāʾ* **59, 116**

Miskawayh. Extract of *Taḥdhīb al-akhlāq*
Dafʿ ghamm al-mawt **25**
Risālat Ḥikmat al-mawt. Persian translation **36**
Risāla fī ḥaqīqat al-mawt **221**

Theophrastus
Asbāb al-raʿd wa-al-barq **36**

Other Authors

A

ʿAbd al-Wāḥid ibn Muḥammad. *Sharḥ al-Qaṣīda al-ʿayniyya* **236**
Anonymous. *Abwāb fī ṭafyi al-nār* (?) **150**
Anonymous. A commentary on Ibn Sīnā's *al-Urjūza fī al-ṭibb* **7**
Anonymous. A short untitled tract on the creation of Adam **33**
Anonymous. A work on *materia medica* **206**
Anonymous. *Fawāʾid al-makhlūqāt* **33**
Anonymous. *Al-Jawhar al-nafīs bi-sharḥ manẓūmat al-Raʾīs* **190**[**a**]
Anonymous. *Kifāyat al-murtāḍ fī ʿilmay al-abwāl wa-al-anbāḍ* **71, 158.c**
Anonymous. *Kitāb al-Manāfiʿ al-mubayyana fī-mā yanfaʿu fī al-arbaʿ al-azmina* **158.b**
Anonymous. *Manẓūma fī al-kuḥl* **71.b**
Anonymous. *Nubadh al-kitāb manṣūmat* (*sic*) *al-Qānūnchah* **141**
Anonymous. *Qāla baʿḍ al-ḥukamāʾ* **61, 63**
Anonymous. *Risāla fī ḥaqīqat al-rūḥ li-wāḥid min akābir* (*sic*) **181**
Anonymous. *Sharḥ al-Arwāḥ* **191**
Anonymous. Sayings by Socrates, Plato, Aristotle, Ibn Sīnā on the soul **221**
Anonymous. Short tract on the use of Qurʾān *sūra*s as talismans **150**
Anonymous. Three brief tracts on *bāh* **175.a**
Anonymous. Tract on the four seasons **158.b**
Anonymous. Unidentified medical work **175.a**
Anonymous. *Urjūza* **158.b**
Anonymous. *Urjūza fī amrāḍ al-ʿayn* **158.c**
Anonymous. *Urjūza fī al-ṭibb balīgha nāfiʿiyya* **158.b**
Al-Anṭākī, Dāwūd. *Ṣifat maʿjūn* **175.a**

B

Al-Baghdādī, Mūsā ibn Ibrāhīm ibn Mūsā ibn Muḥammad al-Mutaṭabbib. *Al-Jawhar al-nafīs* **33, 196**

Al-Baghdādī, al-Sharīf Bashīr ibn Nāṣr al-Hāshimī. *Sharḥ Risālat al-Ṭayr* **29**

Bahmanyār

Faṣl. Note on numbers as the principles of the universe **61, 63**

Risāla fī ithbāt al-mufāraqāt wa-aḥwālihā **61, 63**

Risāla fī marātib al-mawjūdāt **61, 63**

Risāla fī mawḍūʿ al-ʿilm al-maʿrūf bi-mā baʿd al-ṭabīʿa **61, 63**

Al-Taḥṣīl **134, 146, 189**

At-Taḥṣīlāt (al-Mubāḥathāt) **36**

Taḥṣīl lubāb al-ḥikma **49**

D

Al-Dawwānī

Al-Risāla al-Khalkhāliyya **181**

Risāla fī ḥaqīqat al-nafs **181**

Tafsīr of *Sūrat Kāfirūn* **181**

F

Al-Fārābī

Fī-mā yanbaghī an yuqaddama qabla taʿallum al-falsafa **61, 63**

Sharḥ ʿalā risāla li-Zīnūn **142.b**

Kitāb ʿUyūn al-masāʾil lahū **171**

ʿUyūn al-masāʾil **61, 63, 142.b**

G, Gh

Galen

Extract of *Adwār al-ḥummayāt* **171**

Kitāb Jālīnūs fī al-ʿādāt, translated by Ḥunayn ibn Isḥaq, n. 4

Kitāb Jālīnūs fī al-nawm wa-al-yaqẓa, translated by Yaḥyā ibn Sayyār, n. 4

Maqālat Jālīnūs fī ajzāʾ al-ṭibb, n. 4

Gregorios Thaumaturgos. *Mukhtaṣar fī qawl al-Ḥakīm Arisṭū fī al-nafs* **62**

Al-Ghāfiqī. *Al-Jāmiʿ fī al-ṭibb fī al-adwiya al-mufrada*, n. 4

Al-Ghazālī

Risāla fī maʿrifat al-nafs **181**

Risāla sharīfa **181**

H, Ḥ, Kh

Al-Ḥanbalī, Muḥammad ibn Ismāʿīl. *Al-Tawfīq li-al-ṭabīb al-shafīq bi-sharḥ urjūzat al-Shaykh al-Raʾīs imam al-ṭarīq* **130**

Hirmis al-Harāmisa (Idrīs al-nabī). *Risāla fī al-mawʿiẓa al-laṭīfa wa-al-naṣāʾiḥ*

al-sharīfa **181**
Ḥunayn ibn Isḥāq
Risāla fī al-awzān wa-al-akyāl, n. 4
See Galen
Al-Ḥusaynī, Muḥammad ibn Muḥammad ibn Bāqir al-Dāmād. Untitled **142.b**
Al-Khvānjī, ʿAbd al-Jawwād ibn Abī al-Faqīr Saʿīd. *Sharḥ al-Qasīda al-ʿayniyya* **32** (?), **165**

I
Ibn ʿAbd al-Wāḥid. *Sharḥ Qaṣīdat Ibn Sīnā* **270**
Ibn al-ʿĀmid, Abū al-Faḍl. *Risāla fī al-ḥumrā al-ḥāditha fī al-jaww* **61, 63**
Ibn al-Habbāriyya, Muḥammad ibn Muḥammad ibn Ṣāliḥ. Verse rendition of *Ḥayy ibn Yaqẓān* **29**
Ibn al-Haytham. *Jawāb ʿan suʾal al-sāʾil* **61, 63**
Ibn Makkī, Muḥammad
Urjūza wajīza fī ʿadad al-ʿurūq al-mafṣūda **158.c**
Urjūza fī jadhb al-khalṭ **158.c**
Ibn Māsawayh. *Ṣifat jawāsīn* (?) *al-mutawakkil* **158.b**
Ibn Rushd. *Sharḥ al-Urjūza fī al-ṭibb* **15, 94, 95, 111, 172, 205, 206**
Ibn Sahlān al-Sāwī. Persian translation of commentary on *Risālat al-Ṭayr* **36**
Ibn Sayyār, Yaḥyā, see Galen
Ibn Shāhik, ʿAlī . *Sharḥ Risālat al-Ṭayr* **52**
Ibn Tufayl. *Ḥayy ibn Yaqẓān* **36**
Ibn Tumlūs. *Sharḥ al-Urjūza fī al-ṭibb* **121**
Ibn Yamūn? *Wa-hādhihī Urjūza tusammā Irtiyāḥ al-arwāḥ fī ādāb al-nikāḥ* **158.b**
Ibn Zayla
Sharḥ Ḥayy ibn Yaqẓān **29, 36, 52, 168.a, 181**
Talkhīs li-ṣifāt wājib al-wujūd **61, 63**

J
Al-Jūzjānī. Biography of Ibn Sīnā **36, 116, 162, 171**

M
Maimonides. *Kitāb Sharḥ al-ʿAqqār*, n. 4
Al-Masʿūdī, Saʿd al-Dīn. *Sharḥ al-Khuṭba al-tawḥīdiyya* **99, 191**
Miskawayh. *Min Kitāb Tahdhīb al-akhlāq* **62**
See Pseudo-Ibn Sīnā
Al-Madāʾinī, ʿAbd al-Ḥamīd Ibn Hibat Allāh, false attribution **26**
Al-Mināwī, ʿAbd al-Raʾūf
Al-ʿAlq al-nafīs ʿalā Qaṣīdat al-Shaykh al-Raʾīs **122, 166**
Commentary on Ibn Sīnā's *al-Qaṣīda al-ʿayniyya* **126**

N

Al-Nābulusī, ʿAbd al-Ghānī. *Taʿbīr al-manām*, n. 4

Q

Al-Qawṣūnī, Madyan ibn ʿAbd al-Raḥmān al-Ṭabīb
Hādhā muntahā al-ghāyāt fī taʿrīf al-layla 7
Qāmūs al-aṭibbāʾ wa-nāmūs al-ābāʾ 7
Al-Qawl al-anīs wa-al-durr al-nafīs ʿalā manẓūmat al-Shaykh al-Raʾīs 7
Al-Qurashī, ʿAlī ibn Abī al-Ḥazm. *Al-Jawhar al-nafīs fī sharḥ Urjūzat al-Raʾīs* **86**
Qusṭā ibn Lūqā. *Risāla fī al-wazn wa-al-kayl*, n. 4

R

Al-Rāzī, Fakhr al-Dīn. *Waṣāyā* **181**
Al-Rāzī, Quṭb al-Dīn. *Risāla mushtamila ʿalā taḥqīq maʿnā al-taṣawwur wa-al-taṣdīq* **61**, **63**

S, Sh

Suhrawardī al-maqtūl, *Waṣiyya* **181**
Al-Shahrastānī. *Kitāb al-Milal wa-al-nihal* **36**

Ṭ

Al-Ṭūsī, Naṣīr al-Dīn
Fī wujūd al-jawhār (*Risāla fī ithbāt al-jawhar al-mufāraq*) 62
Kitāb al-Albāb al-nāhiyya wa-tarākīb al-sulṭāniyya **16**
Taʾwīl Qiṣṣat Absāl wa-Salāmān **168.b**, **181**

www.ingramcontent.com/pod-product-compliance
Lightning Source LLC
Chambersburg PA
CBHW032254150426
43195CB00008BA/445
* 9 7 8 1 5 5 8 7 6 2 5 1 0 *